WALKS ON THE WILD SIDE

EXPLORING AN UNFORGIVING LAND

JOHN PAKENHAM

EYE BOOKS
NON-FICTION

Published by Eye Books
29A Barrow Street
Much Wenlock
Shropshire
TF13 6EN

www.eye-books.com

First edition 2020
Copyright © John Pakenham 2020

Cover design by Ifan Bates
Cover photograph by John Pakenham
Photographs by John Pakenham
Line drawings by Mo Pakenham
Design and typesetting by Clio Mitchell

British Library Cataloguing in Publication Data
A catalogue record for this book is available from the British Library.

Printed by CPI Group (UK) Ltd, Croydon CR0 4YY

ISBN 9781785631948

For Mo

Contents

Trek 2 – 'It is Better to Die Without Crossing Mugurr'

Trek 3 – Over the Mountain of God to the Curse of Maseketa

*If you have the desire for knowledge
and the power to give it physical expression,
go out and explore. If you are a brave man
you will do nothing: if you are fearful
you may do much, for none but cowards
have need to prove their bravery.
Some will tell you that you are mad,
and nearly all will say 'What is the use?'*

**Apsley Cherry-Garrard (1886-1959),
Member of Captain Scott's 1910-1913 Expedition to the
South Pole**
The Worst Journey in the World

To Begin at the Beginning

I WAS BORN IN ZANZIBAR in the last days of the Sultans. When I was just twelve hours old, the Sultan His Highness Sheikh Sir Seyyid Khalifa II bin Harib Al-Said bin Thurein al-Busaidi and his wife, Seyyida Nunu, honoured us by coming to the hospital with an armful of flowers for my mother and welcoming me into the world.

Zanzibar has always been a magical island, with its old Stone Town built of coral set in a halo of white sand beaches and whispering palms, surrounded by the transparent turquoise seas of the Indian Ocean. Lying halfway down the east coast, it was the gateway to Africa, and used for centuries by the Arabs to trade gold, ivory and slaves. It was also where the great Victorian explorers, like Burton and Livingstone, launched their expeditions into the interior of this vast, unknown continent.

Pa lived there for 27 years as the senior colonial officer, and was devoted to it, studying its peoples, customs and wildlife; no European ever knew it better. Before joining him there, Ma had spent eight years in a corner of south-west Uganda, where she had started a school, and for her, this shift from Uganda (which Churchill had called the 'pearl of Africa'), to the oppressively hot, humid coast was difficult. She also hated the traditional colonial costumes and the clapping for servants. So, she was happy when, with the final twilight of the colonial era, we returned to England. But here, as I grew up, I remember her watching every morning as the City gents scurried for their London trains, black suits, black raincoats, black briefcases, black umbrellas, black bowler hats. She called them the 'black beetles' and said to me, 'Never have a job behind a desk'. I never did.

My maternal granny was a passionate theatre-goer and it must have rubbed off on me as, to Pa's dismay, I had no interest in following him to Cambridge, but instead went to art school to study theatre design. He lost interest in my education from that moment. He was a brilliant natural historian, however, and inspired in me a love for nature and the wild places of the world. This eventually grew into a desire to escape from the safe, cosy, middle-class world of suburbia. So when my fascination with the art of the Italian Renaissance pushed me to start hitch-hiking across Europe to visit galleries and museums, I carried a small tent. I was happy to sleep almost anywhere, including a graveyard. I discovered that I didn't mind discomfort.

I had been sent away to boarding school from the age of eight, so never had a sense of 'belonging' around my home, feeling something of an outsider. This gave me a rather detached view of the world, and a tendency to dislike Western society and the destructive influence of human 'civilisation' on our planet. I had been brought up with books about Africa, wild animals, tribesmen and remote landscapes of savannah and mountain, which my imagination gleefully inhabited. I was used to frequent visits by Arabian and African friends from East Africa, and our house full of exotic memorabilia: Arab daggers; silver salvers; models of dhows, and an ancient treasure chest similar to those used by Captain Kidd, the famous pirate. Unsurprisingly, I developed a thirst to travel in those enchanted climes. Africa was in my blood.

However, my first adventure after leaving school in 1968 was to set off, aged seventeen, with two friends in an old Land Rover, to spend six months driving 20,000 miles to Afghanistan and Pakistan. For the first time I found myself in truly wild areas, sometimes at risk of attack by Pathan bandits. In the tribal areas of south Pakistan the police insisted we take an armed guard with us, but we irresponsibly ignored them and pressed on, even becoming hopelessly lost in semi-desert, only to find the people kind and generous. Although I often had a hollow pit of butterflies in my stomach I discovered that if someone in a dangerous area gives you food and shelter, you are his guest and he will protect you. I liked these wild people of the mountains and deserts.

Ten years later I saw some of the Middle East and was astonished that people could live in such brutal desert lands. I wanted to understand the austerity and wilderness for myself. So in the winter of 1979-80 I spent three months in Southern Algeria around the Hoggar Mountains, the very centre of the Sahara Desert. I was determined to make a journey by camel – not a tourist jaunt, but with a real sense of exploration – so, with a Tuareg guide and three camels, I rode almost 150 miles north through the desert. I was a hopeless cameleer and have rarely been so uncomfortable. The fear was still there, but so was a curious thrill, which fired through me a strange enjoyment of the discomfort.

I had read a book about a camel expedition around the east side of Lake Turkana in north-west Kenya a short while earlier, the first substantial European expedition since the early explorers, and it set my brain alight with curiosity to discover it for myself. I was then lucky enough to be introduced to the remarkable explorer, Wilfred Thesiger, famous for his extensive travels in the Empty Quarter of Arabia, probably the harshest sand desert in the world, and came to know him well. He had 'retired' to Samburu tribal district, south of Lake Turkana – further proof to me that this must be a fascinating area. I make no apology for discussing Thesiger at length in the following pages. He is an almost mythical figure, whose life remains an enigma to most people.

During the period of the journeys recounted here, 1979-85, I was working freelance in the film industry, creating special effects. Extended down-time between contracts gave me plenty of opportunities to disappear into the void of the unknown land which forms the subject of this book. With such a wide range of potential places to explore, and very little knowledge of the area as a whole (partly because much of it was essentially unexplored) I was guided simply by guesswork and my sense of curiosity. North Turkana, on the north-west side of Lake Turkana, struck me as probably the most remote area, so I decided to head there. Halfway down the west coast of the lake, at the end of a long dust road, on a bay named Ferguson's Gulf, was a large village called Kalokol. This seemed an ideal starting point for a circular walk. On the map I picked out names that seemed to mark a possible route and decided to attempt that. My idea was to take loaded donkeys and find tribesmen as guides, but it was all very vague; I did not really know what I was doing. I was very nervous although I took care not to show it.

I became increasingly fascinated by the other-worldliness of this region, unlike anywhere I had ever seen, and the more I witnessed the more I wanted to see. I eventually covered 1,200 miles on foot (the distance from England to Greece) around both sides of the lake. Writing a book about my trips never crossed my mind at the time, but friends who found my stories extraordinary pressed me to record them, so I made detailed accounts of all four walks. And then left them on the back burner for over 30 years.

Since my walks the world has impinged on the wildness of the region. Population has exploded, Kenya's 17 million in 1980 becoming 45 million by 2016, and villages of about a thousand or so in the Northern Frontier Region sometimes expanded to tens of thousands. There is still tribal raiding, but tourism is creeping into what was a wild and often very dangerous area – an inaccessible land which very few then knew of and fewer still had visited. Where I walked, vehicle access is now comparatively normal. But travelling by car totally changes the nature of the interaction with the local people, their harsh lives, and the solitary, silent emptiness of the African dry scrub and desert. For me, travelling on foot – this intimate contact with the land and its people – was paramount to the whole endeavour.

I look back now on the arid solitude of the great African Rift Valley and see in my memory the visions of those enormous skies and the scattered thorn trees across its empty, barren wastes. In the throbbing heat of a stone world I see a flash of red from the decoration of a distant lone warrior, the wild lightning storms, glorious flaming sunsets, and the visions of my time by a jade-coloured sea. It was a unique time in a unique place. My memories still pulsate with the wildness of it all. My tribal companions may now be long dead but the pulse of those days still runs in my veins; days before mobile phones, PCs, GPS and social media, days when travelling in remote places was only achieved with loaded animals and a map and compass. And the thrill of its dangers.

When I saw them, the most far-flung parts of North Turkana had probably changed little since the Stone Age. Looking back at my old trip notes, I realise that the era I knew, the era of my walks, has ended, and now that the world is at last waking up to the damage we are doing to our planet, it feels timely and important to share this rare record of a different world at a different time. This, then, is a book I have to write, a story that needs to be shared, from a world that has vanished away in the thirty-five years since I travelled in it.

In today's climate of 'political correctness', it might be construed as high-handed, even 'imperialist', to hire tribesmen to walk through areas where water was so scarce and where we were frequently at risk of being attacked, even killed, by bandits. However, the realities of life in this area were often brutal, and people were used to digging for water and avoiding bandit attacks. My companions were rarely more at risk travelling with me than in their own *manyattas*, which might be raided at any time. And they were always keen to accompany me. I could never claim to be as tough as they were, and although theoretically I may have had the casting vote, in practice we lived entirely as the equals we actually were, as the book repeatedly shows. I would be sad indeed if such retrospectively applied judgements were to impinge on the ability of modern sensibilities to engage with the adventures told in these pages.

I have included a glossary of local words but, as there was little written heritage at the time, spelling was often unreliable. Sometimes I have referred to a Swahili dictionary, but generally accepted the spellings given to me by local people who surely have a right to be the custodians of their own culture. Consequently you might find different spellings in other places. I also relied on their versions of the 'truth' and have described things accordingly. If you find something to be inaccurate I am sorry; accuracy and truth have been my priority throughout.

I really hope you enjoy making the journeys through these pages, sharing the adventures, pleasures and hardships, and 'footing' at my side over the burning, sandy wastes and strewn volcanic rubble of the Northern Frontier District of Kenya.

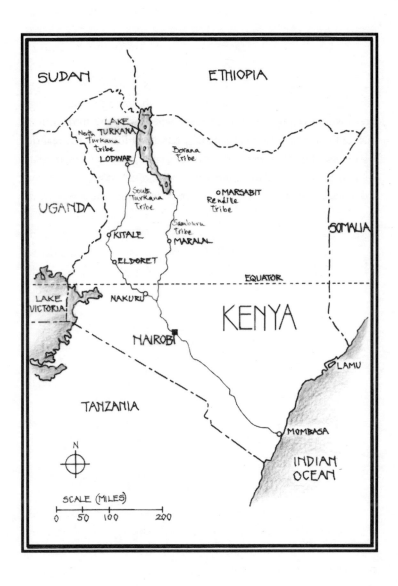

'*Of the gladdest moments in human life, methinks,*
is the departure upon a distant journey into unknown lands.
Shaking off with one mighty effort the fetters of Habit,
the leaden weight of Routine, the cloak of many Cares
and the slavery of Civilization, man feels once more happy.'

Sir Richard Burton KCMG (1821-1890)
Zanzibar vol. 1

Trek 1

North Turkana:
A Land Lost
in the Mists of Time

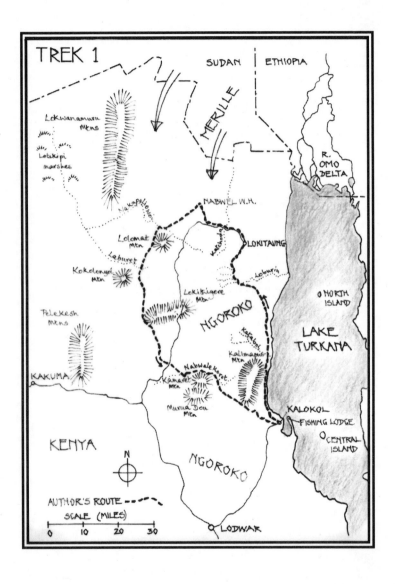

Meeting my inspiration

WHAT DO YOU WEAR to meet a world-famous old-school explorer?
I felt a bit conspicuous in a Prince of Wales-check suit and tie as
I rang his doorbell in Tite Street, London, one April morning in
1978. The intercom by the door crackled drily, 'Yes?'

'Hello, it's John Pakenham'.

The voice warmed, 'Oh yes, do come in. Take the lift to the top
floor. We are number 15.'

The lock buzzed. Inside was one of those old cage lifts with a
sliding concertina door eager to trap unwary fingers, and open to
view from the surrounding stairwell. Arriving at the top, a door in
the corner of the landing was open and outside stood a tall, deeply
tanned man of about 70 in an old sports jacket. Wilfred Thesiger
came across with a firm handshake. 'Come in and have some tea.'

I was not feeling very confident. It is a bit intimidating meeting your hero. I was reassured by the homely smell of old leather from a bookcase which he said contained first editions by the great explorers of the past; people like Burton and Doughty.

Thesiger offered me a chair that faced the window overlooking the Chelsea Physic Garden, and he sat opposite, silhouetted by the light. Behind him on a round table was a large pad of handwriting in pencil which I assumed was a new book. In a quiet but formal Edwardian voice he asked about my own plans, which at that time were starting to focus on a trip to the Sahara, but very vague and uncertain. I simply was not sure how to start.

'You just need to find a lorry or Land Rover going to the very end of the road and then look for a man with camels to be your guide. That's important, without local knowledge you won't get anywhere.'

It sounded so obvious! He started to talk about some of his own long treks in Arabia, where taking local guides had been vital, changing them at the limit of their knowledge for someone who knew the next region. As he spoke his hands emphasised his words, his gold signet ring catching the light. His voice was rather ethereal and detached as his memory cast back through the years. It was a sunny spring day but the old two-bar electric fire was on full, throwing a warm glow across the rug; he was obviously used to warmer climes. He talked easily and I wanted to pinch myself to make sure I was really there, listening to this extraordinary traveller who had spent much of his life in wild places with wild peoples. I was enthralled.

Soon his housekeeper, Molly Emtage, came in with a tray of tea things and biscuits. Thesiger leapt to his feet and his great crocodile mouth cracked into a broad smile beneath the crag of his broken nose, a memento of his boxing days at Oxford. He continued his stories of Arabia and Africa, talking about a journey he had made down the Tana River, Kenya's longest river, in two dugout canoes lashed together. He slept on sandbanks and had to stay vigilant because, as he said, 'River crocs are more dangerous than lake crocs. I think they feel more vulnerable in a restricted space.' He smiled as he told me that years later a sophisticated expedition with inflatables and helicopter drops claimed the 'first' ever navigation of the Tana. We sat with Molly at the kitchen table for some soup and Thesiger glugged sherry into our bowls. It was all rather homely and I looked forward to future visits to Tite Street.

I had always been fascinated by the books of explorers and, as I was working at The London Coliseum for English National Opera, it was not far to walk to Foyles bookshop on Charing Cross Road, where I spent lunchtimes browsing through the travel section on the top floor. One day a book called *Arabian Sands*, by a man named Wilfred Thesiger, had grabbed my attention but I assumed he was another of the long dead Victorians who had wandered across the face of the earth searching for unknown places and peoples. So, when one day an old cousin, Rose Verner, had offered to introduce me, I leapt at the chance. Rose had been lady-in-waiting to the children of the Emperor Haille Salassie during the war, so had connections with Abyssinia (now Ethiopia), where Thesiger was born. What extraordinary luck! So he had kindly invited me to tea to 'talk trips', as he always called it. It was the beginning of a long friendship during which he mentored my own travels, and without which I may never have made the treks described in these pages.

I was thrilled when he also proposed me as a Fellow of the Royal Geographical Society, who had awarded him their prestigious Founder's Medal in 1948. A member of the staff later said to me, 'How on earth do you know Thesiger? When he comes here we feel almost too overawed to speak to him!' Apart from the number of difficult and dangerous treks he had made, the thing that really set him apart was that he had made them all without any modern comforts or gadgetry, just a map and compass and using camels or donkeys. I was determined to do the same.

Some time after I met Thesiger, my brain still full of deserts and camels, a friend suggested making a tour of parts of the Middle East through Jordan, Iraq, south-east Turkey and Syria. This was too good to resist, and, auspiciously, it was there in Aleppo that my treks around Lake Turkana in Kenya really began. Let me explain.

On a stifling hot August day in 1978 I was sitting in a rundown old minibus when a powerful sandstorm blew into Aleppo from the desert. The city came to a standstill, with visibility reduced to arm's length. All the windows were slammed closed until the heat inside was unbearable and everyone was pouring sweat, and when they had to be reopened the sand stuck to everybody and everything, including the book I was trying to read. This was *Journey to the Jade Sea* by John Hillaby, his story about a lengthy trek using camels along the eastern side of Lake Turkana in north-west Kenya, an area that was completely off everyone's radar at the time. The sand of the Syrian desert in my teeth and the dryness of my throat made a perfect backdrop for such a story. The lake had been discovered in 1888 and his was the first significant expedition since the early explorers. I was fascinated by the lake's remoteness, the harshness of its volcanic desert landscapes and the fact that in some weather conditions its water turned jade green. I immediately made up my mind that I wanted to go there one day.

But first, the Sahara.

Saharan preamble

THE FOLLOWING YEAR, having spent nine months working on the second *Stars Wars* movie, *The Empire Strikes Back*, taking care of the eight different versions of R2D2 during the shoot, I flew to Algiers. I set off south on one of the only two sand roads crossing the Sahara, which is actually a vast conglomeration of different deserts merged into one; huge sand seas and endless gravel plains. After a couple of long days in a series of buses I reached Tamanrasset (south of the Hoggar Mountains) in southern Algeria, dead-centre of the Sahara. Amazing that from there to Algiers is almost the same distance as from Algiers to London, yet Tamanrasset is only halfway across the Sahara. An absolutely vast expanse.

I wanted to make a journey with camels up the length of the Teffedest mountain range, which reaches north from the Hoggar mountains to its northern peak, Oudane, also known as Garet el

Djenoun (the turret of the demons). The local Tuareg peoples, who have a brave and blood-soaked history, were terrified of these fearsome demons, the Kel Asouf, so no one would go near it. For weeks I searched in vain for a guide.

At last I met a Tuareg called El Ghamis in the tiny village of Hirhafok, north of the Hoggar mountains, who agreed to take me through the desert to Oudane. He was 38, heavily turbaned, in long, flowing robes, and had spent his whole life working with camel caravans, trading immense distances across the desert, remembering lengthy routes like the back of his hand. Those hands were like the bark of an oak tree, almost brittle with dried, gnarled skin; as were his feet, which had spent a lifetime in scalding sand by day and sub-zero temperatures by night. We had no tent – just wrapped ourselves in camel blankets with long turbans wound round our heads, shuddering with cold. Inside my Icelandic sleeping bag, under the blankets, I was fully dressed, still chilled to the bone, yet El Ghamis' bare feet were always outside his inadequate covers. By contrast the midday heat was extreme. No wonder the rocks shattered with expansion and contraction.

He agreed to take me to the closest point to Oudane that he considered safe, and from there I would have to go alone on foot. To Oudane from Hirhafok and back is almost 150 miles. We took three camels, all of which I found agonising, totally unlike riding a horse. My back was on fire and my bottom was bruised and numb. The Tuareg dictate the speed of their camels by gently jabbing the toes of the left foot into the back of the camel's neck with each step to maintain the rhythm, non-stop, all day long. As a result, experienced cameleers like El Ghamis developed disproportionately large thigh muscles on the left leg.

There was no way I could do that, and after 30 minutes my thigh was screaming. Consequently I tended to lag behind and would sometimes need a light flick with the camel stick to make up speed.

But this was dangerous as the camel sometimes broke into a gallop and on one occasion I was thrown. It is about eleven feet from head-height to the ground, but luckily I landed in the only small patch of sand we crossed that day in a plain of endless shattered rock. No broken bones, but one of my two aluminium water bottles was crushed flat, which would be a serious handicap.

We met very few other Tuareg travellers en route, sharing camp whenever we did. They all thought El Ghamis was taking far too great a risk making this journey to Oudane, and that I, of course, was simply nuts. Conversation was limited as the Tuareg speak an unusual language called Tamasheq, as well as some Arabic, in which I had limited ability. El Ghamis also had about a dozen words of French which were a bit risky as they often did not mean what he thought; such as saying 'cinq' while holding up three fingers. I learnt that *'Mange le chameau'*, was not an invitation to eat one of our camels but a signal that it was time to feed them. But we coped. El Ghamis sang lengthy Tamasheq ballads as we rode along, hauntingly enchanting in the vast emptiness.

Oudane, which rises to over seven and a half thousand feet, seemed little more than a hillock on the horizon when he stopped. That was close enough, he would go no further. We were still 20 miles away. There was nothing else I could do, so next morning I set off on foot with a little food and my remaining one-litre water container (all other water was in goat skins on the camels' loads) to spend the day trudging through the sand. Absolute emptiness – just a few tracks of wild dogs. The nearest settlement was about 60 miles away. My heart thundered. The map marked a well but El Ghamis had said it did not exist. It was a thirsty walk. Close to the base of Oudane I found a small desiccated scattering of old trees and stopped for the night. Their discarded branches allowed me to keep a blaze alive all night to ward off any wild animals. Perhaps it also warded off the Kel Asouf demons.

The next morning I considered scrambling up the lower slopes of the mountain, but with my limited water ration I should already be starting back. And might El Ghamis' terror of the Kel Asouf make him lose his nerve and abandon me? As I skirted some mountains to the south I took a wrong turning and ended up in a blind valley over a mile from my intended route. That really scared me. To be lost in such solitude was terrifying; a death sentence. Shuddering with fear, I retraced my route and at last came across my tracks from the previous day. By now I was dangerously parched and very little water remained. I was increasingly worried about how long it would last. I had read statistics about water requirements at these high temperatures – closer to a litre an hour than a litre for two days. A little further on I came across the tracks of a small pack of wild dogs who had found my footsteps left in unblemished sand and picked up my scent. It was unnerving to see how they had turned to follow my tracks. I thanked God for that fire.

In the early afternoon a movement on the horizon disconcerted me as I believed I was quite alone. I had heard stories of dangerous smugglers trading illegal firearms into Libya, but as this shimmering blur gradually took shape it morphed into El Ghamis and our three camels. He had been so frightened for me among the Kel Asouf that he had not slept, and despite his own fears had bravely come to find me. It was a happy reunion, albeit after a separation of only two days, and we immediately stopped to make tea and bake the leaden Tuareg bread, *targilla*, which is baked in hot sand under the fire. I drank and drank.

After three months in the Sahara I returned to London, much wiser about travelling in desolate places, also having learnt about my own tremulous reactions to the dangers. I had loved it and an intrepid traveller was developing in me. It had been my first trip with animals and I longed to do more, far from 'civilisation' and remote from roads and vehicles. That, I felt, was the real world.

Nairobi: terrifying travellers' tales

I WAS STILL IN BLISSFUL ignorance of exactly what to expect in Turkana when, on 20 November 1980, I flew to Nairobi. Throughout the year I had been planning the trip as much as I could, while working on a film called *Dragon Slayer*. Researching things in those days was much harder than today as there was no internet or personal computer, and little written information about an area that was almost totally unknown. As I disembarked, unsure what to do next, someone suggested I stay at the Hurlingham Hotel. I loved it: a delightful ex-colonial bungalow built in 1922 with very simple rooms opening onto a terraced walkway under a typical red-painted corrugated-iron roof which drummed loudly and excitingly when the rain was passionate. This overlooked an extravaganza of hibiscus, lilies and agapanthus. Heavy scent from the spiralled petals of frangipani hung thickly and voluptuously in the tropical warmth, and everywhere was bougainvillea in a fanfare of colours. This was perfect and although a long walk from the city centre, without electricity during the afternoons, with phones which died with every rainstorm and window catches a burglar would have loved, it was a haunt of old Kenya 'hands', and I was lucky to be there.

Bruce, who owned the Hurlingham, was intrigued by my plans and said, 'You're in luck, the chap in the next room is Arthur Scott who used to be the manager of the fishing lodge at Kalokol where you're headed. He'll have lots of useful information and contacts.'

So Arthur and I pulled up chairs overlooking the garden and pored over maps together while he started to lay out the ground for me. 'You have to understand that Kenya is like two different countries. There are the savannahs of the south with the famous game parks and the tourists, and the little-known deserts of the north, called The Northern Frontier District. This area is still very wild, with traditional tribal conflict and continual raiding of animals.'

Arthur leaned back in his chair and explained, 'Security issues change all the time, depending usually on whether the rains failed or not. At times of drought the amount of raiding intensifies as, if animals are dying, the easiest thing to do is pinch someone else's. Now, after a few good years, there's a serious drought again, with famine in the north, so it's much more dangerous.'

I cleared my throat rather nervously. I could understand the logic of this but was shocked to hear him continue, 'However, that's probably the least of your problems. The real dangers are from *ngoroko* and *shifta*', and he went on to explain that the *ngoroko* were an assortment of Turkana bandits who might raid in small groups or in hundreds, stealing animals and often attacking people just out of sheer sadism. They attack their own tribe as well as neighbouring ones, and are greatly feared, being numerous on the west side of the lake. I swallowed hard, this was not what I wanted to hear.

'The *shifta* are a slightly different proposition, being originally politically motivated. Since the British drew out the national boundaries in East Africa, Somalia has claimed that a large chunk of north-east Kenya should be theirs, so they began sending bands of raiders into the area. This led to what were called the *shifta* wars, and since then they have continued to be a menace. Like the *ngoroko* they wander about in bands, stealing animals and killing large numbers of people. Fortunately they are all on the east side of the lake. So far.'

The Nation newspaper carried reports almost daily of attacks and murder on an increasing scale and automatic weapons were now commonplace. 'Only yesterday the police shot dead six *shifta* at El Wak in the north-east,' Arthur added. 'To cross to the east side of the lake now would be suicidal. Just the other day a group of Turkana fishermen, asleep under their sails, were all shot in the head.' Did I detect a glint in Arthur's eye? Was he enjoying this? 'You'd need a permit anyway to travel on the east side now.'

'Good heavens, thank God I'm heading for the west side.' This was serious stuff and my mouth was dry.

Arthur agreed with my plan to travel in north Turkana on the west side, which he thought had recently become safer, although now the south of the region had taken an opposite turn. 'But don't go too far west as the Ugandan army has been raiding there, stealing herds and killing anyone in the way. And in the south, the Karamajong tribe from Uganda have also been crossing the border to raid. They are related to the Turkana and share the same bloodthirsty traditions.' Even the West Pokot tribe south of Turkana were attacking the occasional lorry heading north, and sometimes killing the driver. Unfortunately that was the only road which entered the region, so I would be on it. This was all a bit of a bombshell. Was anywhere safe there?

I chewed over my plans with Arthur, starting from Kalokol with some local tribesmen and donkeys, and walking north to Lokitaung, perhaps even Todenyang on the Ethiopian border if we made good speed (two names on the map about which I knew absolutely nothing, but imagined to be pretty wild and desolate). Then to cut down south-west away from the lake towards Kakuma (a name of which I had at least heard), and finally loop back to Kalokol via Lodwar, (the tribal capital). As I knew so little of the country the route was not terribly important, so long as it gave me a good insight into the region and its people. I also had little idea what sort of terrain I would be crossing, although the map made it clear it was essentially volcanic desert scoured by dry riverbeds. The journey itself, whatever it held, would be full of interest and undoubtedly exciting.

Arthur said that this would be a pretty lengthy excursion at the hottest time of year, but how donkeys would cope or what speed they would maintain he had no idea. It could only be a blueprint, subject to change. It is easy to draw out grand schemes on a map, but another to actually cover the ground. Fortunately my only time restriction was how long my cash would last. There were, of course, no banks in the wild north of the country, so I would be carrying a lot of cash. A prize target for *ngoroko*.

It was still my first day in Kenya and I was exhausted, so with this startling news swirling around my brain I headed to the bar for a glass of White Cap beer. I had come to Kenya full of curiosity to explore a remote area, not to get myself killed, but that now seemed a terrifying possibility. Should I rethink my plans, or even cancel? Of course not, I would never live it down! But I had a night of grotesque and savage dreams.

Over the next days Arthur gave me more useful information about the risks of crocodiles, and the names of some useful contacts in Kalokol. He also told me where the Nairobi Map Centre was, as

I needed to find the charts I had failed to locate at Stanfords in London. But once I got there they told me that as they showed sensitive areas I needed the permission of the Director of Survey. So I walked up to his office near the university, where a disinterested clerk told me that all applications must be made in writing. Off to find a stationers for paper and pen. Once back, the clerk took delight in saying, 'You are now too late... It is now lunchtime.'

'Damn!'

Just then the director's door opened and a plump bureaucrat emerged. I smiled pathetically at him but he hurried past. I followed lamely. Outside he swung into his old Peugeot, turned the key and I heard the grinding of a dying battery. He cursed and sat uncertainly. Lunch was calling. I seized the moment and put my head through his window.

'Can I possibly help?'

'Damned flat battery!'

'Let me push-start you,' I volunteered, feeling that perhaps the odds were changing.

'Oh that would be frightfully decent of you,' he smiled. 'And by the way, did you want to see me about something?'

I explained briefly about the permission that I needed and in a matter of moments I had the signed form in my hand before I gave him a good shove. He got his lunch and I got my maps. I liked this city! However, this permission still did not extend to maps of the highly unstable borders themselves, so when in the extreme north I had to resort to vague Kenyan road maps.

Nairobi was rather an attractive city with some good modern buildings, clean streets and many fragrant flowering shrubs and trees. Lines of tall jacarandas heavy with their lavender-blue flower trumpets stretched up from colourful pools of discarded petals. The streets were lively and bustling but beset with conmen at every turn, each with a hard-luck story to extract money from the unwary foreigner. Newly arrived tourists were easily spotted by their pale skins so it was important to be vigilant, but once I had earned my sunburn and dusty clothes I was largely ignored.

The currency was the Kenyan shilling, the same value as the old British shilling, so 20 shillings were the same as one pound sterling. Arthur had given me some clues about the price of animals: 'A donkey will set you back about 150 shillings, a camel probably 350, and about 80 for a sheep.' I never really discovered whether Arthur's figures were a bit out of date or whether, more likely, my white skin always upped the price. Foreigners are fair game the world over.

Before setting off north I wanted to visit Sheikh Mohammed Abeid El-Haj, an old friend of Pa's in Mombasa, who had been his assistant for many years in Zanzibar, but had fled from the revolution in 1964. The first-class sleeper to Mombasa was a delight, with the cabins panelled in East African mahogany, *mvulu*, and the dining car was of restaurant standards with smartly uniformed waiters and crisp white linen tablecloths. It rumbled along slowly, allowing time for a good night's sleep, and arrived in the lush coastal strip with rain hammering down and the ground just dancing mud.

I spent a few delightful days with Moh'd Abeid and his family, who treated me royally. 'Why do you want to go to this crazy place? Don't go with these naked savages, stay here and be comfortable!' It was a tempting offer. Turkana was clearly off the edge of the known world. He put me in touch with his son Omar who owned several of the best restaurants in Nairobi and we became great friends. Whenever in Nairobi I used to stay in his beautiful house surrounded by exquisite gardens. I was very lucky.

Into Turkana and 'going native'

SOMEONE INTRODUCED ME to an American missionary on leave from Kalokol, Dale Beverley, who was about to return there. 'Sure, I have a spare seat in the Land Cruiser and could give you a lift to Kitale, maybe all the way to Kalokol. But I'm leaving tomorrow.' So I repacked hurriedly and next day he picked me up and we set off in the late morning.

Not long after leaving Nairobi the road reached the great escarpment of the Rift Valley, clearly visible from space. A smattering of corrugated-iron roofs glinted in the sunshine far below. This view would soon be transformed, as the population would increase rapidly in the coming years. We passed the famous lakes of Naivasha, Elmenteita and Nakuru and, late in the day, climbed towards Eldoret.

I was all eyes, soaking up this marvellous country, the rich red soil and lush green vegetation. My first crossing of the equator was a thrill, and it was long after dark when we rolled into Kitale.

Dale somewhat quietened my concerns about the aggression of the Turkana tribe: 'Don't worry too much about that, it's just their natural trait.'

'What a relief to hear that their penchant for widespread murder and mayhem is such a harmless trait,' I said quizzically.

He laughed. 'But they have no social niceties whatsoever. Anything you need you'll have to beg for and likewise they won't ever stop begging from you.'

Kitale was a small town, a relic of British days with a smart club and restaurant, now thoroughly African, and after a night staying with a friend of Dale's, we continued north. I had managed to pick up a couple of sacks of *posho*, the local maize flour, for which I had needed written permission from the District Officer (DO), as we were entering a famine zone and there was likely to be a shortage. Strangely though, it turned out to be easier to find *posho* in Turkana than Kitale. Somehow we managed to squeeze the sacks in on top of all Dale's paraphernalia: foodstuffs, motorcycle parts, things for the generator and a new fridge. As far as I could see, American missionaries did not exactly survive off the land!

The road north curled through the low forested mountains, with Pokot tribesmen panning for gold among huge tumbled boulders in a river below us. Once over the Marech Pass everything changed abruptly to the flat sun-baked plains of south Turkana. Soon there was little but acacia trees and the chimneys of termite nests towering over the scorched dusty ground, crisscrossed by dry river beds carved out by infrequent flash floods. Not a hint of moisture. The Land Cruiser left a dense plume of suffocating dust in its wake. From now on we would see no more tarmac: the few roads in Turkana were all sand and stone, sometimes washed away by rare deluges. Although I said nothing, I was feeling a bit anxious, as I saw at last the kind of terrain that I would be walking through.

It was already aggressively hot, and as we drove north it became hotter and hotter. Night had already settled when we drove through Lodwar, the administrative capital of the region, where Jomo Kenyatta had been imprisoned during Mau Mau days, and we pulled into Kalokol, at the end of the road, an hour later. It was too dark to see much, but the headlights revealed a little shanty town with some shops no bigger than garden sheds, behind which were tribal *manyattas* of grass huts.

The mission house of concrete blocks was outside the centre and we quickly unloaded, soon sitting down to a communal supper with Dale's wife, a mission pilot, a couple of nurses from the hospital and a visiting ornithologist. (Surely a perfect cast for an Agatha Christie murder!) It was not long before we were laying out our sleeping things on the cooler verandah outside.

In this intense heat the lake evaporated a quarter of an inch a day, and with very few seasonal rivers feeding it except the River Omo from the Ethiopian mountains, it was gradually losing the battle to survive. Consequently, when the ornithologist and I went down to the shoreline in the morning we found it had receded over a hundred yards so that the jetty was now a long walkway to reach it. I lugged my bags into the open boat which took people across Ferguson's Gulf to the tip of the long sand spit encircling most of the gulf, where the fishing lodge stood. It was a great position, commanding lovely views across the lake, and we settled down with a beer to absorb this marvellous sight.

The lodge was a venue for extreme fishermen who sometimes caught Nile Perch of over 400lbs (181kgs). Tiddlers of under 100lbs were not even recorded. The crocs must be well fed; a man would be just a snack! My friend was going to stay here, but it was quite expensive and I did not want to waste cash as the nearest bank was back in Kitale. But I was not sure what to do for the night.

A tremble of excitement to be here at last ran up my spine as I sat gazing across the silence, this great sheet of sparkling water stretching across a magical land; the world's largest desert lake, 160 miles long and roughly 25 miles wide, had earned the nickname of Jade Sea because in different weather conditions it would change from sapphire blue, through bluish grey, to jade green. Constant evaporation of this captive water with no outlet had made it increasingly brackish with dissolved mineral salts, to a point where most Europeans could not drink it. Even Thesiger refused, despite his ascetic tastes. However, I assumed that if local people drank it, it must be potable, even if the saltiness left you feeling thirstier than before. Throughout my future treks it sustained me for long periods.

A local Turkana lad wandered over. 'How are you? My name is David Jumale. What is your name?' He had an intelligent face and wore a blue tee-shirt with green school-uniform shorts, and said he lived with his mother in a *manyatta* about a mile along the same sand spit. When he suggested I stay there I suspiciously wondered what would be the catch. But I had nowhere else to go so gratefully accepted. I bought him a beer and we all sat watching pelicans, storks and herons, flamingos, pied kingfishers and sea eagles. An occasional fisherman paddled past on a small crude raft of four or five palm logs lashed together, using rough poles as oars. It struck me as a precarious sort of boat to float over the heads of submerged crocs and short-tempered hippos.

When the sweltering heat subsided, we hoisted my three tubular nylon bags and the metal camera case and said goodbye to the ornithologist. He was concerned. 'Are you sure it's safe to go and stay in a native village on your own?' If this was unsafe, so close to a tourist lodge, how would I cope in really dangerous areas where there might be a real risk of having my throat cut as I slept? Sometimes you just have to trust your instinct and rely on the goodness of people.

As it turned out, David's mother and sisters were delightful and made me very welcome, despite having no common language. The *manyatta* was a collection of about fifteen grass huts on the hot sand of the beach. The water of the gulf lapped a few yards away where a couple of the log rafts were pulled up and almost naked men mended their nets (*see photo* 5).

The women all wore goatskin skirts, naked to the waist but with great heaps of beads around their necks and arms, while the skinny children with swollen bellies were all stark naked, with just a few beads round their necks. There was no sign of David's father or any brothers; perhaps away fishing. Almost everyone was barefoot.

The family's hut, like all the others, was tiny, about six-feet wide and five-feet high, and they had added a curved windbreak to shield the opening; all made entirely of grass with nothing to close the entrance (*see photo* 6). How they all fitted inside I had no idea. There was certainly no privacy. They cooked on small charcoal fires with the pot balanced over the flames on three stones, a system used the world over which prevents rocking, like a three-legged stool. Seven or eight paces away, a similar hut was going to be my bedroom and to store all my stuff (which seemed an obscene quantity compared with their own lack of possessions).

The neighbours naturally turned out to stare at this interloper from the lodge, and were soon bringing things to try and sell me: spears; wrist-knives; bead necklaces; head stools; walking sticks and fish-vertebrae aprons. These aprons were made of strings of fish vertebrae laced together over a goatskin, decorative and unusual but heavy to wear, and presumably for ceremonial occasions (*see photo* 3). After I had bought a spear, which I thought would be useful on the trek, they drifted off.

We ate together, my first meal of *posho*, which was to become the staple diet of all my treks, a rather tasteless, leaden, mashed-potato texture, made from maize flour and eaten throughout East Africa. At first I hated it. To relieve its boredom it is usually eaten with a meat or vegetable stew called *mboga*, but sometimes also made runnier with added sugar, which they called 'porridge'. As the sun dived for the western horizon the girls began to dance and sing, something they did every evening, before surprising me by coming together for family prayers. The missions had clearly made their presence felt even here along one of the country's most far-flung roads, Turkana's only tenuous link with civilisation.

The following morning David found a man to row us across to Kalokol so that I could start arranging the safari. I wanted to find David Biwott, who, Arthur had said, could help find guides for my trek. But first David and I got stuck into my shopping list and, going from one *duka* to the next, gradually tracked down sacks of *posho*, dry beans, rice, sugar, tea and salt. David was a great help with constant advice: 'This price too high,' or, 'This one good man, he make good price,' or again, 'This is too bad, very old, we find other place'.

The *dukas* which lined the dusty street usually sold much the same things as each other, depending on what the last lorry had delivered. They had cement floors and wooden walls with a crude counter, behind which were shelves and sacks of everything from foodstuffs to plastic jerry cans, cheap mirrors, blankets and garish tee-shirts. A cacophony of cheap and mostly useless ephemera hung from nails in the walls and ceiling. I picked up other items such as aluminium cooking pots without handles (called *sufuria*) and a *panga*, the local style of machete.

It was very important to take a pound or two of chewing tobacco, much loved by the Turkana, who, even in times of famine, would beg for it more than food. Powerful jets of yellow saliva were often squirted in long arcs and half-chewed balls of tobacco were kept tucked behind the ear for later use.

The washing powder 'Omo' was everywhere as were, surprisingly, packets of spaghetti, although these were viewed suspiciously by the rural people, who understandably assumed it was made of worms.

Back at David's *manyatta* we ate tilapia fresh from the lake, the scales scraped off with a wrist knife, before being dropped into the pan where they fried alive, flapping about in the simmering fat. It horrified me, but was it my place to try to impose western values? I was here as an observer not an evangelist. In tribal Africa there was precious little understanding of, or concern for, another creature's torment. Again we watched the girls dancing, increasingly silhouetted by a fiery sunset sinking into its liquid reflection on the water of the gulf. I felt a glow of confidence that things were under way at last and slept soundly on my sleeping bag with a gentle breeze whispering through the grass wall beside me.

Gathering men and beasts

DAVID BIWOTT SENT ME a note to say he had found some people to be my companions. I was keen to meet them and went to the compound behind his *duka*. Biwott was a nice chap from one of the tribes downcountry, probably Kikuyu. He introduced them, two traditional tribesmen who had their own donkeys, and a 'learned man' who spoke a little English.

I was immediately wary of the learned man, who was dressed in western clothes with a bizarre sort of Australian bush hat and sunglasses. He seemed nervous, especially when I outlined my plans for the route to walk. 'I must need 40 shillings every day,' he said. £2 a day may seem outlandishly cheap in today's context but in those days, in that world, it was out of the question and he knew it. The look of relief when I turned him down lit up his face.

But the other two inspired me with confidence, tribesmen from the bush, dressed in simple shabby clothes, who seemed relaxed and comfortable in their own skins. Of course they spoke no English, but they smiled easily and we seemed to understand each other. They were familiar with some of the areas we might be going through. Biwott translated, 'This *msungu* will pay you 15 shillings a day, and he also wants to hire some of your donkeys.'

The concept of hiring was unknown to them so I suggested buying three donkeys and selling them back afterwards, but they did not want to sell any. I had an idea: 'I will pay the donkeys a wage.'

They roared with laughter at this daft idea and came back almost immediately, 'Donkey carry like two men, so *msungu* pay wage of two men to all donkey?'

We all laughed together. Cunning – I admired their style! We threw the idea back and forth a few times and settled on a fixed sum of 150 shillings (£7.50) for each animal, irrespective of the length of the walk. Almost as soon as I had agreed to this I remembered that it was the value Arthur had given me to buy a donkey outright. They had won the first round, and followed up their advantage by asking what would happen if a donkey died.

'If a donkey dies I will increase the price to the same as a new donkey.'

They agreed too easily so I wondered what arguments would ensue over the value of a new animal, but hoped it would not come to that.

I told them I would pay them an advance to leave with their families while they were away. Western thinking! This mystified them. 'Why does he give money when we do no work?' Our first meeting had gone well and I was sure that they were capable country men well used to life in this harsh land. And importantly, with a sense of humour, which would be good when times were tough. I liked them.

Edung was the taller of the two, with wide-set, slightly mongoloid eyes and high cheek bones. He had an aquiline nose with wide nostrils, and very prominent collar bones. His skin was more bronze than black and pendulous earrings swung from each earlobe, with a large orange bead above a filigree of fine chains. His movements were elegant in that tribal way a Westerner might think effeminate, but he was certainly not that (*see photo 2*).

His friend Ekadeli had a lighter build, but turned out to be the tougher of the two. He had the same burnished complexion as Edung but a more oval, finely featured face, ending in a small pointed chin sporting a tiny, wispy beard (*see photo 1*). They both had an often-impish sense of humour and would easily break into radiant smiles, which endeared them to me.

Edung was in a grubby vest and old khaki shorts while Ekadeli wore a worn bush shirt and a loin cloth that might once have been white but, like most clothes in the bush, had gradually taken on the colour of the dust. On their feet they both had tyre sandals, the standard footwear of East African rural people, the sole cut from the tread of a tyre with straps made from strips of inner tube nailed into its edge. Simple and almost indestructible, and if a nail came out it could be tapped back in with a stone. They were lean but not thin, fit and supple with closely cropped hair, and like all Turkana tribesmen they always carried a fighting stick and a head stool.

The following day Biwott found me another 'learned' man, this time a tall chap called Thomas Esekon. Like his predecessor he liked smarter western clothes, obviously a bi-product of a rare primary-school education. (There was no rural education beyond this level, which usually took place during teenage years.) Thomas asked how we would be travelling and when I said 'walking with loaded donkeys' he looked disappointed. 'So we go by footing,' he said, crestfallen, presumably having dreamed of lolling in a comfortable Land Rover. But he was a great improvement on the last applicant and asked for 20 shillings a day (for which I suspected he had been primed). Thomas was blacker than the other two, with a grizzled beard and a broader nose, also slim (no one in Turkana carried an extra ounce of fat), and had that frequent characteristic of taller people, a slight stoop, which made him look up from under clenched eyebrows, unfortunately painting him rather like a Dickensian villain.

My daily commute across Ferguson's Gulf in whatever boat I could hire had become rather tedious and Biwott kindly suggested I move into his house in Kalokol until the safari started. That evening, when I told David's mother that I would be moving across to the town she implored me to take David on the trek as well. He was only sixteen but had worked hard, and his English was better than Thomas's. However, I worried he would find the long walks difficult.

'No, I walk all day, I can walk very hard, and I work.'

He asked for 10 shillings a day and I agreed.

Most people in the towns now had 'Christian' names, the influence of the missions. It annoyed me that they obviously considered their proper tribal names in some way inferior. Personally, I questioned the right of the missions to be there at all, promulgating the teachings of a two-thousand-year-old Middle Eastern prophet from a culture so different from African tribal life, and so abrogating their own traditional beliefs. My own grandparents had been missionaries in China, and after retiring from the Colonial Service my father had joined the staff of a Middle Eastern mission. Consequently, I was brought up influenced by missionary attitudes, about which I increasingly had grave doubts.

However innocently, missionaries were arrows in the quiver of white supremacy, and had softened the path for early traders, as there were many perks to be gained by local people accessing the trappings of the affluent society from which they came. The missions were, however, the only source of medicines in isolated places, and some of the Irish and Italian missionaries I came across in wild areas had seriously interacted with the tribes; one splendid Italian priest I met thought nothing of grabbing his rifle and setting off with his parishioners to do battle with marauding raiders. I discovered later that Thesiger refused to use Christian names, insisting on proper tribal ones. He was, however, a great inventor of nicknames.

I discovered that Thomas and Edung were brothers, but as they were so dissimilar I wondered whether that was a 'bond brotherhood' in some way. Thomas rarely wore the traditional *shuka* (a colourful rectangle of cloth loved by the tribesmen of the NFD, usually worn with two corners knotted together and thrown over a shoulder.) He prided himself on his Western clothes, while Edung was quite at home with the life of a semi-naked herdsman. But they did have one thing in common, a habit of whingeing when things did not go their way. This had already started about my decision to take David. 'The problem is the boy, he cannot come.' Why were they being such a nuisance? Were they trying to keep the money between themselves? I insisted that David would come.

I was slowly getting used to this aggressive heat, which by 9am was already 32°C (90°F) and rising to about 40°C (104°F). The donkeys were on their way, but where from and how long would it take? I was already learning that estimating distance was an extremely flexible science, like using an elastic tape measure. But while I was dispensing our supplies into sacks suitable for the donkeys' loads Edung turned up, having come on ahead, leaving Ekadeli to bring the donkeys in the evening. I assumed correctly that Ekadeli was the most proficient animal handler.

David and I wandered in the shade of a forest of doum palms north of the town. These multi-stemmed palms were rarely over 12 feet high here because of the dryness of the ground, but could sometimes look more like the tall swaying palms of picture postcards when conditions were right, and the Turkana loved to use their edible black fruits as large beads in their decoration. The ground below was a pink/grey gravel scattered with small white stones which led down to the shore of the lake.

A man walked towards us at great speed along the shore of the lake having quickly covered about 20 miles. He was dressed in just an old *shuka*, the colour of the surrounding dust, and wore tyre sandals. He carried no food or water. According to David, 'In old days men walk long way, even 80 miles, carry nothing. They hope they find, but they walk fast.' The younger Turkana, as in most cultures, admitted that their forbears were made of tougher stuff.

We stopped at a little tea house called the Molo Hotel where bottles of beer were almost too hot to touch. Why had they not blown their tops off? Thankfully they also served much more thirst-quenching tea. Inside was Edung, now rich on the advance I had paid, eating *posho* with his wife. She was dressed traditionally in just a goatskin skirt with the usual strings of beads piled round her neck, and I found it reassuring to see that they were proper country people from the deserts rather than from the town. It was meltingly hot.

The donkeys had arrived and Thomas took me to the *manyatta* to see them. They had brought six from which to choose the best three, and Thomas explained that some were stronger than others although they all looked exactly the same to me. Anyway, Ekadeli would make the decision. There was also a heap of donkey panniers to hold our things, an ingenious traditional design made of four ovals bent out of flexible laths, each cross-strung with rawhide cords like very large tennis-racket heads. Their longer sides were tied together at their centres alternately so that, viewed from one end, they formed a 'W' shape, and so sat astride the donkeys' backs with the outer 'wings' opened outwards to fill with luggage. Their tops were then tied in towards the centre to grip it tightly and below them the donkey's backs were protected by several layers of sacking and dried goatskins, the whole assemblage being held in place by a rope girth and a strip of rawhide looped round the rump under the tail. I sorted through them and chose the three which looked the sturdiest, as they would be a vital part of our kit. Tomorrow we would leave.

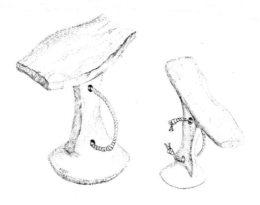

Slow steps into a harsh new world

NEXT MORNING I was up early, feeling secretly apprehensive, making final alterations to the packing. As usual a crowd of villagers assembled to stare, and finally after a last breakfast of *posho* porridge, we loaded up and set off. It was 12 December 1980, 22 days after I had arrived in Kenya. I was 29.

Once we were past the last of the of the *manyattas* surrounding the town I secretly felt almost shaky with excitement to be underway at last. I had dreamed of this for ages, and it was finally becoming real. What would the future hold? Or the *ngoroko*? It was impossible not to feel flutters of lurking fear.

We walked north, about a mile from the lakeshore. My first impression of the terrain was its relentlessness; grey gritty gravel tinged with buff, occasionally with faint patches of darker grey, and sprinkled with pale stones. It was dotted with clumps of doum palms or stunted, broadleaf trees, and between them I glimpsed the lake to our right. Graceful acacia trees with spreading canopies gave a hint of grandeur to the drab colour. Where the land did undulate a little, for some reason the slightly higher ground was often covered by knee-high grey-green spiny scrub, a few bearing small dusty-pink flowers (*see photo 7*).

We infrequently saw small *manyattas* of six or seven grass huts, and herdsmen watching groups of a dozen goats. They always carried a thin stick, usually held across their shoulders like a yoke, their loincloths and *shukas* blending with the landscape, invariably a sandy sack-cloth hue from long years in these dusty desert conditions. A woman walked past, dressed as usual in a goatskin skirt with heavy necklaces of beads and carrying a large cloth bundle on her head, balanced on a coiled grass circlet.

The distant mountains to the north hung in a grey-blue curtain along the horizon under an unremitting dome of unblemished blue. This was not an environment for birdsong, the only sounds an occasional rustle of the breeze and the constant animated chatter of my companions, interjected by little high-pitched yelps as they reacted to the conversation. The ground was unmarked by vehicle tracks or animal prints, apart from the wiry thread of a goat track showing paler in the greyness. The tremble of heat wobbled over the ground and small dust devils cut across our path.

The donkeys plodded along, unconcerned where we were going or how far. Already I was worried how slow they were, slowing or stopping unless continually encouraged by the little clicks of the tongue which the Turkana use. I had started off with the stick rather than the carrot approach, completely inappropriate, and they would have been justified in resenting me. I soon mended my ways and hoped to earn their respect. I doubt that I ever did but they certainly earned mine as time went by. Thesiger had told me that donkeys walk at about 2mph but ours were going a bit slower than that and we seemed unlikely to cover the entire route I had hoped for. My budget was not unlimited.

I could only talk with Edung and Ekadeli through the interpretation of Thomas or David, which I always had to ask for, as they had obviously not been interpreters before. I wondered how much of their conversation was about me, and whether it was disparaging. Was I being neurotic? Thomas returned to his theme of why David could not come with us. 'The boy is the problem. He is too much young and he cannot make long walk.' Already I was finding Thomas irritating and even wondered about sending him back instead.

That first evening I bought the catch of a fisherman, including a very large catfish and, although it had been an easy day, I decided to turn in early. Using my sleeping bag as a mattress I slipped inside the liner as I often did. Edung was shocked: 'If *ngoroko* come in night we run very fast, but you stuck in sack and they cut your throat.'

'Thanks for such encouraging advice!' But I knew he was right. 'OK, in future I will sleep under it, not in it.' The thought that *ngoroko* could even be active so close to Kalokol was a shock. Was nowhere safe from them?

That triggered a conversation not only about the *ngoroko*, but also the Merille raiders from Ethiopia. The *ngoroko* were apparently quite different from inter-tribal raiders, ne'er-do-wells who would attack anyone anywhere to murder, rape and pillage for the sheer sake of theft and destruction. Although usually moving in small groups they could sometimes attack in hundreds. A most unsettling subject for the first night of the trek, and all night I tossed and turned under a bright moon, plagued by images of blood-curdling killers creeping up on me.

Probably the most important preparation for making a trek in a dangerous area is the re-evaluation of our own lives, learning to dispense with the cosseted importance we Westerners imagine that we deserve, and accepting our own fragile mortality. This is essential if we are to feel at ease in this potentially hostile environment, and it always took me a few days to adjust to this different risk assessment. Thesiger said to me years later (spontaneously quoting Meinertzhagen), 'I have absolutely no belief whatsoever in the sanctity of human life', an attitude formed of necessity over a lifetime in wild places.

Next day we passed a small mission bungalow near the Kataboi River, which of course was dry as dust, so, for the first of countless times, we used a waterhole dug by local people (*see photo 9*). This one was 18 inches deep. Ekadeli dropped into it with one of our enamel mugs and repeatedly filled our largest *sufuria* for the donkeys to drink from, while more water trickled in to puddle round his grimy toes. Only then did we fill our plastic jerry cans. The donkeys were always our priority, needing to drink every day if possible. I discovered that ground water is always sweeter than that from ponds or rivers, filtered through the sand and gravel...despite grimy toes!

Our safari was of course a bit different from how nomadic Turkana travelled, mainly because a *msungu* (white man) was paying, so everyone expected a regular supply of goats for the pot. Already there were mutterings about finding one, so Edung and Ekadeli went to look for a herdsman. He wanted 100 shillings – above Arthur's estimate – so I refused and the others agreed. But a gnarled old shepherd sold us a sheep – impossible to tell how big it was under all its wool. As it was already getting late we tied the poor creature to a tree and went to bed, intending to spend the next day preparing and cooking it. I had mixed feelings about the impending slaughter.

In the morning, as Edung tried to lead it on a tether to where it was to be dispatched, the sheep sensibly had other ideas. Soon it was trying a range of escape tactics, tugging for freedom, digging its hooves into the sand with legs rigid, or making dashes into dense thorn scrub where we could only follow painfully.

'Catch it!'

'Oh no, not in there!'

'Ouch!'

'You push, I pull!'

'Lift the back legs, then no running!'

'Argh, it's kicked me!'

My Turkana colleagues were completely outclassed by these Houdini-esque gambits, feeling uncomfortable and embarrassed, trying to unknot it from its tangle of thorns while it pushed in further. Eventually extricated from the barbs it played its trump card. It sat down and would not budge.

'It is too much heavy.'

'Drag it!'

'Try roll it?'

At last it was pulled over onto its left side, Thomas held its muzzle while Edung picked up my hunting knife and deftly cut through the loose skin of its throat to reveal the jugular vein which he cut through deeply. I was appalled and fascinated equally by this gory event. Strangely ashamed. How often do films show us someone's throat being cut? Have any directors ever seen it? The powerful spurting blood flooded the gaping wound and poured into a *sufuria* which David held to catch it. The poor creature was so exhausted that it made no attempt to struggle and died quietly and quickly.

I was shocked by the callous matter-of-fact attitude of the others, grinning and joking. But for them this was a frequent procedure, carried out countless times since childhood. Over time I would be responsible for the deaths of many goats, but while I almost got used to it, the sense of guilt never quite left me. There is nothing macho or impressive about taking life, but it is sometimes necessary.

Ekadeli laid it on a bed of palm fronds and within the hour it was skinned, topped and tailed, gutted and hauled up by its back legs to the branch of a tree to be split in half down its spine. The meat was teased from the legs and cut up in a zig-zag fashion so that each strip ended up about six feet long to be dried in the sun, looped like macabre Christmas decorations over cords strung between trees.

As always happened, a family had turned up to sit and wait hopefully for some presents from the carcass, and was rewarded with half a bag of *posho* together with the blood and intestines, and later the bones to crack for their marrow. This might seem a mean gift to our Western eyes, but in this hungry land they were all acceptable foodstuffs, full of nutrients. Normally only males were slaughtered, the females kept for breeding, and the only parts considered inedible were the skin and bone casing, horns and hooves, and the spleen and penis. I have often eaten every other part.

The offal was always boiled or fried first as it would not keep in the heat, and the ribcage stewed or roasted on the fire. The entire head and the fatty tail were set to roast slowly on a fire of dried palm fronds, its open, staring eyes seeming to follow me reproachfully. Rather ghoulish. Cooking fat was always bought in large tins called Kimbo and was the only additive other than salt and sometimes a spicy sachet called Mchuzi Mix sold in every *duka*. After sharing the boiled offal, which was always tasty, I found before me some ribs, large lumps of fat from the tail, part of the brain together with half the tongue (looking exactly like half the tongue cut straight from the back of the mouth), and an eyeball. I was not one to turn away from a challenge but this was a bit daunting! The tongue tasted good as long as I could disassociate it from the continual tap-tap as David beside me chewed the gums from the teeth of the lower jaw.

Looking up at Edung he grinned as he held the head, still clothed in burnt wool, and tore the cheeks from it with his teeth, the nose on one side and an ear swinging on the other. I chewed slowly on the eyeball. Oh God, would this macabre scene be repeated often? Of course it would. I dozed, feeling a little green.

In the evening we made *posho* again, and ate the remaining ribs. David said, 'The Turkana, they know how to eat meat.' They certainly did; they never stopped. They also knew how to eat *posho*, which was available in two grades, a cheaper refined white maize flour which had lost much of its goodness, and the wholemeal 'brown' flour supplied by American aid projects. Although healthier, the people did not like the wholemeal version as they considered its colour an impurity and its slightly nuttier texture was unpopular. I did not like any of it, but forced to choose I would have voted with the Turkana for the blander white version.

When cooked to a thick mashed-potato consistency with added salt, small handfuls were kneaded into balls and a deep dent pressed in with the thumb to make an edible spoon. Filled with meat or vegetable stew – *mboga* – you just pushed it into your mouth. If there was no *mboga* you scraped it from the *sufuria* with your finger tips and threw it into your mouth dry. An acquired taste, but very popular throughout East Africa. Slowly I learned to like it, which had never been true of the leaden *targilla* bread of the Tuareg in the Sahara.

While still near the lake we sometimes swam. The water was much warmer than any swimming pool, almost like a bath. I can perhaps be forgiven for assuming that my companions knew if it was safe from crocs; an idiotic assumption in the most densely crocodile-populated lake in the world!

Starting off again, the chance to graze had briefly rejuvenated the donkeys, but it did not last long and soon they were back to their usual dawdle. This was worryingly slow progress. I had imagined that our two five-gallon jerry cans would be ample, but in this heat we needed to drink frequently, and the perpetual *posho* used up a lot, so it was not long before we were low on water again. But when we came to a large mud pool overhung by doum palms, Edung said, 'We take water.'

I was incredulous. 'It isn't water, it's mud!'

Edung just grinned.

I waded through knee-deep sludge to the middle, wondering if there were leeches, and drank some. It was hotter than a bath tub and so not at all thirst-quenching, but we filled the jerry cans with this brown soup anyway and decided to have a meal. The tea and *posho* were all the same colour; mud. Even gritty. But beggars cannot be choosers. We ate the rest of the sheep too, equally unappetising with cindered wool and raw inside, under a carpet of flies.

Suddenly Ekadeli whooped and leapt in the air. Between the grazing donkeys a puff adder lay coiled in a hole; a dangerous threat to them. The adrenalin surged. Keeping our feet well back we dug it out and chased it off with our fighting sticks, which it staunchly resisted; my first encounter of many with these very poisonous creatures. Over a yard long and very fat-bodied, they rely on their excellent camouflage and stay put, making them easy to step on accidentally. Untreated, their venom often causes death, and of course, without refrigeration facilities, we had no antidote. It pays to keep your eyes open!

One of the donkeys had already developed an open sore from the rubbing baggage, despite the covering of goat skins and sacks. This turned out to be a constant problem, and I did my best to dress the wound with Fucidin (an antibiotic cream) and covered it with a dressing, to the amusement of my companions. At the same time a revolting smell drew me to a rotting hole at the base of another donkey's ear, with flies festering inside. It was stomach-churning; how had I missed that before? Another thick layer of

Fucidin kept the flies off and eventually cleared it up.

My bags were not locked and I soon realised that in this tribal society possessions were not seen as private property, but casually shared. Thomas had found my stand-by wristwatch and started wearing it proudly as a prop of Western affluence. However, I was horrified to find that he had fiddled with it and, already, on only our second day, it had no glass, no winder, no minute hand, and was useless.

He calmly handed it to me, 'This is not work. You need mend.'

'But if you pull bits off it, of course it won't work. It's very complicated!' I swallowed my fury.

But then he started again with his moans about David. 'He cannot come, the boy, he can do no walk with us.'

This time I erupted. 'God, I am sick of you moaning on about David, he is coming or we all go back to Kalokol and then no safari, no money!'

The threat of lost profits did the trick, and at last he shut up. I simmered.

Heading inland: snakes and spiders

THE FINE GRAVEL had now changed to a gritty sand underfoot, with the same sporadic clumps of doum palms, and for a while the sky glowered ominously. But after a few large spatters of rain it relented and passed us by, leaving the sun to flay my pale skin again. It was time to turn inland from the lake towards the hinterland of north Turkana, heading north-west in the direction of Lokitaung. Water would now become scarce.

Having left the lake behind it was important to travel by map and compass so I started to fix our position by triangulating from mountains the others recognised. The ground rose and we toiled through broken, rockier country. This was more interesting than walking on the plain, now crossing gullies, dry, rocky stream beds and low hills with longer views across the rugged land. Edung pointed to a mountain silhouetted ahead and claimed emphatically,

'Lokitaung behind this. Tonight we sleep there,' but a glance at the map showed that at this speed it might even take three days. My map and compass became increasingly indispensable. We had so far only covered 35 miles –painfully slow.

Edung, David and I walked on ahead of the donkeys and hardly noticed the distance pass as we talked. 'Have you been to this place before?'

'Yes, but long time. Too much Merille here, very bad.'

'They come all this way from Sudan to raid?'

'Many many here, kill too many people and take goats.'

Crikey, this was scary stuff. 'Could they be close?'

'Always too much close.'

As we walked, the sleepy heat settled thickly over a wide gully where children loitered lazily in the boredom of tending goats. Nothing else moved except the throbbing heat haze rippling the stagnant air. This lethargic mood shattered the instant we were spotted. Sand flew from spurring heels as they sprinted, and dust rose in their flight for the safety of the *manyatta*. At a whelp of alarm adrenalin raced also through the goats who joined the scramble to flee, the voice of terror leaping the barrier between species – a single language of the universe. In the moment of panic we had been mistaken for Merille raiders. Our empty hands waved to show we had no weapons but the stampede was headlong and we watched impotently. The *manyatta* was fortunately unarmed or a defensive shot might have felled one of us.

We sat on the edge of the gully to await the donkeys, and first a woman, then a man, appeared, hanging back warily. She repeatedly shouted, 'Where is my son? You kill him'. Her son had not returned with the others. Calling back that we were Turkana and unarmed we slowly approached, when suddenly, like a flushed hare almost under our feet, the lad exploded from the cover of some rocks and dashed to his mother who scolded him furiously. As the brittle terror subsided she began to talk, explaining the frequency of the raids they suffered. She asked if I was a Somali. She had only seen two or three white men before, always in vehicles, and assumed that they came from the furthest country of which she had heard. This was a wild place.

The Merille camped in the mountains and came at night with Kalashnikovs to steal flocks and kill the villagers. In Turkana all tribes from Sudan and Ethiopia were called Merille, a collective name synonymous with Daasanach, just as on the east side of the lake northern raiders were called Shangalla. No one was absolutely sure where they came from, and even Thesiger admitted he was uncertain of the difference and called them all Merille. They were all greatly feared.

As dusk was settling heavily we decided to camp at the next *manyatta* we came to and found a collection of low biscuit-coloured huts, naturally camouflaged amongst the gravel and dust of the desert floor, which was thinly dotted with spreading acacia trees and a scant ground cover of low grey-green scrub. Edung stopped the donkeys.

'We sleep here.'

But David chipped in, 'It is safer inside the *manyatta*'.

I disagreed, 'But the *manyatta* is where the Merille will attack, so it would be safer to stay hidden in the bush, at a distance'.

'They find us, they kill us. In *manyatta* plenty peoples to help fight'.

Neither case was reassuring and as often happened we did the easiest thing, camping where Edung had first said, a hundred yards from the *manyatta*, where we were clearly visible and completely helpless. 'In that case we will operate a series of watches through the night', but my logic fell on deaf ears, and after sharing out some chewing tobacco with our inevitable audience we all went to sleep, hoping for the best.

Finding ourselves alive in the morning we continued across broken country crisscrossed by gullies and dry stream beds. Very occasionally we came across local tribesmen, and here a young lad of about twelve, alone in this wilderness and dressed only in an old loincloth, stared at me, mesmerised. Even my companions were at first puzzled by his language.

'What did he say?' David giggled.

'He ask if that the colour of your body or if you take off your skin,' Ekadeli said, then told the boy, 'This is *msungu*, white man.'

The boy came closer to peer intently and David said to me, 'He says he hear people talk of *msungu*, but he not seen one.'

He came and sat beside me and gently stroked the hair on my forearm like a kitten. In this land where body hair is unknown, children were always fascinated by this. I was thrilled to be in such a remote, unvisited place. How many places remained in the world where people had never seen a white man before?

We would sometimes exchange tobacco for milk, but due to the drought no one kept cows, so this was from goats or camels. Any trade was always a lengthy process and would try my patience. The required etiquette involved approaching a *manyatta* and then sitting and waiting 40-50 yards away. We knew that we had been seen, but there would never be any immediate reaction. They probably hoped that after a while we would move on without disturbing them. After ten or fifteen minutes, someone would wander out of the village and sit down about ten yards away, usually with his back to us, pretending not to have even noticed us. After another long delay of several minutes he might shout across to us without turning to look, 'What you want?'

After another pause, one of my group would call back, 'We want milk'.

'We have no milk'.

'We seen your goats on the hills and know you have milk.'

This would eventually produce the answer, 'We only have little and not to give'.

So it would go on until slowly and grudgingly a gourd or two of milk would be produced. Inevitably their begging for tobacco would follow promptly. Never was there any mention of such unknown words as 'please' or 'thank you' – just 'give me'. When I was with the Samburu tribe later on, their friendliness and good manners made a remarkable and refreshing contrast.

We were joined here for half a day's march by a man whose spindly legs and swollen belly were evidence of great hunger. He wore a dashing red *shuka* and a faded orange loin cloth, his hair made up with clay into a sort of thin helmet to support feathers in the traditional style of the Turkana men. The front of his scalp was shaved so that the mud skull-cap sat further back, the first broad band of it stained orange, behind which a decorative cluster of ostrich feathers on the crown of his head pointed vertically five or six inches in a flamboyant and attractive plume. He carried himself with great pride and no doubt could claim opponents killed in battle.

Everyone in this area wore wrist knives, and as well as the ubiquitous fighting sticks they also carried their spears, although these were impotent against the AK-47s of the Merille. Wrist knives were worn like bracelets, disks of thinly beaten steel with a central hole for the wrist, and a sharpened outer edge. Ekadeli demonstrated how to fight with them, facing the palm of the hand outwards and swiping the blade upwards across an opponent's face, or bear-hugging him with both arms and raking the blade up and down to sever the muscles in his back or chest. Very close combat.

The fighting sticks which every Turkana man carried along with his stool were made from acacia wood, always carved to have a harder knotted head shaped a little like an axe. Its use was self-evident: a good skull-cracker. At the end of the trek Ekadeli made me a present of his own, which I still treasure. The head stools, simple curved supports five or six inches tall with just one leg, were carved as a single piece and supported their heads as pillows while they slept (principally to hold their mudpack hair decorations off the ground), but were at other times used to sit on or to rest a knee or elbow as they lay on the ground. They were always put to use somehow, and were always carried along with the fighting stick. As well as wrist knives, thumb knives were occasionally used; a small blade which curled off a steel ring slipped over a thumb or finger. Only very occasionally did I see someone carrying a bow with arrows, and hippo-hide shields had disappeared.

Coming over the crest of a small hill we dropped into the lovely river course of Loburin, flanked by spreading trees festooned with fleshy stemmed creepers, among which families of monkeys bounded away from us. About 100 yards wide, the banks were sometimes stacked with heaps of water-polished rocks, shimmering in the sunshine. After digging for water to fill our jerry cans we came to a series of rock pools, clear water reflecting the deep blue sky, some even with small fish. The gritty sand at the water's edge was pockmarked with the prints of camels and goats and our grateful donkeys drank deeply. Here the low cliffs of the river valley were formed of deeply split slabs of dark basalt, sometimes weathered into huge screes of rubble, yet somehow tough little thorn trees still sprang from rocky fissures. A shepherd dressed in ragged skins drove past a couple of dozen goats, mixed colours of black, brown and white. Set in a craggy gorge, a thin rivulet cascaded down the rock wall, the dampness decorating it with mineral deposits in intricate marbled colours of blue, white, yellow and red. We followed it uphill, sometimes climbing steeply where it narrowed into a trickle, bubbling down the centre of its pebbly bed, and I wondered how Ekadeli managed to coax the donkeys to follow us up the slippery rock with no obvious track. Even so, sometimes it became too difficult and we had to backtrack or make detours to the south.

On a desolate hillside of barren rock a solitary girl stood motionless in the simmering heat, dressed in goatskins, and apparently quite alone. Presumably she was minding goats (although there was no sign of them), while subsisting on milk and blood for weeks at a time. She was the colour of the dust, almost invisible in this vast stone wilderness, and completely ignored us as we snaked our way below.

We finally camped near some fallen trees but soon found the area was alive with hunting spiders. These very large-bodied, biscuit-coloured spiders make no webs but run at alarming speed to catch their prey, having a poisonous bite that the local people told me was more painful than a scorpion sting, and could even kill. Occasionally as we slept I had felt one run across my bare chest, but assumed that as long as I did not roll on it in my sleep there was no cause for alarm. However, on this occasion one appeared in the middle of our camp that was so huge that Ekadeli yelled, 'We must kill this one. He too much big, much poisonous', and I chased it with a stick until eventually annihilating it. Afterwards I measured it and found it to be over seven inches diagonally from foot to foot, with mandibles so large that I could slip my pencil between them. Not a cosy sleeping companion.

Late next morning we left the riverbed, scratching myriad bites from clouds of mosquitoes which had feasted on us during the night. Our path was a narrow animal track through dense, chest-high green scrub, and in a careless moment I had a real fright, almost treading on a four-foot-long, sandy-coloured cobra slithering across the path under my feet. Accompanied by whoops and yips my companions set off with a hue and cry, raining down rocks as the poor creature tried to escape, moving at a jogging speed with the front half of its body held almost vertically and its impressive hood spread wide. I crouched to take a picture but the others pulled me away in case it spat its venom: 'Too much dangerous, you stay back'. When they had killed it they insisted I join them in performing an ancient pagan rite. After pulping its skull with the end of my stick they buried the battered head in a small hole, and each of us in turn shuffled slowly across the still-writhing body with our heads lowered and eyes closed, spitting as we went. 'This keep us safe from snakes on our safari'. It obviously worked.

Snakes were always a risk, and in dense vegetation we would knock our fighting sticks against branches to make a commotion, as cobras prefer to get out of the way if possible. Their venom attacks the nervous system, and although more lethal than puff adders, the chance of an adder bite is much greater, as they stay put, relying on their camouflage, and so are easy to step on. Adder venom thickens the blood, which can cause a heart attack. One day I had a huge shock to find I had stepped within a couple of inches of a young coiled puff adder, which mercifully gave me the benefit of the doubt and did not strike. I much appreciated its courtesy! Although we were within the range of black mambas, whose venom is usually lethal within 20 minutes, they generally prefer forests to such desiccated rock desert. A choice I found reassuring.

By now some of my clothes were becoming adopted communally, an osmotic process I had barely noticed and did not care about as long as I still had something left. Edung was rather dapper in a white canvas hat and usually carried my map case, while Ekadeli ignored the intense heat with a blue tee-shirt pulled over his bush shirt. Thomas carried my heavy, metal camera case and only David still retained his school uniform of pale blue tee-shirt and green shorts, although by the end of the safari he had claimed a shirt and some long trousers. This became the normal state of things on all my walks and I learned to take extra clothes accordingly.

Lokitaung: starvation and desolation

As we approached Lokitaung the signs of drought and famine became more pronounced, lots of children with distended stomachs, and boreholes had been drilled with long crank handles to pump up clean sweet water in abundance. A constant stream of women came to fetch it in large square paraffin tins, on the top of which they floated sprigs of leaves to reduce spillage as it sloshed about, carried on their heads. We refilled our jerry cans and had a cursory wash. Everyone we passed was asked how far it was to Lokitaung and almost without exception one would say, 'near', while the next said, 'far', then, 'near', and so on. Hopeless. A young boy carried a newly born lamb with its afterbirth wound round a stick and Thomas explained, 'When people very hungry they eat even this thing'. Among gently undulating and thinly wooded hills we passed a great many cairns of sticks and stones marking the sites of killings by Merille, and added our own tributes. We were in lawless country.

A fine-looking young couple we passed were very friendly to me and took delight in having their photographs taken. He was wrapped in a large brown *shuka* from the neck to just below the groin and like every Turkana man he carried his fighting stick and stool. He had the traditional shaved panel across the front of his scalp from ear to ear, the short hair behind it still carrying the remains of an old mud skullcap, while his wife followed the unfailing custom of the Turkana women in shaving each side of the head, leaving a broad band of short, tousled, twisted plaits in a central ridge. She had large brass earrings and the usual heavy mass of bead necklaces piled from shoulders to chin. Below these a wide strip of leather hung between her bare breasts to below her waist, decorated with large roundels of red and white beads, and in front of her goatskin skirt was another panel of leather, similarly decorated. The goatskin skirt itself was ankle length at the back, but above the knees in front, so as not to impede walking. She carried a round gourd plugged with a long, hollow wooden stopper used for milking camels. The milk carried in these gourds often had a burnt taste from the hot coals used to purify the inside. They were a delightful and mutually affectionate couple (*see photo10*), and I felt inadequate with my inability to talk to them, as the others had continued ahead.

Lokitaung, which we reached just before dusk, had the usual collection of *dukas* and a Catholic mission station on a hilltop. Close enough to the Sudan border to need a substantial defensive presence, there were rows of small police accommodation buildings, always known as 'police lines'. By now we had all become the colour of the land through which we walked, skins and clothes alike 'too much dirty', so I walked up to the mission, only to discover that the American missionary was away in Lodwar. However, someone sent for the clerk, who invited us to use an outside tap. Much later we were moderately clean and sat down to eat the ubiquitous *posho* with meat *mboga* before going to our stony beds at the bottom of the hill.

Stories of donkey rustling had unsettled Edung and Ekadeli, so when ours all disappeared they were alarmed and searched for them throughout the night and next morning. We became increasingly worried by the implications of losing our transport in this remote spot, but in the end it turned out that they had found some good grazing, which they desperately needed. This scenario was repeated often on my treks, and was hard to prevent as the donkeys worked all day and needed to eat at night, so could not be tethered or confined in a *boma*. I never knew when they slept.

In the alarm Edung had reassembled the spear, which we kept hidden in towns. Like all tribal spears it was made in three parts, a long narrow steel tail shaft and another steel bar terminating in a blade at the front, with a handle of acacia wood between the metal sections. Different tribes used spears of different lengths with different-shaped blades, and different lengths of wooden handle, but all had to be well-balanced in the hand for throwing. The blades of spears and wrist knives would sometimes have a simple hide cover over the cutting edge to preserve its sharpness, being used for all manner of tasks other than hunting or fighting, usually to butcher meat. Turkana spears have smallish leaf-shaped blades while the Maasai and Samburu ones are longer with narrow parallel edges. The wooden handle was glued into flared flanges at the ends of the steel sections, traditionally using the sap of a particular acacia tree which was heated over the fire to soften and then hardened as it cooled. However, modern times had made new materials accessible and now Edung assembled the pieces using molten sugar.

The acacia tree, being the most common source of hard wood, was used for many things, different species for different tasks, not least of which was the use of its sap as a popular chewing gum. This probably came from the acacia-like Commiphora tree, the ancient source of myrrh in Arabia, which scientists have recently discovered to have many medicinal properties – although this has long been known in the desert.

As my companions had romped through our supplies of *posho*, powdered milk and sugar, never attempting to ration anything, we were very lucky to find that, although in a famine zone, the *dukas* still had plentiful supplies. As sugar was comparatively new to them I would often catch them with the sugar sack, lifting handfuls straight into their mouths. I could hardly blame them, as when the *msungu* had gone, the sugar sack would be empty.

The American missionary came down for a chat when he returned from Lodwar, and explained to me how mission policy these days now urged the Turkana to retain their own culture and not to emulate Western values. This was good to hear, although I noted they were still clearly intent on replacing traditional beliefs with Christianity.

It was only 17 years since Independence and, because of its dangers, the frontiers of Turkana had been opened several years after that, meaning that in other parts of Kenya few people knew much, if anything, about this, their largest tribal district. Similarly, few Turkana knew much, if anything, about what went on outside their own tribal boundaries, and often not far beyond their own villages. Despite this inevitably inward-looking existence I was amazed how at night, as we lay staring up at the great panoply of glittering stars, undimmed by pollution, my companions would be fascinated to know what they were, why they moved, and why the moon was so much bigger. They asked lots of questions, a few of which I could answer, and always listened spellbound, finding the things I told them incredible and often hilarious.

The idea that the earth was round and circled the sun was of course totally daft, and when I explained in detail how the Americans had gone to the moon and walked about on it there was an awed silence broken only by little cries of astonishment, until after a long time Ekadeli broke the spell saying, 'You tell us a joke,' and they all collapsed in laughter. Why not? The whole thing seemed perfectly barmy in the reality of their lives. Actually, it still does to me. But they continued to wonder and question and doubt, like most of us. Thomas once amazed me by saying, 'I know what is the smoke behind aeroplanes', referring to the vapour trails. When I asked, he explained, 'People inside roast meat'. More logical than walking on the moon!

As we left Lokitaung I begged a large dressing from the mission clinic for the increasingly open wound on the ailing donkey, and we pressed on westwards towards the Kachoda River. It was time to start swinging round towards central Turkana and continue our circuit. Feeling refreshed after our two-night stay, we had an easy start on one of Turkana's few vehicle tracks, slipping a rope through a hole long-since cut between the lead donkey's nostrils to help pull him along. The land was becoming increasingly arid, and digging for ground water was fruitless, so after a couple of days, when we were told about another water pump at Nabwel our parched throats persuaded us to veer north to find it. In an area of scattered trees, whose roots must have found water somewhere, there were in fact two pumps, one thronged with people and the other with a broken handle. I replaced the handle with one of our fighting sticks and we drew the water both we and our donkeys so desperately needed. But I was sad that when we moved off no one repeated what I had so easily demonstrated.

'The land God gave to Cain'

HEADING BACK SOUTH-WEST to resume our circuit we spent all day reaching a pass through the hills which gave onto the true desolation of the north Turkana heartland. It was a spectacular vista in all directions. A land of volcanic rock and dust, a place from another world, even another planet. We stopped to camp on its brink – what you might call the watershed if there were ever a drop of water. The cruel landscape was set alight by a glorious sunset which lit the mountains behind us in a soft apricot glow and threw warm shafts across the weakening cerulean sky. The grey shapes of the Lokwanamoru Range to our right and the jagged summits of Lolomat ahead silhouetted darkly and faded steadily into the inky night. I was moved by the immensity of it all, surrounded by emptiness, stillness and silence, remote from the world. We had been walking for nine hot days.

The donkeys wandered far during the night, scavenging what few dry wisps of grass they could find. It took another extensive and worrying search to find them before marching on to the Nakapeliowoi River bed, where we successfully dug for water. I always assumed that any accessible water would lie beneath a river bed, probably below its deepest points, so it was a mystery to me that it was usually found somewhere under the banks, often higher even than the water level when infrequently in spate.

The search would begin by repeatedly driving the rear haft of the spear into the sand and looking for the dark stain of moisture, or grains of damp sand clinging to the steel. If there was a clue we would dig into the sand with the *panga* or our hands and with luck discover a thin trickle dribbling into the hole. It was often very sluggish for this to make a puddle we could bale out with a mug into a jerrycan, or into a *sufuria* for the donkeys. Thirsty donkeys drink a lot. This might take over an hour, and often needed repeating the next day. With our limited time and resources we could only dig down a couple of feet, and some water holes we found were six or eight feet deep.

When water was scarce local people often filled in the holes they dug after drawing water to prevent evaporation and to hide them from others. This hidden water supported a smattering of trees along the riversides, and we stopped for lunch under the writhing trunks of a spreading tree that rare flash floods had tried to tear from the ground. It had survived the drought by reducing its transpiration by producing only tiny leaves. Everything fought for survival in this desperate land.

A woman and her daughter sitting dejectedly nearby asked for medicine for their painfully red dribbling eyes. Probably trachoma, and I had nothing but ordinary eye ointment. I felt ashamed and realised that travelling in wild places bears a responsibility to carry large stocks of medicines in future, and learn how to use them. My English GP generously gave me copious advice.

We continued into the heart of this wasteland of dry rock and gravel, taking water again the following day as we approached the mountain of Lolomat, and camped at its foot. We were now deep in an unvisited region, a perilously parched, empty and wild country; truly the land God gave to Cain. Today, looking at satellite images of the area, I am astonished by the harshness of this savage land; a remorselessly cruel, dry, rock desert stretching great distances across undulating plains of grey-buff to the threatening, drab outline of surrounding mountains (*see photo 8*).

These were the strongholds of the Merille, used for lying up between raids, and also the haunts of *ngoroko*, far beyond the reach of any kind of law. We doused our cooking fire at dusk to avoid attracting attention, although secretly knowing that we would have already been spotted as we crawled like worthless ants across this never-ending moonscape.

Often at night I would wake to see Edung sitting up, staring intently into the darkness. It was eerie and hollow, particularly at first light, the time favoured for their attacks after encircling their quarry in darkness. The pit of my stomach would churn at sunrise, half-expecting to be torn apart by a sudden volley from AK-47s hidden among the surrounding rocks.

To add to our misery the nights had become bitterly cold on the higher ground. Powerful gusts threatened to blow away my companions' *shukas*, the meagre coverings which protected them, tucked under their feet and pulled taut up to their shoulders. The summit of Lolomat is 2,898 feet, almost the height of the Scottish Munros. Despite Edung's strict warnings I was glad of my sleeping bag liner, and twice in the middle of the night, aching with cold from the bitter, cutting wind, I even climbed into the down bag itself. How the others coped I could not guess, but their hard lives offered little choice other than to suffer in silence. I hoped that this was also inclement weather for nighttime murder.

The days between these icy nights were as hot as the nights were cold, the enormous differences in temperature somehow exacerbating the cruelty of the pitiless wind, and the grilling of the unforgiving sun. Edung knocked down a flying dove with a stone, and when he began to pluck it I gasped, 'For God's sake kill it first'. They indulged my strange request. Its little life provided a tiny meal to share between five.

We walked south towards the rounded shape of Kokolonyoi, with the distant mass of the Pelekech mountains beyond it. The Lokwanamoru mountains to our right loomed closer, along with the risk of attack from hidden assassins. After more than two days walking through this dusty wasteland Edung said, 'This night we sleep Kokolonyoi', but of course we did not and stopped after dark like sitting ducks on a low hill halfway to it from Lolomat, where the vicious wind tore at us and froze us once more.

We could not afford to loiter in these nightmarish conditions and next morning set off at 5am. Three hours later we came to a waterhole eight feet deep and almost dry. A family living in some huts close by (what they lived on was a mystery) told us, 'No water till Pelekech mountains. Two days footing'. They added, 'We make this well, you give tobacco', which seemed fair to me at least. Passing up cupfuls of water one by one, and waiting for more water to filter slowly into the hole was painful, but eventually the donkeys were satiated and our jerry cans were full. It cost us a lot of our chewing tobacco. We were in the Laburet River, part of a substantial river system which theoretically drained any non-existent rainfall north-west to the marshes of the Lotikipi Plain. All of the rivers here died of thirst even after rain, vanishing in the deserts long before finding an escape, and even the marshes were just a dead end, leading only to evaporation.

The donkeys were now exhausted and when we reloaded, the one carrying the jerry cans collapsed three times. I found it pitiful to witness and felt dreadful. Thomas voiced the obvious, 'This donkey too much tired'. So as soon as we came to the thin shade of some straggly acacias we stopped for our midday break to let them nibble at any stems of dead grass they could find. We were soon surrounded by the inevitable gaggle of people begging for tobacco, tea, and *posho*. The entire landscape appeared as barren as the face of the moon and as we walked we would not see a soul for many hours at a time, yet the moment we stopped and produced food they seemed to materialise out of the ether. Here, once again, I encountered people who had never before seen a white man, and again I faced the same curious questions about whether I had peeled off my skin.

By 1980 the modern world had forced its way into almost every nook and cranny of the planet, and to find myself among people who were still as unknowing of the outside world as their Stone Age forefathers was extraordinary and curiously humbling. They were mostly women with the usual tangle of twisted hair on the crown of their heads, rows of large brass rings pierced through several holes around the edge of their ears and great heaps of beads around their necks, whose colour was sometimes barely visible through deeply ingrained dirt. I dreaded to think what infections or parasites might be harboured in that inaccessible mass. Some wore bracelets of doum palm seeds, as well as the usual beads and bands of various metals (*see photo 11*).

As the women did not carry wooden stools like the men, they sat in the dust, one hand crooked across their foreheads to shield their eyes from the blinding sunlight. In this faraway place their goatskin clothes were often so ragged and thin that they resembled little more than old, brown felt. Few people wore any kind of footwear.

These must have been some of the last people in Africa, among the last in the world, never to have looked into the face of a European. Having walked through their harsh and inhospitable land I could understand how the world had been held at bay, but even so, 'progress' was approaching with relentless speed and I felt honoured to have been allowed to witness this inaccessible wilderness before it changed forever.

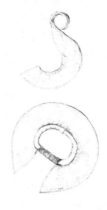

Bestial Christmas: a tide of ants and a torrent of urine

CONSIDERING THE difficulties of finding water, and the slowness of our progress, I decided that we must shorten our route, missing out the Pelekech mountains and Kakuma, and start to turn back towards the lake. I was bitterly disappointed, but perhaps we were lucky as we later heard that the Karamajong tribe from Uganda were raiding in the area around Kakuma. We would have made a good target. So during our break I took fresh compass bearings and we set off in a new direction heading south-east.

As usual we found ourselves crossing a wide arid plain of gritty sand liberally scattered with small rocks and stones of shattered basalt, whose rocking made our footsteps unsteady. Our legs were scoured by the fine thorns of low scrub reaching to our calves, although this irritation was forgiven for the gift of their tiny yellow flowers in this monotonous landscape. Strangely, the powerful wind had persuaded what little vegetation survived to form up in lines, each in the wind shadow of its neighbour, giving the land a striated effect in a palette of sombre pastel creams and browns like a dirty cirrus sky. Trees, where they existed at all, were stunted and strangely out of place. We passed a group of about twenty emaciated cows, obviously raided from a greener homeland and now slowly dying without reliable grazing or drinking water.

Next day the dome of Kokolonyoi disappeared over the horizon behind us as the smoky ghosts of the mountains to our east gradually grew bolder. Short of water as usual, we stopped in a riverbed but found so little that it would have taken several hours to fill one jerry can. The usual congregation of 'visitors' materialised out of thin air, all with their hands outstretched. I knew that the tradition was to beg for just a small gift of tobacco, but confronted by a *msungu* they came demanding everything they could think of, calling out, 'Cook *posho* and tea for me.'

Even my companions were infuriated by their rudeness. 'This people not true Turkana. Very bad thing.'

Increasingly I felt that they were nothing but a nation of beggars. Even more insulting was that if we gave them food they would eat it without comment and then either demand more or just stand up and stalk off in silence without a backwards glance at us. The lack of any words of gratitude in the Turkana language summed up their attitude. The complete lack of initiative in the people around me was exasperating. But perhaps I was expecting too much. If I pushed my way into their lives with my alien ideas about timescales, haste and stress, that was clearly my problem, and in their eyes I was a gold mine to be excavated for as long as the opportunity remained. Only on later treks did I really understand that it was my impatience that was at fault, and that life so far from our own hell-for-leather society is perforce lived at a very different pace; that of the natural world.

Failing to find water again, we set off to try to reach a waterhole near the hill of Lokithigere before dark, long since inured to our constant nagging thirst. The donkeys must have been suffering more than we were and it was a joy to find an ample source of sweet water for them when we arrived. The darkness settled around us as they drank and drank and drank, more than I would have thought possible. Exhausted, we hurriedly made camp and only after lying down did I realise I was on a slope with my head lower than my feet, a sure recipe for a bad head in the morning. I swung round and was asleep. It was Christmas Eve 1980.

I woke blearily in the first hint of sunrise to a disconcerting tickling all over my body, and as I opened my eyes, found to my horror that I had slept with my head resting on the entrance of a large ants' nest, to which its inhabitants had understandably taken great exception. Like Lilliputians they had emerged in vast numbers to investigate this interloper, and the inside and outside of my sleeping bag, as well as my entire body, was a grey, moving carpet of inquisitive ants. It made my skin crawl, literally. Thankfully they were not a biting species, unlike the local, small, red ants with a bite like a wasp sting, but it was a creepy start to Christmas Day and I ran down to the waterhole to bathe from one of our cooking pans and part company with my inquisitors. The others naturally thought it hilarious.

We made a new ant-free camp close by in the dappled shade of a tree and soon the inevitable visitors began to arrive. Despite their non-stop begging we eventually succeeded in buying two calabashes of camel's milk, and David and I set off to find a goat. The sun hammered down from an implacable sky, its heat claustrophobic and suffocating, draining us of energy and moisture as the running sweat traced patterns through the dust of our bodies. We wandered from one tiny *manyatta* to another making enquiries and at last we came to an isolated and shabby hut from which a very tall man appeared. He glowered at us through deeply bloodshot eyes, veins throbbing on his temples, brows clenched in a threatening expression, shining with sweat and absolutely stark-naked. He seemed very aggressive and I felt nervous that a nasty situation was about to arise. In a way it did.

Feeling vulnerable with his menacing face only inches from mine I asked him if we could buy a goat. As he answered he turned imperceptibly and, while continuing to speak, suddenly pissed copiously, missing me by a whisker. I stayed motionless, good British sangfroid, but very nearly damp sangfroid! This was becoming a Christmas to remember! It was clear that we were now in as unrefined a corner of the country as we were likely to come across. However, he did indeed have goats. 'You come when sun is high. Goats in shade of big tree.'

When we returned at noon he offered us a huge black animal, an absolute beauty with the stance of a prize bull and a magnificent pair of handlebar horns. The goat gave us a good run for our money, and when we tied him to a tree he reared up and snapped the rope with one lunge, but Edung dived to catch him and dispatched him instantly. While he and Ekadeli butchered him, David and I drew more water for the coming feast.

We cut up the offal as soon as it was removed, straight into the frying pan, heart, liver, lungs, kidneys, windpipe, assorted fat and gristle and last, and definitely least as far as I was concerned, the testicles. We ate it immediately, and after the bland *posho* we had lived on for several days I found it very rich and quickly dozed off.

It turned out that Ekadeli's home was only a couple of hours' walk from here and suddenly we were joined by his brothers. How they had found out about our presence in the vicinity, and then managed to locate us, since we were not following any roads, was a great mystery to me. I gathered news travelled fast, even in such remote places. Nomadic communities were always on the move; naturally, they took the latest gossip with them and, as David had explained, people could cover immense distances very quickly, so the news must have got through.

Despite this, I was often amazed how people knew, or sensed, each other's whereabouts. Several times on these treks we split up and met again on some solitary goat track half a day's journey further on. How? Conceivably they still retained something of the unconscious telepathy of our ancient forefathers, their minds not yet bombarded by all the 'noise' of TV, radio and so on, still unclouded by the effects of microwave, internet and other forms of electro-magnetic radiation.

I was impressed by the remote wildness of Ekadeli's origins, but I was also struck by how coolly he and his brothers took this unexpected, unannounced meeting. Family relationships seemed less important to them than they are to us, although when it came to the remains of our goat, Ekadeli predictably told me, 'It good to give stomach, blood and head to my brothers'. Then, as usual, the skin was scraped clean and pegged onto the ground to dry in the sun. I had promised this exquisite black skin to David for his mother so was irritated when Edung bullied him into handing it over. The women brought us more camel's milk which was so acrid that it completely overpowered the coffee and sugar.

I went to sleep to the staccato lullaby of cracking bones as my companions noisily sucked out the marrow. Images of Christmas in England loomed in my brain, but I was quite happy where I was.

Last legs: from drinking blood
to a baked-bean feast

IT TOOK EKADELI four hours to find the donkeys in the morning as they had searched far and wide for non-existent grazing. However, we made good time despite the strong gale now buffeting us head-on, trying hard to push us backwards and stabbing us with the sand it carried, while the dust painted us in beige-brown desert camouflage. We found a place to draw muddy water and let the grateful donkeys drink, then struggled on through patches of desiccated thorn bush about eight-feet high which reached out thin branches to plant rows of needles into any unprotected flesh.

Close to the equator, sunshine is short but regular, 6am to 6pm, and as the last glow seeped from the night sky towards 7pm we stopped to camp. Thankfully, the strong wind now dropped at night and in the morning we were underway quickly. I set a more southerly course, looking for water as usual, and the scorching wind renewed its flailing attack, any signs of vegetation long since withered away, so that when we stopped for a midday break the wretched donkeys just stood statuesque and starving in the burning sun, waiting nobly with an air of stoic indifference.

The only water hole we found stank so diabolically that Thomas grimaced, 'This thing too much very bad', and even the animals turned away in disgust. The others had again romped through the sugar, tobacco and tea, so we were lucky to find some Somali *dukas* here, just simple grass huts standing alone in the emptiness, and replenished our stocks. After a long march into the evening we slept heavily on the rough bare rock.

We bought another enormous goat which again snapped its tether and we struggled to steer it by its huge horns until we found a good water source in the leafy Nabwalekorot River and killed it. It was so powerful that even after its throat was cut it roared furiously until it died. I look back with sadness and regret at those moments. If we eat meat we must be honest with ourselves about what that entails, but I believe that taking a creature's life should be done with compassion. The blood which we collected in one of the cooking pots was immediately whipped up with a stick to take out the clotting agent, forming a great cluster of bloody membranous bubbles like a bunch of grapes. The stick was thrown away and the process repeated until all the 'bad' blood had been removed, and then Ekadeli stirred in a cupful of sugar and we divided it between our mugs. The goat had not been dead five minutes and the blood was still hot, but although in my diary I noted that it 'tasted very good', my memory is not so convinced. A pair of tawny eagles landed in the thorn tree above our heads and stared down haughtily for a long time; a refreshingly different sort of begging visitor.

As we ate the offal I found that I had been treated to one of the testicles. Failing to get my teeth through it I passed it on to Thomas, who was a devotee of all the more dubious parts.

When we had removed the stomach and intestine he had asked, 'Will you give me one part which I like too much?'

I had immediately replied, 'No, you know the rules. We share everything equally without favouritism.'

'But this thing is only one,' he had insisted.

'What thing is that?'

With a lick of his lips, 'The anus.'

'It's yours,' I had heard myself say, before my brain had even considered the question.

Later I discovered that the intestine, when properly squeezed out and washed thoroughly is pleasantly sweet, although rather gristly like the windpipe, which I was already used to finding in my bowl. However, it was sometimes best not to know too intimately the contents of our cooking pan.

I remember one occasion when, removing the organs from a goat, David cut out the bladder and, to my horror, emptied its contents into the pan. 'Why the hell did you do that?'

With a grin and an unrepentant shrug he replied, 'It is part of the goat,' with which it was hard to disagree.

As David struggled to lever the jaw from the baked head using my Buck hunting knife, it slipped and cut deeply into a finger, exposing the moving tendon. I immediately washed and bandaged it but he was quite unconcerned and next time I noticed his hand the once-pristine bandage was covered with filth and goat gore. Any concept of hygiene was quite unknown among the rural Turkana.

The Nabwalekorot River was delightful, its banks hung with trailing limbed trees, groups of doum palms, rocky outcrops sheltering small clear pools, and views of the north-east facing crags of Kamaret mountain nearby. We waited at one of the pools as a girl was watering her goats, but I was surprised when her father told her to stop and water our animals instead. Afterwards the father demanded tobacco in payment, which Edung steadfastly refused. As the man worked himself into what became a violent rage we loaded quickly and set off pursued by volleys of threats, and while within earshot his curses continued to rain down upon us. I suspected there must be some old smouldering feud and felt it prudent not to intervene.

At the next waterhole some girls told us this was the last water for a long way, but looking at the map I was unconvinced and sure enough we came to another much larger one only half an hour further, 25 yards long and brimming with clear, sweet water. But there we were beset by visitors begging for food and medicines so aggressively that I considered dishing out overdoses of laxatives to see them off! And when we lay down to sleep the mosquitoes arrived in squadrons to feast on us, so I unrolled a large mosquito net to cover us all in a row. Blow me down if two of the visitors did not force their way under it as well. It was a crowded night.

In this area many men wore blankets in place of *shukas* and one tall, slender man with a silver goatee beard was particularly elegant, with strings of beads around his neck and around his naked waist. He sported a fine mudpack hair decoration topped with a small curl of ostrich plume. His hands moved slowly and balletically when he spoke. He was clearly a man of distinction and was treated with deference and respect (*see photo 12*).

I felt sad that our safari was nearing its end. We had just one last ridge of hills to climb, but by now the donkeys were on their last legs and we had to physically push them up a steep rocky slope. Poor creatures, I hoped they would never have to make such a journey again. I looked forward to unloading them for the last time. We crossed the final rocky hills, an attractive rust colour with dry river beds full of doum palms rustling in the wind, and late in the day glimpses of the Kalimapus hills near Kalokol appeared. We knew that next day we could reach it.

At the last waterhole a family of nomads was on the move to better grazing, the girls doing all the work with the donkeys (*see photo 13*) while a little way off the men sat and talked, one wearing an exceptionally fine mudpack skullcap which he was proud for me to photograph; a broad strip stained pink and the rest pale blue surmounted by a carved piece of bark holding small ostrich plumes. From this a loop of green beads hung over his forehead while around his neck was a string of black doum palm seeds interspersed with pieces of bark. Behind his ear was lodged a half-chewed ball of tobacco. I wondered whether in days of yore all the warriors had worn decorations as fine as this (see photo 4). If so they must have been a remarkable sight, particularly when going into battle with their spears and large hippo-hide shields. As usual everyone assumed I was a Somali, more understandable now with my deeply tanned skin.

Edung and Ekadeli were keen to have their money before we reached Kalokol. 'If peoples see we have money all will begging for us.'

So at our last break I divided up the spoils and the last of the medicine.

This hilly country was increasingly rich in goats, sheep and camels, an indication of how close 'civilisation' was. Reaching the escarpment of the last hills a panoramic vista unrolled before us of Kalokol, Ferguson's Gulf, Lake Turkana and Central Island, and beyond to the hazy mountains on the east side. This distant view across the lake was a tantalising glimpse of what was currently out of bounds, too dangerous, but which I was already yearning to see.

As we dropped down onto the coastal plain the temperature soared and the donkeys settled into a slow fatigued trudge. We were all worn down, utterly exhausted. The throbbing heat pounded us with its merciless assault until it became almost unbearable as the afternoon progressed, and the further we walked the more Kalokol seemed to recede before us like a mirage. We were a motley assortment of human beings, ragged, exhausted and dust-coloured, patterned by running sweat, and with a jagged, cloying thirst. Ekadeli and the donkeys trailed behind and I wanted us to arrive together, but more important was to reach the *dukas* before they closed for the night.

At last we struggled into the welcome shade of the doum forest on the north side of the town and were soon among the first outlying *manyattas*. Our gnawing thirst got the better of us and we sat in the shade to share two large Kimbo tins of *pombe*. This local beer was frothy and yeasty, densely cloudy and full of debris, but just what we needed. Glorious. It was almost 6pm, when the *dukas* would close, so we pressed on and suddenly saw the corrugated-iron backs of the town buildings and the Cooperative Society shop before us. Two *dukas* were still open and I bought what we agreed would make a celebratory feast.

Our march that day had taken 12 hours in temperatures sometimes around 40°C (104°F) and I was hardened now to living with a raging thirst, something I could not have endured three weeks earlier. I had been forged into a tougher creature.

The night soon engulfed us. We waited, but no Ekadeli. Thomas suggested, 'Maybe he camp outside town and come in morning?' I hoped not. Our cooking materials, together with the *posho* and dried food were in the donkeys' panniers so, no donkeys, no feast. It was extraordinary that even here in his home Thomas had no cooking pans or basic food supplies whatsoever. What had his family been eating?

Edung managed to beg some tea which refreshed us while we waited. Just as I was giving up hope there was a rumpus at the edge of the *manyatta* and Ekadeli appeared with our triumphant donkeys. Their hot, sweat-soaked, steaming backs were quickly relieved of their dreadful loads for the last time, and I hoped that their pains and exhaustion would soon be forgotten as they disappeared into the darkness in their desperate search for grazing.

We dined luxuriously on an entrée of baked beans followed by a plat principal of *posho* and spaghetti, complemented by repeated top-ups of grand cru tea. It was a grand feast. We slept on the sand outside Thomas' grass hut, and as I drifted quickly into a dreamless sleep of utter exhaustion, the last thing I was conscious of was a large hunting spider running across my bare chest to bid me farewell from the wilds of Turkana. It was New Year's Eve 1980.

Several days later when I arrived back in Nairobi I took a taxi from the bus depot to the Hurlingham Hotel. The Kikuyu driver asked me where I had been, probably expecting me to say Maasai Mara or Tsavo, but when I said Turkana he asked me to repeat it. Then he thought long and hard and said 'Ah, you mean in Sudan,' so I told him that actually it was in north-west Kenya and was the largest tribal district of his country. He reflected for a moment and then smiled at what he thought was my ignorance but refused to believe me. Seventeen years after Independence Turkana was still lost in the mists of time.

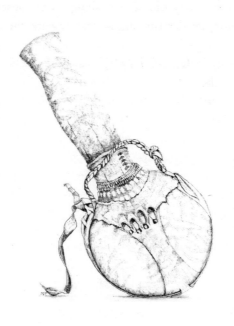

'It is not the goal but the way there that matters,
and the harder the way the more worthwhile the journey.'

Sir Wilfred Thesiger KBE (1910-2003)
Arabian Sands

Trek 2

'It Is Better to Die Without Crossing Mugurr'

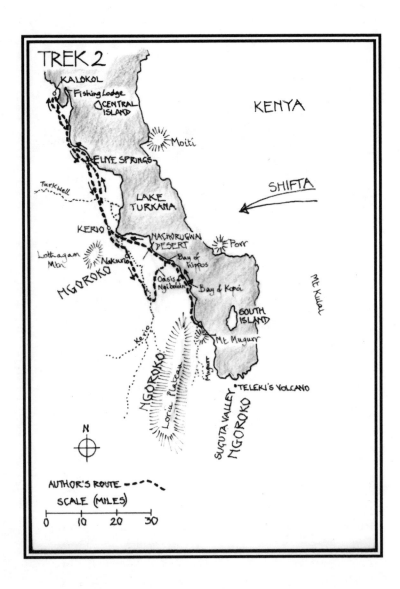

A joyful return to Kalokol
– but two's a crowd

AFTER NINE MONTHS of working at Pinewood Film Studios on a picture called Krull it was wonderful to land in Nairobi on 12 September 1982, heading for Turkana once more. I knew where I would rather be. Last time I had been all nerves. But this time I had the quiet confidence of someone who knew what he was doing. Or thought he did...

If possible, I wanted to reach Teleki's volcano, below the southern tip of the lake. This was remarkable only for having erupted as Teleki's expedition had first arrived and discovered the lake, but it thus marked a significant moment in local history. I had heard that, being in lava desert, it was threateningly hot, and the Suguta Valley immediately to its south was uninhabitable, so had become a *ngoroko* stronghold. That could be a problem. We would see.

On my last trip the south-west of the lake had been dangerous and unstable, but maybe things had loosened up since then. My companions had learned that I honoured my promises and we had gradually built a relationship of trust. I had even come to like Thomas and he had written to me in England to answer questions about who could come with me on another trek. Things were looking promising.

But this time I was not alone. After hearing stories about my last trip a friend I shall call M wanted to join me for this trek. I was worried whether he would cope with the heat and discomforts, and I actually jealously guarded the thrill of being alone in these wild places. The great travellers and explorers have had a certain masochistic streak which has helped inure them to the inevitable hardships and risks of their journeys. An English companion might easily jeopardise that. After a bloodthirsty attempted coup in Nairobi the month before we flew, M's father pressed me to be responsible for his son – but how could I guarantee his safety?

Wilfred Thesiger, who had been born in 1910 yet was often described as the last of the Victorian explorers, had continued to take an interest in my travels, and in May 1981 had proposed me as a Fellow of the Royal Geographical Society (FRGS). He had been awarded the Society's Founder's Medal in 1948 among many other honours, but he sadly reflected, 'There are so few real explorers these days; the Society is full of geography teachers.' So I knew I was very lucky when he suggested, 'Why don't you come up and stay with us at Maralal in Samburu district and I'll help you set up a trek from there.' I lunched with him several times at his flat in Tite Street, or at his club, during his annual spring visit to England, and we discussed the possibilities. In the end I decided I would join Thesiger at Maralal after my coming trip to south Turkana.

Once in Nairobi M and I moved into the Hurlingham Hotel on Argwings Kodhek Avenue and went for lunch with Omar at his newest restaurant, 'The Paddock', overlooking Kenyatta Avenue. It was great to see him again – always a delightful host. Afterwards I walked down to the Acamba Bus Service to book the next day's tickets to Kitale. In reality the bus station was a scruffy little office on a road of broken tarmac along which down-at-heel buses rolled periodically throughout the day, not to be compared with the smart buses which serviced the commuters and shoppers of Nairobi.

In the town centre I saw plenty of evidence of the attempted coup of 1st August; lines of bullet holes in the sides of buildings. Stories and rumours abounded of what exactly had (or may have) happened. The coup was short-lived – an attempt to overthrow President Daniel arap Moi by elements within the Air Force. It had begun at midnight and been defeated by the army with the General Service Unit (GSU, a special forces section of the police) by the morning. A popular though unproven rumour was that truckloads of air force personnel were taken out to Wilson Airport at first light and machine-gunned. Several people thought that Moi had been tipped off, and I spoke to some who claimed they had seen the presidential limousine speeding away from State House late at night. Looting had been chaotic and it was believed that one of the reasons for the failure of the coup was that revolutionaries were too busy breaking into shops and houses instead of carrying out their orders to overthrow the State. Many Asian women were raped and there was still great fear in their community. My Arab friends were doubling up the security on their houses.

Among all the various rumours I heard a delightful illustration of splendid old colonial spirit in which an ancient English lady drove into Nairobi the following morning, when bodies were still scattered about, and was stopped by armed soldiers preventing anyone from entering the centre.

'What on earth is going on?' she asked them.

'The road is closed, ma'am. There has been a national emergency.'

'Never mind about that, young man. On Sunday mornings I always play bridge with my friend Miss Simms and I have no intention of being late today.'

With that, she drove on, leaving the bemused soldiers standing speechless by the kerb.

Next morning our bus surprisingly set off on the dot of 10am. The engine screamed loudly all the way until drivers changed at Eldoret and the new man discovered there was in fact a gear above third. Just before crossing the equator it had started to rain hard and soon torrents of red mud were cutting a gully beside the road.

M had set his sights on staying at the Kitale Club, which I saw as a last-ditch attempt to delay facing the reality of Africa. But it turned out that this was for members only, so, to his unspeakable disgust, we booked into the Kamburu Silent Lodging and Boarding where I had stayed before. Personally I was quite happy to be back in the simple concrete-floored courtyard surrounded by small rooms with corrugated-iron roofs and iron bed frames. One communal shower cubicle next to the exit to the street sometimes even had running water.

We did, however, go to the Kitale Hotel for a drink and dinner. The only other diner turned out to be Arthur Scott who had given me so much advice before my previous trip to Turkana. Arthur was now General Manager for Hill Barrett, the transport company which also owned the fishing lodge on Ferguson's Gulf of which he had been the manager. We talked for a long time about what had happened since I had left north Turkana.

'The raiding in the north has got worse again. You wouldn't want to be going up there now. Very dangerous, you were lucky! But now south Turkana, which was a nightmare then, has quietened down.'

Doubly lucky. We arranged to meet him in the morning, as a lorry would be leaving for the Kalokol fish factory on which we could probably find space.

Back at the Kamburu the watchman gave us the pleasing and surprising news that there was not only water but hot water in the shower. Even the light bulb in our twin room was working and the sheets were spotlessly clean. I, at least, was very content.

After an extraordinarily English breakfast of bacon and eggs in the Bongo Bar at 7am we found Arthur, who told us the lorry was due to arrive at 8.30am, but that it would take an hour to load. This entire hour was taken up withdrawing money from the bank – the last we would see for about six weeks – and during interminable delays I slipped out and bought three jerry cans, some clothes for Edung, who was coming again, and various items of food.

By 10.30am we were swaying and bouncing along the road atop a mountain of flour sacks and cardboard boxes under a partial canvas awning over the open truck, with a distant cloudy view of Mount Elgon to the west. At first the landscape was level and grassy, with groups of very British-looking cows. We climbed into the wooded hills and saw more and more *manyattas* of the round thatched huts of the Pokot tribe. The hills grew into small mountains with valleys sometimes draped in cloud, and for a while it tried to rain.

As we rolled north it was warming up and by the time we climbed over the Marich Pass and dropped down onto the great plain of south Turkana the sun was beginning to peep through the clouds and toast the land. Quite quickly the forests became thorn scrub and even the acacias turned from green to dry brown. Then the thin yellow grass disappeared, leaving just dust and sand and long, dry river courses cut into the landscape. The sun, still blinking blearily through the veil of cloud, was now becoming hot. As the lorry rumbled on endlessly, the veil finally parted and the hammer of sun started to pound the anvil of Turkana for a new day.

In the late afternoon we reached the range of small black hills at Lodwar, where a *matatu* lay on its side across the road. They crashed regularly, often with considerable loss of life, because they were poorly maintained, if at all, and the passengers were crammed in so tightly that the boy who took the money – and occasionally even some passengers – were left to hang perilously and illegally onto the outside. Fares were cheap, though, and they weaved excitingly though the traffic with horns blaring. In Nairobi I enjoyed using them, for speed and convenience.

I felt nostalgic when the shape of Kalokol and the fish factory became discernible in the failing light, with Ferguson's Gulf behind. We climbed out stiffly as the plume of dust settled around and upon us. I had told M about the fishing lodge and he was keen to get to its comparative luxury as quickly as possible, but by now there would be no boat across the gulf. As we stood awkwardly beside our pile of bags Thomas appeared, and told me his news. 'I am now weigh clerk at the fish factory so every day I earn money.' But not much.

Dale Beverley, who had given me a lift from Nairobi to Kalokol before my first trek, had suggested we stay with a Danish engineer from the fish factory called Peter Schmidt, and Thomas knew where he lived. So we shouldered bags and followed him past the padlocked *dukas*, through the tribal *manyattas* and, after what seemed a long way, arrived at a little compound of European houses. They were new since my last visit. Kalokol was growing.

The Schmidts were having supper, but welcomed us. 'You must come and sit and eat something.' Thomas felt awkward – Peter was his boss – and he accepted just a cold beer before hurrying away. After our day in dehydrating wind, M and I drank lots of iced water as we talked, and then accepted the offer of a shower, shedding a beach-load of sand from clothes and hair, blown into the back of the truck from the dirt road. We settled down to sleep on the balcony of the unused house next door. At 11pm it was still 33°C (91°F).

Safari preparations
and a touch of tourism

THE FLIES WERE OUR alarm call at 6.30am, and after Hanne Schmidt kindly gave us breakfast we went to explore the little town's collection of small one-room wooden shops with cement floors and roofs of often-leaky corrugated iron. At the edge of the road, tailors sat on the ground, winding the handles of their ancient sewing machines. Their ability to quickly make or adapt almost anything was a vital part of what made life sustainable. Around the *dukas* had sprung up some bars, tea houses and a few concrete administrative buildings, while a scattering of traditional tribal *manyattas* – grass huts in tiny compounds of grass fences – clung to the edge of the town.

Peter took us to look around the fish factory, a large building full of expensive machinery in which more chaos than efficiency was evident. Thomas was there so I handed over a package of clothes for him and Edung. 'This is too much good, very happy,' he beamed.

Peter drove us down to the jetty, now enormously long in order to reach the shoreline, as, unbelievably, the level of the lake had fallen more than ten feet since I had left only 20 months earlier. The rains had failed in the Ethiopian hills, meaning that the River Omo, which supplied the lake with 80 per cent of its inflow, had shrunk to a fraction of its former breadth, and Ferguson's Gulf was now so shallow that, apart from a deep central channel, it would be possible to wade across. Wading would have been a bad idea, however, as the shallower water was now a popular breeding ground for crocodiles, who had multiplied profusely, and claimed human victims only recently.

At the lodge we spent the afternoon on the verandah, gazing over the wonderful panorama of the lake and watching the fishermen on their log rafts, the leisurely water birds, and the hippos cooling themselves in the shallows. Today the lake was a quiet, silver-blue sheet streaked with darker grey-blue bands, and the mountains of the eastern shore faded slowly from palest grey until they sank into the darkening sky. M felt comfortable here.

We walked down to David Jumale's *manyatta* in the morning but discovered from the covey of children that soon surrounded us that he was working for some Luo fishermen on the other side of the lake. A pity, as he would have loved to come again. Thomas had also told me that Ekadeli was away at Kakuma, but he had found a replacement called Ekele.

I suggested to M that we should move into Thomas' *manyatta* but discovered that moving him from his comfort was not going to be easy. Perhaps this was not working too well. Had he expected a sort of South Pacific island holiday? So I took the boat back to Kalokol alone and found Edung already wearing his new shorts and tee-shirt. It was a good reunion and I was pleased to be on my own with him and Thomas. As the night settled in we sat to eat by the light of a hurricane lamp I had just bought, while the women played with toys I had brought for the children, who did not seem to understand how to play. Our bed was the sand outside the hut. 'Too much good to be with you again.' Happy memories.

The Norwegians next door to the Schmidts had arranged to hire the lodge launch with its driver to visit Central Island, which, being totally undisturbed, was a prolific breeding colony for the lake crocodiles. Lake Turkana has three islands named – without imagination – North Island, Central Island and South Island, the remains of old volcanos which abundantly populate the Rift Valley. No doubt they had always been sanctuaries for the crocodiles, as when Count Teleki first discovered the lake and named it 'Rudolf' in 1888, a party that was sent over to South Island was never seen again. The lake was renamed Turkana in the process of Africanisation following Independence.

I very much wanted to go to Central Island, so I agreed to join the Norwegians, and we went to collect M from the fishing lodge before setting off on the one-and-a-half-hour trip.

The island contained several small lakes in its extinct craters, surrounded by cliffs or steep rock screes running down to the water's edge where the crocodiles bred. We took the paths the crocodiles used to reach the main lake. I noted in my diary that the smell was like a cross between ferrets and rotting meat. We kept a wary lookout as we walked.

Climbing higher, the view down into the crater lakes was beautiful, with sapphire blue water ringed crisply by narrow white beaches (*see photo 16*), yet sinister with lines of crocs just under the surface, their noses close to the beach like moored canoes. I assumed that this ambush position must have been habitual rather than practical, as being in such numbers they must have long since denuded the island of any edible mammals. I guessed the longest were about fifteen foot. Flamingos traced delicate patterns of white and soft pink as they flew over the water, and a lone pelican flapped past. We went down to the water's edge at a quiet spot, but when two crocs started swimming determinedly towards us we beat a hasty retreat.

After two and a half hours on the island we took the boat back, reaching the lodge at sunset, too late to return to the *manyatta*, so I joined M for dinner and decided to sleep the night there. I at last persuaded him to move across to Thomas' *manyatta* in the morning so we could make a start on our trek. The drone of the generator died at 11.30pm and the lights instantly died with it.

Thomas treated us to an unexpected lunch of spaghetti with pieces of mutton. I recognised the cooking pots from our first safari. Today was for buying provisions but first, going up to the Schmidts', we fell into conversation. Peter had been a 'big white hunter' in his younger days and was full of anecdotes. 'One day a rhino turned and charged me, and my gun-bearers sprinted for their lives. But as I was always a bit overweight I slipped in the mud and fell flat on my face. I thought that was it, and expected to be gored to death at any moment. But rhinos have very bad eyesight and it charged almost over the top of me to chase after the Africans.'

The obscenity of trophy hunting became illegal in Kenya in 1977, only three years before my first trip to Turkana, but since then the destruction of Kenya's wildlife has accelerated rapidly with poaching. In just the years that I spent there the elephant population was decimated by more than 90 per cent. A hideous tragedy for which we should all feel deeply ashamed on our watch of this precious planet.

Peter had experienced a lot in the bush. Knowing that I was going on to Samburu tribal territory next, where game was more plentiful than in Turkana, he passed on all manner of advice. 'Don't underestimate the hyena. They get bad press but are courageous and cunning animals with a much stronger bite than a lion.' I had read about hyenas dashing into the light of campfires, grabbing food and vanishing with it into the night. On at least one occasion a hyena reportedly bit the face clean off a sleeping man in camp. Peter added, 'They can easily sever a leg with one bite.'

He particularly warned about hippos for when we were near the lake. 'You think they are fat and slow, but they can outrun you for a long way. And they have very bad tempers. At night, when the hippos come out of the lake to graze, getting between them and the water is an extremely dangerous place to be.' Many old hunters have said that hippos are potentially the most dangerous animals in East Africa, but Peter's most constant saying, in a quiet voice while wagging his finger menacingly, was, 'The most dangerous animal of all is the human being.' We were duly warned.

We moved our bags to Thomas' hut and started to add the provisions for the trip. We ate later with the Schmidts before returning by torchlight to Thomas' hut. M was by no means happy with the idea of sleeping there. When we arrived everyone was at a dance with bells and drumming, and there we met Ekele, dancing enthusiastically with bells round his calves. He knew how to enjoy himself! He was thicker set than Edung, sporting a grizzled moustache, and he had long, powerful arms, sometimes adorned with a wrist knife. He wore a very soiled white vest and khaki trousers, which he liked to roll up above the knees, and often tied his head in a sort of white turban, into which he sometimes stuck a white feather. He turned out to be an expert at managing the donkeys.

I had warned M about hunting spiders, and within five minutes of getting into his sleeping bag he sat bolt upright and gasped, 'There's one in my sleeping bag!'

I found it hard to control my scepticism, but suggested, 'Open the mouth wide and ease yourself out very slowly to give it a chance to escape.'

He began carefully, and then suddenly flew into a whirlwind of panic. Never did a man leave a sleeping bag faster! When we shook out the bag there was nothing there. Perhaps it had left the bag even more rapidly than he had, but despite his protestations I could not contain a wry smile.

When it came to negotiating the price of the donkeys Edung had become more demanding. Thomas whispered, 'His uncle he tell Edung to ask more money.' I thought his profit last time was excessive, but now he wanted ten shillings a day per donkey. Thomas only earned 12 shillings as a weigh clerk. I beat him down to eight and a half. We shopped with a vengeance, and the heap of bags increased. Eventually we seemed to have covered everything.

The Schmidts told us there was to be a big festival to welcome a Norwegian Aid Scheme, and after lunch we heard the singing begin. There were photographers from the Kenyan press and even a small TV crew, so people had been told they must allow pictures to be taken, and the police were there to enforce it. By mingling with the press I got some photos. They were very finely dressed, a jazz of colour as they danced, horsehair fly whisks waving and ostrich plumes swirling. The bead necklaces were as bright as new, and the men's mudpack headdresses were spectacular (*see photo 14*), leg bells and wrist knives looking dramatic. I even spotted some bows and arrows. Everyone thoroughly enjoyed the day.

But gradually I began to have doubts. The *shukas* were mostly kangas and kikois from the coast, and the women's hairstyles were all down-country fashions, not the style of the local people. Was this the thin end of the wedge of tourism? I already knew that the Maasai dances laid on for tourists in Nairobi were often performed by Kikuyus and not Maasai and I was concerned about the veracity of what we had witnessed. Sadly, with time these displays can only have become less authentic.

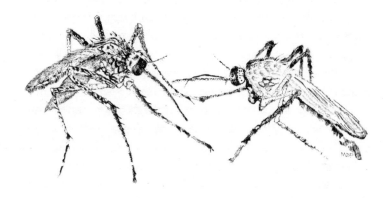

Idyllic days, tormented nights – and farewell to M

BECAUSE OF OUR delays we had decided to start our trek that evening. But before leaving we went to eat *posho* and, just as I feared, it proved totally inedible to M. He could not just ignore the taste and eat it anyway. How would he cope without the mainstay of the local diet? Even the *mboga* stew he found barely edible.

The donkeys arrived at 4.30pm with Edung. There was a lot of stuff to load and it took a while to find a place for everything. It was 22nd September and suffocatingly hot as we set off south, about three-quarters of a mile from the lake edge. A dramatic lightning storm lit up the early night sky to the west but no rain. Yet. I was amazed how even after dark the heat did not start to relent, and soon we were slippery with sweat and shiny in the moonlight. Remembering his father's anxieties I mentioned to M, 'Might be a good idea to walk behind the donkeys just in case of a puff adder.' I felt his apprehension mount.

Small sand dunes became heavy-going in the dark, and after two-and-a-half hours of stumbling and sinking into this difficult surface we decided to call it a day and make camp. Making tea and preparing a meal was slow, as no one had learned where things were stowed among the panniers. It was 11pm before we eventually turned in, but at least we were underway.

The next day, we continued along the beach of sand, whose igneous origins sometimes coloured it grey, while tall palm trees swayed in the breeze. We walked through flocks of flamingos (*see photo 17*) who took to the air in their thousands, circling round to land again like exotic aircraft, and a group of goats dashed in and out of the small waves to cool down. Black-winged stilts stalked stiffly along the water's edge, balanced delicately on their improbably long, stick-like pink legs. It all seemed idyllic.

The lake water here admittedly tasted pretty foul. M scowled, 'I just can't drink this muck'. He continued his abstinence, too, from the midday *posho*. He even refused to drink from the same water containers as our tribal companions, so always carried a separate one-litre flask on his belt. In the mid-afternoon we found a spring of clear, sweet water bubbling up on the beach and filled a jerry can, but the suppurating flamingo guano which surrounded it added it to M's blacklist. How long could he survive this self-imposed denial?

The real dangers of this land were as yet unknown. It was a long time after dark when we stopped for the night among some doum palms and drank delicious tea made with the spring water, followed by spaghetti flavoured with Mchuzi Mix. But when we bedded down the mosquitoes attacked in force, and even after spreading my large net over us, any point where it touched our skins was a furious pincushion, the focus of a ferocious and sustained attack.

We were absolutely miserable and built up the fire as a deterrent, the mosquitoes' numbers so dense that flames actually licked a yard high into the air through their swarms, but it had no effect whatsoever in reducing their attack on us. At midnight Ekele came to the only conclusion: 'We go high for wind'. So we gave up the unequal struggle and went to the lengthy and frustrating process of reloading the donkeys in the dark and setting off for higher ground, where a wind might protect us from our torturers.

A mile away among the dunes we found a breeze and made a fresh camp, free of mosquitoes. As soon as we were settled again it began to rain. Finally convinced that this was not just a passing shower we packed up yet again and set off in search of a tree that might give some shelter. The moon had set, and in the pitch black it was hard to choose a suitable spot, but eventually one met with everyone's approval. Predictably, just as we settled again the rain stopped, but by then everything was sodden. A wretched night. Throughout the entire escapade, however, M had only received one bite. Perhaps the local mosquitoes could not tolerate a *posho*-free diet. After less than three hours of soggy sleep the morning chorus of flies was extremely unwelcome at 6.30am.

It was an easy stroll to reach Eliye Springs, where there was a small lakeside lodge, our last chance of any kind of comfort. Ekele and the donkeys were left far behind and soon the early clouds cleared to allow the sun to resume its attack. We sat on the lodge verandah with a cold beer apiece and waited for the others. M had inevitably decided that at this last contact with a navigable road he must find a way of turning back. He intended to head to the coast for a conventional holiday, which was just as well: our hardships had not yet begun.

The lodge was delightful, on the beach surrounded by palms, and it was hard to leave. I bought an attractive walking stick as a souvenir for M, and later he found a particularly good spear for 100 shillings which he bought from a tiny, wizened and deeply wrinkled old man who was absolutely stark naked in the sunshine. For some reason we could hardly enquire about, he was entirely missing his penis.

We camped on the sand under a spreading acacia tree near the house of the local manager of the Turkana Fishermen's Cooperative Society, who told us that a Society lorry was expected next day to collect dried fish for the fish factory at Kalokol. The timing was perfect. Thomas bought a couple of traditional ostrich egg necklaces for M and me, made from pieces of shell threaded onto a string and then rubbed over with an abrasive stone until formed into a flexible tube.

Next day, as I haggled down the price of a goat, M climbed onto the lorry and he had disappeared in a cloud of dust and black diesel fumes before Ekele had killed the animal, hacking open its throat so deeply to the spine that Thomas walked away in disgust, shocked by his brutality. All ways of killing an animal are unpleasant, but cutting just the jugular vein to bleed it to death is more normal – and comparatively humane compared with the way Ekele had slashed through the entire throat. The poor creature then sucked in its own blood through its severed windpipe and literally drowned. But sadly, this was not so unusual. We are conditioned to being squeamish about the letting of blood but animals are not, and seeing their own blood spilled does not seem to horrify them as much as it does us. Pain, on the other hand, is something we all understand.

Ekele mixed the blood with goat's milk and sugar and handed us all a mug. It tasted predominantly of the milk, which had been flavoured with doum fruit. He hung the carcass from a branch by its back legs and skinned it quickly and expertly before removing its organs, which we fried with vegetables for a very tasty meal. Edung commented that 'The peoples here south Turkana not beg like north Turkana,' and so far that was perfectly true; the crowd which arrived during the bargaining for the goat had all left by the time it was killed. The people further north were much poorer so famine cut more deeply.

We swam in the lake and enjoyed another beer in the lodge before wandering back as a truckload of young Europeans on an overland adventure holiday roared past, discovering the 'wilds' of Turkana from the road.

The carcass was split in two to roast, and long after dark it was pronounced cooked. Luckily it was impossible to see the cindered fleece on one side and the meat inside, still cold and raw. I gnawed on some ribs but Edung and Ekele ate the rest, as well as both back legs, after which I spent the night driving off village curs who crept up incessantly to chew the bones, tossed far and wide. Because of rabies I was not keen to fraternise with these pariahs.

Next day I paid a woman to fill a jerry can from the lake, perhaps an unfair request as it took her so long struggling under the weight that we only set off at 9am. The bush became denser and a mile or two before we reached the Turkwell River (in the past a major provider of lake water) we entered an area of well-spaced, large, stately acacia trees and mature doum palms growing on a sandy floor; bizarrely like a Turkana interpretation of Capability Brown's planting of great oaks in parkland. The dappled light they offered was very pleasant, the sensation of Englishness enhanced by the cooing of doves and the rasp of a crow. Less English, though, were the remains of the goat tied to the side of one of the donkey's loads and swarming with flies. It was fried with potatoes for lunch.

When we emerged onto the bank of the Turkwell, almost a mile broad, there was not a drop of surface water due to the irrigation projects upstream, which I was told had been established by the missions, and which now further contributed to the falling level of the lake. In the wide river bed were several large waterholes, about five feet deep, and at one we repeatedly filled our largest *sufuria* for the thirsty donkeys to drink their fill (*see photo 18*). The wind picked up the talcum-fine alluvial dust and covered us all in a thin coating until we became ghosts.

The river bed was haphazardly marked with strange designs drawn by the incessant wind picking up or dropping its cargo of dust, and thin pale lines where animals favoured the same paths. The low cliffs of the river banks surmounted by the surrounding forest were frequently lost in the haze of blown dust. When the donkeys were finally satiated we filled the jerry cans and continued to the long shadows of the south bank, rewarded by a splendid view up the river to palms silhouetted against an ethereal golden sun plunging from a burnished copper sky, finally doused by inky night. We camped soon afterwards.

Bandit country, dust and drought

IT WAS DISCONCERTING to wake up, open my eyes and find myself looking up at a circle of people staring down at me. I felt at a bit of a psychological disadvantage. One of them tried to sell me his walking stick for 20 shillings, and failing that made a joke of offering me his attractive teenage daughter for a shilling.

Once we had dispelled the crowd and packed, we headed for the Kerio River, where we found a crank-handle pump, which made watering the donkeys much quicker. Already the wind had coated us all with fine dust again. I walked on with Thomas, amazed by how much he had changed since the last trip; he was now so helpful and hardworking. Leopards could indeed change their spots. A real friendship grew between us.

In the village of Kerio we needed to restock already, especially with chewing tobacco, but it was not long before we were besieged by a throng of the great and the good of Kerio, so I felt obliged to make presents of tobacco to these half-naked dignitaries, after which our supply was drained again. We bought another goat and tied it to a tree overnight with the donkeys, as Edung was concerned about thieves.

All night long it blew a gale and the fine dust found its way into everything, even to the very bottom of my sleeping bag. I could taste it, smell it and feel it in my lungs. My ears and nostrils were full of it, and when I woke I had to scrape it off my eyelids before I could open them. So buried in dust and sand were we that we had almost become part of the landscape, only high points showing as islands above its surface.

Once dug out and cleaned up we slaughtered the goat (*see photo 15*). Curiously, only Edung and I drank the blood, into which I stirred sugar while he added milk as well.

Not far from us was a long, rounded mountain called Lothagam which, until only two months previously, had been a stronghold of *ngoroko*, raiding widely and brutally. Now they had been flushed out, with many killed, and villagers were returning to their *manyattas* from wherever they had fled to. But we heard stories of the north, now once again a cauldron of savagery with continual raiding. Where we had bought the large black goat two people had just been killed. My guardian angel was obviously hard at work, and from now on the main topic of conversation with everyone we passed was the *ngoroko*. The Suguta Valley to our south, inaccessible by road, still had its dangerous reputation as a route by which *ngoroko* could raid or escape both east and west. That was where we were heading.

Thomas told me a horrific story. 'A classmate of my school went with *ngoroko* gang which attack *manyattas* south of Lodwar. They very bad men and, all together, rape a poor girl. Then this horrible man push his rifle inside her and pull the trigger. The bullet he come through her neck. Very bad thing.'

Death was hopefully instant. Fittingly, he was shot and killed soon afterwards in a gun battle with the administrative police. (By the 21st century, bands of *ngoroko* were sometimes being organised by corrupt elements within the government and police for cattle-rustling and gun-running at a handsome profit, with a big increase reported in 2016.)

As we were finishing preparing the goat, I received a message to call on the administrative police post in Kerio. Dutifully I went to see them. It seemed that among all the rumour and nervousness after the attempted coup in Nairobi I had imaginatively been reported as a possible plotter now in hiding in Turkana. I produced my passport, probably the first one they had ever seen, and with no idea what it actually was or where to look, they put more effort into play-acting knowledgeable sleuths than looking for the date of my entry visa. In the end we all decided that I was probably not a dangerous threat to the president and they gave me their friendly permission to carry on with my trek.

Before nightfall we built substantial barriers against the wind, but with only limited success, and the fine stuff still found its way into our lungs until our chests ached. Edung woke us with alarm in the early hours to announce, 'One donkey he stolen', but when I inspected the rawhide strip with which it had been tethered its fibrous ends showed a break, not a cut, and soon the escapee sauntered nonchalantly back out of the darkness. Edung tended to over-react.

So far we had only walked 40 miles and really needed to cover some ground, although the donkeys were delighted with this speed. We managed to set off the next morning by 7am. We passed a crocodile skull, presumably killed for its meat, which tastes like fishy chicken. The crocodiles of Lake Turkana are blessed with having small pieces of floating bone in their skins called 'buttons' and considered undesirable by the fashion goods industry, so they have never been hunted in earnest. With teeming numbers of tilapia and Nile perch in the lake, together with a human population which had traditionally despised the eating of fish, so offered no competition, their numbers were burgeoning. A few were killed for food, particularly by the small El Molo tribe in the south-west of the lake, but generally they were left undisturbed. I hoped that they would display a similar respect for us when we went into the lake to take water.

We pushed through dense young doum forest, hoping not to come head to formidable head with a rhino, and noticed the fresh spoor of hyena, who feed on local livestock. I mentioned to Thomas, 'I have heard that hyena can crush a man's head in their jaws.'

He casually added, 'They crush donkey skull – and donkey he has hard head!'

Their faeces are even white from all the bone in their diet. The idea that hyena are cowardly scavengers is misguided. I had recently read a report from the Serengeti with evidence showing more lion stealing hyena kills than hyena scavenging from lions. Worthy of respect.

My map showed the Kerio estuary as an area of marsh, and we had been told that the main river was broader than the Turkwell, with water chest-deep. In fact it was half as wide and dry as dust, like its surroundings. But as we crossed we saw a group of camels with a male in season, or *musth*. In this state they blow great membranous balloons from their mouths and can be highly volatile and aggressive. Seeing this had an electrifying effect on my companions, who became very agitated and immediately swung the donkeys round in the opposite direction and kept a constant lookout behind as we headed off at the double. Thomas explained, 'They attack with no reason, bite and kick very bad, even continue to death.' We hurried along.

At one point we came to a short stretch of running water, like a moving pond, which disappeared back into the sand. In its shallows stood a line of a dozen spur-winged plovers. That was the only hint of damp at the mouth of one of Kenya's longest rivers. The dryness of Turkana was extreme.

While in England I had read *Another Land, Another Sea*, describing the first intrepid circumnavigation of the lake by Stephen Pern, an ex-Para, about three years before I had first come to Turkana. With two Turkana and three donkeys from Loyangalani he had walked round anticlockwise, but what he saw was very different from what I was seeing. There had been recent dramatic flooding, the level of the lake was unusually high and the rivers were in spate. Fresh grass and meadows of wild flowers had blossomed everywhere for the animals to graze, and with it had come a host of wildlife. The air was full of birdsong. It sounded joyful, and even the dangers from *ngoroko* seemed much diminished, and were not the constant topic of conversation they were now.

Over the course of my walks I covered most of the same ground as Pern had, much of it barely recognisable from his descriptions. I also ventured much further from the lakeside; extraordinary how a drought can so dramatically and savagely change a land and increase the appetite for tribal raiding. The only section which was not so changed, even then bone-dry and dangerous, was where we were now heading, perhaps in a permanent rain shadow.

We followed the dry course of the Kerio upstream for the rest of the day, leaving it only to enter the nearby village of Nakurio. There we visited its only *duka*, a little store of corrugated-iron and thatched grass, and treated ourselves to some sodas which, absurdly, had been standing in the sun and were almost ready to explode.

I wanted to get up this dry river as far as we could find waterholes, and then cut east across the mountains of Loriu to get back to the lake. The worry was that Loriu was well-known as a *ngoroko* stronghold, but I was counting on them also having been driven away by the drought. Our surroundings were becoming more desert-like – large expanses of sand with occasional rocky outcrops – and Edung became increasingly tetchy about our chances of finding water. 'It is no water here and donkeys will die. If donkeys dies, we dies.' Did he have a point?

We camped where we found one tiny spring, not too badly soiled by camel and goat dung, oozing a limited sluggish discharge that we decided was drinkable, but I restricted myself to tea that evening to give my stomach a rest from its normal daily ration of gastrointestinal bacteria. I was fortunate on my treks in Kenya not to suffer from this extraordinary diet. On one occasion in north Turkana we had to sweep a large slick of floating camel dung off a stagnant pond before filling the jerry cans, and afterwards everyone else was curled up with stomach pains and diarrhoea while I was luckily unaffected. Sadly, I had not been so fortunate in Asia.

Next day we continued upstream in a strong wind which rippled the sand, filled our eyes with fine dust, and was an assault of tiny needles on our legs. Even the wind was excruciatingly hot. Walking became shattering work, as the dried surface crust of the sand was not quite firm enough to support our weight and with each step we broke through and sank in. Because of the limited trickle from the spring where we had camped we had only collected a meagre offering, and after a first cup of tea when we woke we now carried no water in our jerry cans. I felt increasingly parched, my heart was pounding audibly, the dust in my lungs made them ache and my spittle had dried to a sort of gum that I could almost chew. For a moment I even found myself wondering why I was there…

Edung became increasingly angry with me for continuing on this route: 'We all die soon, no water.' My map marked more waterholes ahead but I had learned that it was by no means reliable. My hopes of reaching Teleki's volcano, due south of the lake on the edge of the

Suguta Valley, might be putting us at considerable risk of attack. My goal and the extent to which I could allow it to endanger the lives of my companions were constantly in the balance. In my diary I noted, 'Worth a go anyway', but was this unrealistic?

As we unloaded at a new waterhole I was overwhelmed by a sickening smell of rotting meat coming from the remains of our roasted goat, tied to the outside of the panniers. Luckily it was so thickly encrusted with sand and dust that only a small area remained for the flies to crawl in and out. Anyway, this was no time to be picky, as it was shortly to be our lunch and, in the event, once the shiny green rot had been scraped off and some of the remainder was fried, it tasted edible. We were so short of food, however, that we only cooked half of it and the rest would have to provide us with a future meal, while also breeding a new generation of blow flies.

Dehydrated donkeys and waterside woes

EDUNG'S COMPLAINING had started to disconcert me about continuing into the Loriu mountains, so we had been asking local people about waterholes. Everyone insisted that the only way from here was to head for the small oasis of Ngiboloin, the only possible water source. This was a real setback, partly because it meant heading backwards north-east, thus wasting a day or two's travel, but also because it was in the Nachorugwai desert. This was surely foolhardy?

The donkeys were exhausted and already desperately thirsty, so we made the decision to lighten their loads by taking very little water. At a push we would reach the oasis that night. We drank as much as we could hold and set off with just three litres between the four of us. We had already walked nine miles that morning in the searing heat and now would have to cover at least the same distance again, some of it through sand dunes. And we had to trust that the oasis really did have water. It was undeniably dangerous.

I set a new compass bearing and we set off again through broken sandy country along the edge of the desert. The powerful dry wind persisted from the east, the heat was brutal and the donkeys were at their absolute limits. Soon we also had raging thirsts. But Thomas was unfaltering in his support, and Ekele at least kept any doubts to himself. Just Edung: 'The donkeys are die, and we all die.' Such cheery company! When the sun set it was fortunately replaced by a good moon to light our way, but the heat remained. We walked on and on (*see photo 19*).

Our spirits lifted when a black silhouette of palms came into view and we eventually arrived, deep in the night, soaking with sweat. Eighteen miles in extraordinary heat with barely a sip since midday. Water was our priority and we split up to search for it. After an hour we had still found nothing more than a patch of muddy grass, soggy from some underground ooze. We must find water or the donkeys really might die – and perhaps us as well.

We unloaded, and Thomas and Edung took the *panga* to try to dig out some water. After a long time they returned with a little liquid mud the colour of boot polish, and when we started to drink it we tried not to retch. Edung remarked with unnerving accuracy, 'This smell like goat's stomach.' It was sickening. So sickening that everyone agreed not even to try cooking with it, preferring to go hungry and even thirstier. The wind continued to blow strongly throughout the night and once again we were covered with grey dust.

Next day started cloudy. We were ravenously hungry, but much more importantly we were now dangerously thirsty. Our throats were like gravel and there was barely any saliva to swallow. The poor donkeys were even more desperate. In daylight we could see that the sand dunes were gradually burying this oasis, together with its water source. There was nothing here. I wished we had continued towards Loriu. We had to press on. Only four miles remained to the lake, but these were over a small range of rocky hills. It was an act of cruelty reloading the wasted animals; I felt despicable. We all ached with thirst.

The going was desperately slow, the hills covered with black-brown rocks of iron ore which rolled underfoot and threatened to sprain an ankle. This was the third day since the donkeys had last drunk but they plugged on stoically. God, how I admired them. After all, they were not the ones who had chosen to come on this scatterbrained safari.

The first glimpse of the lake produced a longing to plunge into cool water and drink and drink until we burst. Thomas and I pressed ahead, setting off down a little dry valley which led from the hills to a grassy beach with a couple of small *manyattas* of grass huts. Just as we began to race into the cool water we saw, to our horror, a family of hippos feeding on weed in the shallows. Thomas' tone was one of anguish: 'This too much dangerous,' and I remembered Peter Schmidt's warnings. Just as we crept cautiously to the water's edge a crocodile surfaced close by and we retreated.

Thankfully I found a small rock pool and we drank for several minutes. Very soon the others arrived and it was a joy to watch the donkeys drinking fit to explode. But once Edung and Ekele saw the hippos they also lost any desire to enter the water. The fishermen thought our reticence hilarious. 'We come with you, hippo not problem.' Even the crocodile did not worry them unduly, and with all the communal splashing it eventually sloped off.

The largest hippo had meanwhile wallowed closer to us and the fishermen began throwing stones to drive it away, which seemed absurdly antagonistic to me. Edung enthusiastically joined in this fusillade and when, with a large pebble, he hit it smack on the end of its great bulbous nose, the huge bull hippo reared up with a terrifying roar and smashed down in an explosion of murky foam. I waited with bated breath, but when it resurfaced it was further off, as they had predicted. One of our hosts swam out to where the hippo had last plunged and shouted back, 'You see – now safe. Come with me.' I quickly declined, as I had heard of short-tempered hippos biting the feet off swimmers above them.

We sat out the midday heat in a disused hut and made tea which tasted as much like tea should taste as I had ever encountered in Turkana. The prospect of spending the next week walking gently along the beach put us in quite a festive mood and I caught myself wondering whether this trek might not be sufficiently exciting. The future, however, had other ideas.

Ekele meanwhile had located the clinically sterile medical scissors and decided to cut Edung's short hair even shorter, which delayed our departure. Consequently we again walked until well after dark and finally stopped for the night on a shingle bank, where we ate the inevitable *posho*.

In the morning we continued along the shoreline for an hour and a half until we came to the point that the fishermen had said would be impossible for the donkeys; a place where a spur of hill plunged into the lake in a great jumbled chaos of rock. After spending a long time scouting around we chose a route which might be negotiable, although a couple of places looked very dangerous, and the bleached bones of donkeys and cattle scattered about in the tumble of black boulders bore that out.

Our admirable donkeys slipped and skated, pitched and shied, but after being steadied and bolstered up as much as we possibly could, considering that our own feet were skidding and sliding helplessly, they got through. Snorting with flared nostrils, sucking the hot air, eyes rolling as they pitted their strength against the loose rocks and severe gradients, they looked heroic, but in the end they coped much better than I feared. If one of them had panicked it might have ended tragically. A broken leg would have been impossible to treat, requiring the immediate slaughter of the animal. At one point among the confusion of rocks I came across a human skull; someone else had been less fortunate. A broken leg for one of us might have been just as fatal; we were about 100 miles from any chance of medical assistance.

One rocky headland led to another past small bays, sometimes with a few fishermen's huts perched near the water, and we continued to scramble over great tumbles of rock. By 11.30am the donkeys were completely drained and we made an early stop for our midday rest. The terrain was going to be impossible for them to continue much further (*see photo 20*) so I made a plan to leave them behind soon with one man and for the rest of us to carry what food we could and try to reach the southern point of the lake. I noted in my diary, 'It might be possible to do it in three hard days of walking, but it will be no joke.'

Edung was incredulous: 'Why you do this thing? Too much hard, too much dangerous. Crazy. Just to see place where *msungu* no see?'

I put in the diary, 'I don't really blame him; sometimes I think I'm rather barmy myself.'

My one consolation was that the fishermen we passed still said most of the *ngoroko* had been driven out of this area. But where had they gone to? Probably to the Suguta Valley where we were headed, with temperatures soaring into the mid 40sC (113ºF). The hottest place in Kenya and sometimes among the hottest in the world.

After carrying on a little further south to the bay of Kopoi it was clear that the poor animals were well and truly done-in and must rest for a few days. This was a good place for them to recuperate, with some decent grazing and unlimited water. There were the windblown remains of four huts where we could store their loads, and which would provide shelter for whoever stayed.

I was still determined to reach Teleki's volcano if at all possible, but now this would have to be on foot without the donkeys. I decided to take Thomas, which he was delighted to hear, and suddenly Edung was keen to come too. Why? I tried to dissuade him but he would not take no for an answer. Odd. So we ate maize-meal porridge, which was wasteful of sugar, but I felt we needed extra energy for the concerted push ahead. Curiously, just as the others were all feeling the exhaustion of the trip catching up with them, I felt exhilarated and filled with a new lease of life and energy. I was to need it.

The madness of Mugurr

WE WOKE EARLY and set off carrying two bags of *posho*, some salt, sugar, tea, dried milk, and half a dozen sun-dried tilapia, with my six emergency freeze-dried rations and a *sufuria*. Not much for three men for over 60 gruelling miles in this heat, but we needed to travel light. In my kit was my Nikon camera with a couple of lenses, my hunting knife and a one-litre water bottle which we could constantly replenish from the lake as we went, with a final thirsty push down to the volcano itself. I of course carried my diary and pen, and a few items from my now-comprehensive medical kit. We started at break-neck speed over one spur of hill after another, rock-hopping along the edge of the water, and floundering through deep, soft sand. The boulders of the giant screes were savagely weathered and sometimes immense, often rocking under foot.

It started cloudy, and a cool wind blew strongly from the lake, but I was dripping with sweat all the same. A boy from a *manyatta* near Kopoi tagged along with us but could not keep up with our forced march and constantly lagged far behind. It felt good to be moving so fast, without the loaded animals.

Suddenly, about mid morning, Edung lost his nerve and said he was going back. He did his best to persuade Thomas to return with him, but Thomas would not hear of it. Edung rounded on us fiercely, 'You crazy, you die soon in mountains. Too much crazy!' and turned on his heel. Did he have a yellow streak, or was he just more realistic than me? Hmm...

So Thomas, the young boy and I pressed on, walking like automatons, one hill after another, one bay after another, constantly twisting and jumping through great heaps of fallen boulders. This terrain was wildly beyond what our donkeys could have coped with and very demanding for us too; sometimes like the mayhem of a war zone. The black rocks soaked up the extreme heat and our feet almost smouldered on them (*see photo 21*).

The fishermen had told us we might reach Mugurr that night but I was keen to try to reach it by midday and cross it in the afternoon. Mugurr was the largest of the peaks which dropped into the lake beside a dry stream-bed of the same name. In the event we stopped for our midday break under a large, spreading acacia tree just a mile before reaching it; a splendid effort. The sky had cleared and it was now gruellingly hot. I felt my nose split open down its ridge in the dry wind and smeared on a little Fucidin ointment to keep the flies off.

We had covered about 13 miles in the morning, although the terrain made it feel twice that much. To reach our destination I wanted to sleep well past Mugurr that night. To my great pleasure I found that the changed man Thomas had become was fully prepared to put in as much effort as I was.

Baboons barked and screamed outrage at us from the rocks

above as we ate *posho* with a freeze-dried chicken ration. At 4pm we started again, still desperately hot, and as we entered the bay of Mugurr the jagged uneven rocks we had been walking over all morning petered out and we found ourselves on small shingle, sand and even grass. Grass that would never be grazed by donkeys – they could never reach it.

We passed many depressions where crocodiles had laid their eggs, and soon we started to see large numbers of young ones three or four feet long in the shallow water. On guard around them were the sinister shapes of many adults floating with just the tops of their heads breaking the surface. This was a substantial breeding colony. On a small sand spit projecting into the lake we noticed a heap of adults basking in the sunshine, literally piled on top of each other, and as we came closer they unravelled, almost unwound, and slithered noiselessly one by one into the dark, brooding waters (*see photo 22*).

I was surprised how shy they were for animals with such a fearsome reputation, but soon saw a reason for them to be watchful of human beings. In a patch of burned grass we found the skull of a crocodile which had been roasted and eaten. I collected some of the less blackened teeth as a souvenir.

The water was a deep, tantalising blue, belying its sinister occupants. A group of four pelicans flapped up from its surface at our approach and a pair of cormorants on a rock eyed us disapprovingly.

On the other side of the bay we came to where the side of Mugurr plunged almost vertically into the lake. Here a group from a *manyatta* nearby told us it was too late in the day to start our crossing of the mountain, that the mountain was much too dangerous, and to be caught on it at dusk would probably be fatal. I asked whether there were hyena in the mountain and was relieved when they said there were not. My relief was short-lived as they then told us that Mugurr was populated by leopard. One old man said in a very grave, quiet voice, 'It is better to die without having to cross Mugurr,' a phrase that was to echo repeatedly through my brain the next day. They said that we should start first thing in the morning, provided only that the wind was not too strong, as we could be blown off the cliff face. It sounded daunting.

We found windbreaks of flat stones erected by previous travellers who had slept here before attempting the mountain, and the ground was scattered with the bones of fish they had eaten. We woke frequently with the strong wind blowing through our thinly wrapped *shukas* (I had left my sleeping bag behind), and restless with worries about the day to come. Every time I turned on my bed of stones I would wake with a start, having been impaled by yet another fish bone. One moment I woke from a dream of leopards to see a dark, stealthy shape move past within a couple of yards. My heart thumped so loudly in my chest I was sure that this creature must hear it. I could hear nothing else. But it turned out to be a nervous antelope, which quickly melted into the night.

We had been told there were two possible routes across the mountain, one for young people, which involved rock-climbing across the face of the cliff with a direct drop to the waves breaking on the rocks below. The other route was for older people, which was safer but longer, climbing over the top of the mountain following stream beds and involving even greater effort and tenacity, scrambling up and down steep gradients of loose shale. The cliff path was the shortest and quickest so we set off that way, the young boy in front as he knew the way, and Thomas bringing up the rear. It involved great concentration as we clambered up and down, in and out of small gullies in the rock face. The consequences of losing my grip did not bear thinking about, with a direct drop to the rocks beneath, and the black water which we had seen was well-populated with crocodiles; survival unlikely, almost certainly impossible.

So great was my concentration on following every step and handhold of the boy in front that it was some time before I noticed that Thomas was no longer behind me. I assumed he was just round the last crag of rock. Shortly afterwards, however, I spotted him about a hundred feet above us, crossing a buttress of rock, and he signalled that he preferred to continue at this higher level. I was concerned as I felt we should stick together, yet there was nothing I could do now.

Moments later I wished I had followed him up the cliff to his higher path. In front was a place where a smooth, flat face of rock was at an angle of about 80 degrees, but seemingly vertical. It was not very large, certainly less than ten feet wide and high, and beyond it there was a meagre level platform. Below it a void dropped to a small inlet which undercut it 50 or 60 feet below, where the waves pounded the black, half-submerged rocks.

The wind was strong and blustered unexpectedly, sometimes threatening to throw me off-balance, particularly when it caught my leather map case, which hung from my shoulder, and dashed it against the cliff or swung it wildly out over the drop, trying to drag me with it. Already I had found the map case to be a liability. When climbing a difficult piece of rock it had been blown out sideways as I swung into a new position and had then become trapped between my body and the cliff so that I could not press against the rock face, making me scrabble madly for a new hold to stop me from falling. My nerves were becoming frayed. This sheer, smooth piece of rock I now gazed at was clearly impassable.

My horror was therefore inexpressible when the boy handed me the bag of *posho* and the cooking pan he was carrying and prepared to cross it. Only then did I notice a tiny horizontal crack about half an inch wide and not much deeper, running two thirds of the way across the middle of the rock face to a small projection the size of an ordinary household matchbox. Beyond that the rock was completely smooth. He was helped by the fact that he was bare-footed and could wedge the side of his small feet into the crack, and flatten his body against the rock so that his finger tips just hugged the top where it curved away from the vertical.

He edged his way slowly along this tiny fault line until he was able to step across onto the matchbox projection, where he steadied himself for a brief moment and then made the final stretch to land on the little platform the other side. As I swung the bag of *posho* and the cooking pot across to him my throat was bone-dry and my brain ached with fear. It might have been a simple challenge for a freestyle rock climber, but I was certainly not that. I knew I could not do what he had just done. I desperately measured the distance by eye to see whether I could jump across, but without a good run-up it was much too far.

I should of course have also swung my heavy camera and map case across to him – even the hunting knife and water bottle that were on my belt – but my brain was not working in a logical way and all I could feel was an emptiness in the pit of my stomach and the trembling of my muscles. I could just press the edge of the sole of my lightweight boots into the crack, my whole foot being cantilevered out into space. My mind cried out that this was crazy, unnecessary, and that I was about to die. My strength had drained away and I was very, very frightened. One tiny slip was all it would take and I would be gone.

I pressed myself to the rock as he had done and, reaching up, could just flatten my palms onto the top curve of the rock. It was quite smooth and offered no grip. My hands hunted around for something better but there was nothing, so I pressed the edge of my boots into the crack, now directly over that appalling drop, clinging like an insect on a wall. I started to shuffle the short distance to the matchbox. It might just be possible. Just then a strong blast of wind seized the map case and flung it out behind me, destroying my balance, and I felt myself being peeled away from the cliff.

As I was losing all control I made a desperate hopeless step forward and surprisingly found the matchbox under my foot, which steadied me for a fraction of a second, allowing me to pull my other foot up to it and make a frantic jump. I landed uncertainly on the small platform beyond the rock. My calf muscles were shaking uncontrollably, but I had survived. My heart thundered in my chest, my very being trembled, and my brain was numb. I did not even dare think about how I was going to cross this place again on the return trip.

In a sort of trance I continued to follow the boy, weaving and climbing in and out of gullies, across stacks and buttresses, and finally climbed high in the mountain away from the lake before dropping down into a small bay with a few acacia trees. It had taken just over an hour to cross Mugurr. We had covered less than half a mile as the crow flies but it felt like a lifetime. We sat to wait for Thomas to appear. We waited and waited. I used the telephoto lens on the camera to scour the side of the mountain but saw nothing. I felt sure that at any moment he would appear, yet he never did. I wondered if he had passed us and had continued ahead, so I motioned to the boy that we should continue, but he signed to say that Thomas must still be in the mountain.

After waiting for more than two hours I decided that he must have had an accident and started up the side of the mountain again to look for him in the area where he might have crossed. It was now late morning and the heat was building powerfully. The boy, still carrying our cooking things, set off back along the cliff path the way we had come.

I stopped frequently to shout for Thomas, but only my echo ricocheted back across the rocky ravines. I did not check the compass and just walked on instinct, guided by the direction of my shadow. It was 38°C (100°F) and rising, and the increasing thirst and tiredness took its toll on me as I slogged up the steep, rocky slope. Loose shale slipped from beneath my feet. At last I came to the top, absolutely exhausted, my legs trembling with fatigue, my saliva thick and my heart pounding in the heat. I looked out across a knot of ridges and gullies. To cross from each to the next meant a steep descent, skidding on loose rocks and torn by thorn bushes, followed by another backbreaking climb to the top of the next, and then another, and another. So it went on, ridge after ridge until I found I had reached a final hilltop overlooking the place where we had started into Mugurr that morning (*see photo 23*).

There was no one, no movement, so sign of life. Neither Thomas nor even the boy, whom I expected to be there waiting for me. My only thoughts were that he had either met Thomas and they had gone on south to wait for me, or that he had found Thomas having had some awful accident and would need my help to carry him out of the mountain. Either way it meant that I would have to cross the mountain again by that awful cliff route in case they were on that path. I chose a steep, dry stream bed leading down towards the lake, which I estimated would take me to join the cliff track beyond that terrifying slab of rock. It was very steep and I had several heart-in-mouth slips towards the sheer drop into the lake a long way below before I reached the little shelf that was the path.

This was no longer just gruelling, it had become a nightmare. I was now so tired that I seriously considered whether I had the stamina to cross the mountain again. But there was no choice, I had to find out what had happened to Thomas. I owed him that. I started moving along that little track again, perched high above the edge of the lake. As I came round the very first rock buttress my heart dropped and my energy drained away. I had misjudged it, and in front of me was that impossible sheet of rock again. I sat down and waited for more than ten minutes until my leg muscles had stopped visibly shuddering with exhaustion, and then went to face it. As soon as I eased the edge of my boot into the thin crack I knew that I could not do it. To try a second time would be to die. There was not a shadow of doubt in my mind.

So I turned back until I found a place where the rock face had weathered sufficiently to provide hand- and footholds, and hoped that from the top of this buttress there would be a place to get past that hellish obstacle. If I found no way forward from climbing this rock face I knew I would not be able to climb down it again. Once more I was overhanging the pounding waves on the broken rocks way down at the water's edge. Mercifully, from the top of my climb there turned out to be a way through and I scrambled up and down gully after gully and eventually came once more to the little bay south of Mugurr.

I was sure that here I must find the others, but there was no one. Silence. Just the vast emptiness of Africa throbbing in the midday heat. Perhaps they had continued south. I was very, very tired and it was now seeringly hot, but I walked across the bay to the next headland that plunged into the lake. Here there was more climbing to be done, and after examining it for some time I decided that it would be foolhardy to waste more energy by crossing it and probably finding no one on the other side. I would almost certainly have to re-cross it.

I walked back to the base of Mugurr again and drank from the lake until I was fit to burst. I had made up my mind that I could not possibly face that cliff path again and that I must climb over the top of the mountain once more. The few clouds had cleared and the sun beat down with venom in its heat. I could only think now about escaping from this mountain with my life, irrespective of what had become of my companions. At this point it was just a matter of raw survival. A lonely, empty survival, many, many miles from any hint of civilisation. Deep in this unforgiving land.

I sat and rested for a long time. As I relaxed, my mind drifted and

I found myself wondering what European might have been here before me. This place was unapproachable by vehicle, and the tiny number of people who might have walked along the lakeshore in the past must have been using animals to carry their loads, forcing them to pass behind the mountain away from the lake. It dawned on me that no outsider had ever been here before. It was a lonely feeling. I wished I had not been there either.

It was now early afternoon and the heat was at its peak. I wondered about waiting until later in the day under the shade of a tree, but if the others were waiting for me somewhere, the longer I delayed the more likely it was that they might give me up for dead and set off again towards the donkeys. I drank again and soaked my clothes and my hair, and set off up the steep rocky slope once more. The pounding in my heart increased from discomfort to the point of real pain, and I started to wonder if I might soon have a heart attack. I began stopping to rest for two minutes after each minute of climbing, and over halfway to the top I found a large rock which cast enough shade to sit in, and rested there for half an hour.

My legs were now shaking uncontrollably from exhaustion and I worried about a serious fall. I picked up a porcupine quill as a crude writing implement in case I should be completely incapacitated, yet knew that no one would ever come to read any message I might leave, scrawled in my own blood on a rock. The absurd melodrama of the situation was not lost on me, but it was all too horribly real even to tempt a wry smile. So I continued to the top in very short stages, taking another long rest under a thorn tree near the summit.

Once over the top I started down a steep stream bed, skidding and tumbling and saving myself by grabbing at thorn scrub, which tore at my hands. I was no longer aware of any pain. Then off again to climb an even higher peak, stopping under a thorn tree again for half an hour to rest. Looking around at my surroundings I noticed one or two natural caves in the rock walls, and for a moment even wondered about spending the night in one. Then I remembered what we had been told about Mugurr being populated by leopard. Such a cave might be exactly where a leopard would lie up during the day. I pressed on.

Reaching the top of this higher summit I found a saddle I could walk along to reach another peak, and suddenly, for the first time, I knew I was going to make it. A strange feeling of triumph burst through the overpowering tiredness. From the next peak I looked down directly onto the bay from which we had set out that morning, a torment ago. However, I was much higher than I had been last time I had re-crossed the mountain and knew that the descent was going to be very difficult.

The rock was mostly brittle and rotten, coming away in my hands, and the scree kept slipping out from under my feet, forcing me to ski in it between each fall. My hands were torn and bleeding and my legs and arms smeared all over with blood, strangely too bright to look convincing. Occasionally I would send a great landslip of stones cascading into the ravine below and I grabbed at anything I could to stop going down with it, often stopping afterwards to pick acacia thorns the size of matchsticks out of my hands. My legs were now impervious to pain or exhaustion and in an extraordinary masochistic way I found myself almost enjoying it; making it an academic exercise to guess where and how badly I would fall next. In a tumble of rock my watchstrap was torn off my wrist but I felt nothing. My mind had somehow become detached from my body and no longer cared, observing its misery with complete indifference. At last I slid to the bottom of the slope and looked around. No one.

I staggered over to the water's edge and took off all my clothes and lay flat in the shallows, not for a moment considering the absurdity of introducing blood into water infested with crocodiles. After the pains had eased I rinsed out my clothes, which had dried into rigid boards with the salt of my sweat where I had discarded them on the beach. This last crossing had taken me over three hours and it felt good and rather unreal to be alive. The previous evening, a lifetime ago, an old man had told me, 'It is better to die without having to cross Mugurr'. Today I had crossed it four times. It still haunts me.

After rinsing the salt from my clothes I sat on a rock with them drying around me, too tired to be able to think what to do next. As I gazed back towards the mountain I saw a movement. Walking very slowly and very painfully across the first rocky outcrop was Thomas. He was at his physical limits with exhaustion. I did not stand up to go towards him and he did not speed his limping step towards me.

Our first words were the same: 'Where is the boy?' Neither of us had seen him. Perhaps he had gone to the nearby *manyatta* where his uncle was staying. Perhaps he had fallen re-crossing that ghastly sheet of rock. Wherever he had gone was where our limited survival rations were. He had been carrying them all. We had nothing left to eat.

Thomas and I began comparing stories. On the first crossing he must have made better time than we did and had gone ahead of us. Thinking that he was behind us he pressed on as quickly as he could, thoughtfully leaving the occasional note on a rock or pinned in a thorn bush, in case we were following behind. I had seen none of them. After some hours he came to a bay where fishermen were camped and they told him that they had seen no one for many days. So he had set off back again. It was as he re-crossed Mugurr that, easing himself down a steep slope of scree on his hands, feet and backside, it had all slipped down with him in a terrible rock slide and he had crashed to the bottom of a narrow ravine. He had slammed hard into the facing rock wall, badly crushing his toes. They were a messy sight, one big toe badly damaged with the nail torn off it, but he said the real pain was in his little toes.

I tore strips of fabric from my shirt and bandaged them up and we hobbled together towards a small group of people we now saw sitting further along the bay. They had not seen the boy return from the mountain, but said they knew his character, and that he would have stolen the food and cooking pan. We called to a woman who was returning from fetching water at the lake to ask if there was any milk we could buy, and she told us to follow her to the *manyatta* by some trees in the valley. First I went to slake my thirst yet again from the lake and bring back water for Thomas, who was in no fit state to walk further than necessary.

Slowly and painfully we followed her up to the *manyatta* and, as Turkana custom decrees, we sat down some way off to wait to be greeted. After a time her husband emerged from a hut. He was one of the fierce bloodshot-eyed men we had met the previous evening, but he now welcomed us warmly as his visitors. He collected three stones and lit a fire between them and, sending for a cooking pan of water and some milk, helped us make tea. In the gathering dusk the details of our day's exertions started to leak out, and hearing that I had crossed the mountain four times he announced that he was going to kill a goat in my honour.

This was generosity indeed, of a kind unimaginable in north Turkana. He led over a medium-sized black goat and asked, 'This big enough?' Under the circumstances it looked enormous, but Thomas told me, 'Two Turkana eat goat this size just one day.' Our generous host then asked whether I would like it roasted or boiled. Never having had a whole goat roasted I suggested that. The wretched goat was led away a short distance, where another, older man selected a jagged stone a little larger than a clenched fist and, holding the muzzle of the goat in his left hand, struck it deftly on the back of the head. It dropped instantly to the ground. But, as a large fire was being assembled and the flames were springing up, the poor creature staggered to its feet once more. The killer blow was repeated more powerfully.

The older man, whose name was Anam, laid the goat on a bed of stones and quickly disembowelled it with the point of his spear so that all the blood remained within it, a delicacy associated particularly with roast meat. When the fire was a fierce blaze he picked up the goat by its four legs and swung it on top, complete with all its fur, which singed in a great cloud of sparks. The muscles of the legs contracted in the intense heat in a ghoulish way, causing the forelegs to curl round until the hooves touched the stomach. Every few minutes it was lifted, turned over, and flopped back into the flames. After a time Anam expertly jointed it with his spear, which must have been razor-sharp, and then the individual pieces were laid back onto the fire to continue roasting.

Quite soon the liver and kidneys were brought over to us and were very good indeed. The only light was now from the fire, and this was starting to die down. Thomas and I sat on the ground in the surrounding darkness without plates or knives, and after a little while large pieces of meat were brought over and dropped on the sand in front of us. It was a bizarre and truly savage experience. Each lump of goat meat, indistinguishable from the next in the darkness, was now covered with sand, the outside carbonated with charred skin and burnt hair and the inside still cold, raw and bleeding. There was soon a huge pile of meat, two or three legs, sections of ribcage, the head and other less tempting morsels. It was a unique feast.

Thankfully my hunting knife was on my belt so we were able to dissect some pieces into smaller portions. We tore away at the charred hide with our teeth and gnawed at the bones. Thomas was up for it and gave it his best, as any Turkana should. I was a little slower, finding all the sand grinding between my teeth rather off-putting, and faced with the sheer quantity of meat I started to lag, despite the remonstrations of our hosts, 'Eat, eat, must eat meat'. I did my utmost to be the perfect guest, but it was a demanding dinner, and I was still deep in shock after the day's hardships. I was very glad it was pitch black so that I could not see what I was eating, much of which was still completely raw, yet under the circumstances it tasted good. It was odd to be alive and able to taste it at all. Increasingly the tiredness was starting to sweep over me in a dark, foggy wave.

It was impossible for us to eat more than half of the goat, and we asked to take the rest with us next day on our return to the donkeys, now that all our food rations seemed to have been stolen or lost down the cliff. We drank more tea before stretching out on the sand to sleep. However, the enormous quantity of raw meat and burnt fur which I had consumed after such a nightmarish day soon began to take its toll and it was not long before I was forced to wander off into the night.

I was determined to walk a good distance as I did not want our hosts to realise that I was being sick, and I managed to get up the valley as far as a distant stand of doum palms. I hardly noticed that all the half wild dogs of the *manyatta* had followed behind me. They obviously sensed that something dramatic was about to happen in the extraordinary way that dogs do, and when I suddenly started to throw up they clustered around me to delight in this shared bounty from above, much of which did not even have a chance to hit the ground, lapped up as it fell.

When at last I returned to my sleeping place I felt very cleansed, but guilty to have wasted so much valuable protein. As I lay down Thomas asked, 'You feeling OK?' I admitted that I had been sick because of eating so much raw meat. He mused over this for a moment and then said, 'So it was raw meat? I thought because you eat both the testicles.'

I was instantly deeply asleep.

Limping back from the dead

ANAM WOKE US AT 6.30am, asking how we could sleep so long. He said, 'I come to donkeys to take *posho* for my wife, and tobacco for me. Three *moran* [warriors] come too, go to Nakurio to *duka*. But now they roast one more goat.'

So we started with Anam on the long walk. He had a weathered, pale-blue mud skull-cap over the back of his head, yet without feathers, and with just a strip of pink in front of it. Large aluminium rings hung from each ear and he wore what looked like a very old, grey army blanket over his shoulder. Now, looking at him more carefully, I guessed this 'old' man was probably in his 40s.

It was extraordinarily hot again and, after the exhaustion of the previous day, we were shattered before we even started. Mile after mile of rock-hopping and ploughing through soft sand took a severe toll on our remaining strength. I was particularly concerned about how Thomas must be suffering with his smashed toes but he bore it in brave silence. His tyre sandals did not offer much protection. We frequently drank from the lake, wetted our hair and clothes, or lay in the shallow waters.

Our discomforts became all-engrossing and the walk itself and the changing terrain went by largely unnoticed. I remember only that it grew hotter and hotter, and there appeared to be more and more spurs of hills to cross. Everything was becoming a haze. After a few hours the young men caught us up, carrying the meat wrapped in palm fronds, and afterwards there were constant stops in the shade of a tree or rock to eat meat.

The conversation as usual turned to the *ngoroko*. Anam told us that although the threat had diminished, he and his family had recently had to flee around the southern tip of the lake after a hideous attack, to escape from further assaults. He said that his previous *manyatta* had been attacked twice, and although the *ngoroko* had rarely killed anyone, their brutality and inhumanity knew no bounds. They took absolutely everything they could – all the animals and all the clothing – leaving everybody naked and shoeless, and of course stealing any money they could find. Anything they could not carry or did not want they destroyed. They beat the older men severely and raped all the women. Even the young virgins were not spared, being opened with knives, during which their fathers had to sit facing the ground, and anyone who looked up at the screams of his daughter was beaten on the head with a hammer by someone standing behind.

This homicidal sadism and torture was quite different from conventional raiding. Nothing that might be done against the *ngoroko* could be too severe, and it was high time villagers were able to defend themselves. Accordingly, a new strategy had recently been introduced called the Home Guard, and it was the main reason why the *ngoroko* were now on the retreat. This plan was to arm a number of villagers so that each *manyatta* stood a chance of protecting itself, not just against the Turkana *ngoroko* but also against other tribal raiders and the Somali *shifta* on the other side of the lake.

The Home Guard were given old .303 Lee Enfield rifles, which were effective and accurate, although slow to reload compared with the modern automatics like AK-47s which were flooding into the country from hostilities further north. Inevitably the threat to wildlife was increased by this policy, as it put guns into the hands of often hungry villagers. Anam told us with considerable glee that over a hundred *ngoroko* had recently been killed in these mountains alone, and that now the handful remaining were more likely to come to the *manyattas* starving and begging for food.

Eventually we reached the mountain of Kopoi and struggled to the top of the headland to look down into the bay to see where our donkeys were. The fishermen's huts were empty and not a soul was in sight. Our disappointment was immense; we were on the point of collapse. Surely they could not be far?

We continued our agonising trudge, dragging ourselves forward mechanically, with little remaining sensation of heat, thirst or even pain. We came to a *manyatta* of goat herders, then another of fishermen, then another. We were too tired to think. The sun sank and slipped from the sky and we slogged on in the darkness. Where the hell had they gone? We staggered on late into the night.

Much further to the north we saw the fires of another fishing village and when at last we arrived they said our donkeys were under some trees a little way from the lake. In a daze we walked on and suddenly everyone was talking, someone was shaking my hand and after a while I realised it was Ekele. Edung also grasped my hand and led me over to where they were camped. We collapsed onto a carpet of goatskins and waited for food. Thomas kept slipping into unconsciousness and I gave him powerful painkillers from my medical kit.

To my great surprise the boy turned out to be there also, and said that after I last saw him he had walked through the night to get there. When *posho* was cooked I insisted our visitors eat first as they had been so generous to us, and when it was my turn I was too tired to manage more than a few mouthfuls. Thomas was showing a fever which he thought was malaria, but which I believed was delayed shock. We talked for a short time and then blissfully passed into oblivion. Somehow we had covered over 20 miles that day. How Thomas had managed it, clambering through the screes of basalt rubble on his broken toes, I had no idea.

We had a rest next day to let Thomas get his strength back, and after Anam had started for home at 3.30pm we continued at a slow pace till we reached the bay of the hippos, where we camped nearby in a deserted *manyatta*. Thomas' fever returned so I made him sleep in my down bag to try to sweat it out.

That night the hippos came up to graze the verdant grass around us. I remembered Peter's warning not to get between the hippos and the water, but there was not much we could do about that and soon we were. Thomas was particularly worried, and despite his fever and his exhaustion he woke frequently to check that they had come no closer, but they remained about 50 yards away.

Next day Thomas felt stronger and we decided to make a push for Kerio. It was a long walk crossing the eastern side of the Nachorugwai desert without a midday break. At the waterside we passed a host of water birds: white-faced whistling ducks; sacred ibis; great egrets; goliath herons; and of course the ubiquitous flamingos and pelicans. Groups of yellow-billed storks, wearing beaks several sizes too large, mixed with spoonbills, also competing for the 'silly beak of the year' award, waded through the shallows.

Further north were increasing numbers of Boran humped cattle, some cooling themselves in the aquamarine waters. We camped in the river bed again at Kerio, sent for *pombe*, and dozed. We had been joined by a helpful chap called Daniel. We rather liked him and he ended up staying with us all the way back to Kalokol.

When we went to restock in the *dukas* at Kerio we became aware of a look of shock on people's faces and soon discovered that a rumour had widely circulated that somewhere between Nakurio and the lake we had been attacked by *ngoroko*, the donkeys and baggage all stolen, and that we had all been killed. It is more than a little disconcerting to hear news of your own violent death, but reassuring to have indisputable evidence to the contrary.

We were feeling lazy and stopped long enough to slaughter a goat, only carrying on at 3pm next day, camping at the Turkwell River again. Everyone was enthused by the idea of heading home, so I was woken at 5am with a cup of tea, a full moon still hanging brightly in the inky sky.

At Eliye Springs we went to the lake for a long overdue bath. News of our deaths at the hands of the *ngoroko* had preceded us here also, so once more everyone was shocked, but hopefully pleased, to see us again. Today's gentle walk of 13 miles, and our overindulgence in meat, meant we slept as heavily as the dead we were reported to be.

After a day resting at Eliye we started on the last leg home. The donkeys set off first with Ekele and Daniel. It was a holiday atmosphere – no risk or urgency. When we caught up with them I was concerned to see that Daniel was carrying a flamingo upside down by its pink legs, more dead than alive. He had knocked it down with a stone as the tribesmen do, and there was really nothing I could do for the poor creature now.

When we stopped at a fresh water spring on the beach he announced, 'Now we cook flamingo,' and he built up the fire. As he was about to toss it onto the flames I stopped him, startled by his callous disregard, and insisted that he kill it first. He found this slightly quirkish but did as I requested before casting his victim onto the fire. The feathers shrivelled instantly, burning up like cellophane into a black tarry mess. Daniel turned the bird a few times, using the long legs as handles, and then pulled it off, gutted it and put it back to continue roasting. Obviously a well-practised procedure when cooking this protected species.

At last he broke it apart and handed us the pieces, which to my surprise tasted very good indeed – a dense, dark meat with a texture like turkey. It was hard for the local people to understand why a species needs to be protected when they see them in flocks of many thousands, especially when they taste so good in an often-hungry land. A common practice was for groups of people to walk along the shore at night while the flamingos slept, carrying flaming torches made from bundles of reeds. The birds were confused and mesmerised by these dancing lights and the men were able to approach close enough to knock them down with sticks.

Embarrassingly, our flamingo was wearing a British Museum ring, so I noted the number, and on return to England I contacted them. They astonished me by saying the bird had been ringed 20 years before. I could hardly tell them that I had eaten it, and felt rather ashamed.

Our last night was among sand dunes, far too hot to sleep, until a breeze finally sprang up. We rose at 5am, and they made *posho*. How they could eat, especially when a *msungu* was paying!

We entered Kalokol at 11am and were met with a rapturous welcome. Happily, news of our deaths had not reached here. The spoils were divided up, Thomas getting the lion's share of cooking things and a jerry can, which he richly deserved. I worked out the wages, as usual adding a handsome bonus.

It was a sad farewell after our adventures together. I had failed to reach Teleki's volcano, yet had earned some even more powerful memories. Maybe there would be another opportunity on my next trek from Maralal.

From Turkana tribesman
to Nairobi tourist

I HAD DECIDED I would like to take Thomas to Nairobi for a day, as a reward for his loyalty. I was sure he would be fascinated to see the capital city of his young and expanding country, and to be able to understand where, as a Turkana, he fitted into the larger picture. He might one day decide to look for work further afield, and I wanted him to understand what other parts of his country were like. I broke the idea to him and he was thrilled. I had trouble finding transport down to Kitale, but when two plucky Danish girls in a Renault 4 ran out of petrol Peter Schmidt helped them out, then leaned on them to give Thomas and me a lift.

On my last evening I went over to the fishing lodge again with Peter and Hanne for a final dinner overlooking the lake. I found it moving to bid farewell to this wild and little-known land.

We arrived promptly at 7.45am for an 8am departure. The Danish girls were very uncertain of their cargo, although Thomas was looking very smart in some of my clothes. Apart from the powerful tribal smell that filled the car and persuaded our hostesses to keep all their windows wide open, the only eventuality on the journey were occasional light showers as we passed from south Turkana into the hills of West Pokot.

Thomas was all eyes as we drove through densely wooded mountainous country – to him an unknown land – with peaks of six or seven thousand feet, and Mount Elgon on the horizon at more than twice that height. His astonishment at entering the metropolis of Kitale was extreme, with so many more than the four or five vehicles a day that he saw in Kalokol.

We thanked our chauffeuses and checked into the New Kamburu Silent Lodging and Boarding where I had stayed before. Thomas very much enjoyed the concept of taps with running water, and even a hot shower, when it worked. With heart in mouth I risked a dinner at the smart Kitale Hotel. It was the first time Thomas had ever been confronted by a knife and fork, but he did his very best to master this absurd way of shifting food from the plate to the mouth. Only once, as he impaled his steak with the fork while hacking at it with the knife, did he slip, and most of the contents of his plate leaped across the table and landed on the starched, white linen cloth.

Luckily the table was laid for four. So, feeling embarrassed about the mess, and announcing that 'I not like to see this thing,' Thomas ingeniously built a pyramid of the unused crockery from the other place settings over the stain to hide it. Throughout this construction I kept catching the eyes of the horrified waiters, who were itching to eject him, but I held them at bay and left a tip sufficient to earn their forgiveness. For the next couple of days we confined our destructive eating habits to the Bongo Bar.

1. Ekadeli on first day of trek I

2. Edung on first day of trek I

3. Turkana girl at Kalokol wearing a fish vertebrae apron

4. Turkana man at Kalokol 'wearing an exceptionally fine mud skullcap'

5. Turkana fisherman on a log raft, with his sons, near the fishing lodge at Kalokol

6. Turkana girls outside David Jumale's mother's hut near the fishing lodge at Kalokol

7. L to R: Ekadeli, a local Turkana man and woman, and Edung on the first day of Trek 1

8. Entering the empty interior of central Turkana

9. Ekadeli filling our *sufuria* from a waterhole in the Kataboi river

10. Near Lokitaung 'a fine-looking couple took delight in having their photo taken'

11. Turkana woman in the remote 'land God gave to Cain'

12. Turkana 'man of distinction...treated with deference and respect' after Nabwalekorot

13. Turkana nomad family at the last waterhole on our way back to Kalokol

14. Old Turkana *mzee* in Kalokol

15. Thomas serving lunch! (A leg of goat.) At Kerio

16. One of the lakes on Central Island in Lake Turkana: a paradise for crocs

17. Lesser flamingos on the beach north of Eliye springs

18. Edung watering the donkeys in the Turkwell river north of Kerio. Ekele behind

19. Ekele with the donkeys entering Nachurogwai desert

20. A hard place for the donkeys. Heading south towards Mugurr, shortly before I had to leave them behind

21. Tough walking to Mugurr, after leaving the donkeys

22. Pelicans and crocs as we approach Mugurr – looming on the horizon

23. View looking north from the top of Mugurr

24. Wilfred Thesiger and Lawi Leboyare near Maralal

25. Finely decorated Samburu girl at the wedding at Oporoi

26. Samburu *morans* waiting to dance at Oporoi wedding

27. Samburu *morans* dancing at Oporoi wedding

28. Samburu *morans* singing at the wedding at Oporoi – one wearing the traditional hairstyle

29. Abdilahi heading north from Parsaloi towards where the *shifta* were killing travellers

30. Walking through the hills towards the *manyatta* with the camels in *musth*

31. In the foothills of Mount Nyiru, home of Nkai, the Samburu god

32. Abdilahi admiring the panorama from the top of Mount Niyuru

33. Our desiccated donkeys at last able to drink after three days and 'feeling cool by the lake after that hellish griddle', although 'my thermometer still measured 43C'

34. L-R: Letipile, Ayoko and Abdilahi leading the donkeys south of the lake towards Loyangalani

35. Looking aross the Rift Valley from the road between Maralal and Baragoi

36. Chukuna, Barnaba (back) and Lopus leading donkeys through a rocky defile north of Moiti

37. In this magical scene we could almost forget that [...] the Shangalla frequently painted this beautiful landscape with blood

38. Downtown North Horr, bordering the Chalbi desert. L to R: the author, Barnaba, Lopus

39. The author with Samburu *morans* and two Samburu girls the day after clitoridectomy. Near Maralal

40. Lawi's Samburu *moran* driving his goats to water near Maralal

Because of my shortage of funds in Kalokol as a result of M's early departure having halved the budget, Thomas had helpfully forgone his wages until we reached the bank here, so I was now able to pay up. As his tyre sandals were highly incongruous with his new clothes, and mine did not fit his broad feet, we were now able to go in search of a pair his own size. I also made a phone call to Nairobi from the post office which, although I had to wait 20 minutes for a line, was a thing of astonishment to Thomas, nonetheless. Stair-rodding rain made the liquid mud in the streets bounce a couple of feet into the air and the corrugated-iron roof of the Kamburu hammered spectacularly half the night. But it kept us dry, which Thomas' grass hut in Kalokol certainly would not have done.

After a final breakfast in the Bongo Bar we went down to the Acamba bus station and set off on the dot of 9am. The journey was uneventful for me, yet a constant source of interest for Thomas. We rolled into Nairobi at 5pm. Thomas was now truly awed by the immensity of his capital city, unimaginably vast.

We took a taxi up to the Hurlingham, where Bruce and Katie were sweet to him. Having travelled widely when they were younger they knew exactly the sort of thing that people freshly in from the bush liked to eat, particularly steak sandwiches, which dispensed with the awkwardness of knives and forks. Thomas was fascinated by the luxury of the bathtub and took several baths, although, curiously but unfairly, it did not make him smell any more sweetly. It must take a long time for sweat glands to finally remove the odours of a tribal lifestyle. Luckily he was not aware of it. There had been no twin-bedded rooms available so, with some trepidation, I had booked two singles, but all seemed to work well, and I heard him heading down the corridor for yet another bath at intervals during the night. Having his own personal electric light bulb was also a very special treat. The Hurlingham was a big hit.

Next day we devoted to exploring Nairobi. Thomas was certainly getting the hang of things remarkably quickly, as it must have been an overwhelming culture shock. He looked quite the man about town, dressed in a pale-blue check shirt, grey sweater, brown corduroy trousers and shiny black shoes. How he crammed his damaged toes into the shoes I had no idea, but he did not complain. It must all have been extraordinary for him, yet a passer-by might have mistaken him for a local business man. We gazed up at the dizzy heights of the Kenyatta Conference Centre, the splendour of the university, the four lanes of traffic on Kenyatta Avenue, and the classical grandeur of the public library. Sadly, it was raining again, but that did not matter to Thomas at all. Perhaps it always rained in a place so far from Turkana. He bought some soap, shampoo and a towel. Washing was now strictly à la mode.

I thought it would be fun for him to have lunch in the Thorn Tree Café of the New Stanley Hotel, where we could have sandwiches again, and see a first-class hotel. He loved it, and was cleary amazed by what a luxurious place his capital city was. I was glad it made him feel so proud to be Kenyan. After lunch I took him into the foyer, which left him breathless with its pictures, mirrors and carpets.

Then we went to a small metal door and pushed a button. The door slid back. He was puzzled why this might be of interest but I suggested that we go inside. As the door closed I told him to have a good look at the corridor outside. He clearly thought I had lost my marbles. I then pressed another button and the little room shook for a few moments, and the door slid open again. He was a bit uncertain, so I asked him if it was the same corridor. He could not believe how they could have changed all the furnishings so quickly, and when I said we had gone up in the air he knew for certain that I really had lost my mind. So I drew him to the window above the street where we had sat for lunch.

Instantly the enormity of what had just happened hit him and he let out a series of great, ear-splitting whoops that sent the chambermaids scattering for cover, and with arms waving wildly he started explaining to them the magic of what he had just witnessed. I wondered if I had overdone it. Quickly he grasped the idea that the little room could go up and down the building and we spent several delightful minutes playing in the lift through all the hotel's various floors. When I felt we were in danger of being thrown out by the manager I suggested that perhaps we should be getting back to the Hurlingham to pack up his things.

While he had yet another bath I got him a supply of sandwiches for the journey, and we walked back to the centre of town, carrying his few things to the Acamba bus station for the night bus. It pulled out at 8pm, with Thomas gazing out of the window, grinning fit to burst. He had come to Nairobi as a Turkana tribesman, but he was returning home as a Kenyan. It had been a great day.

The following day was 18th October 1982 and I was thrilled to be setting off in a few days to Maralal, in Samburu tribal district south of Lake Turkana, at the invitation of the greatest explorer of our age, Wilfred Thesiger.

Sadly I have never been back to Turkana, nor seen any of my Turkana companions again. I wonder now, almost 40 years later, how the passage of time has altered it. What was once Kenya's wildest and most dangerous tribal district has been changed by time and progress. I was lucky to have travelled in some of its remotest places only a few years after it had been a prohibited area, too dangerous even to enter without a special permit.

For several years Thomas and I exchanged the occasional letter, but it gradually petered out. I sometimes wonder what became of all my companions during the following years. Today, if Thomas is still alive, he must be in his mid 60s. I wonder if he ever thinks back on our adventures together. Memories of when an Englishman, for some strange reason, came to his land to walk far across its wildest places, just to satisfy his curiosity.

*'By day the hot sun fermented us;
and we were dizzied by the beating wind.
At night we were stained by dew, and shamed into pettiness
by the innumerable silences of stars.'*

TE Lawrence CB (1888-1935)
Seven Pillars of Wisdom: A Triumph

Trek 3

Over the Mountain of God to the Curse of Maseketa

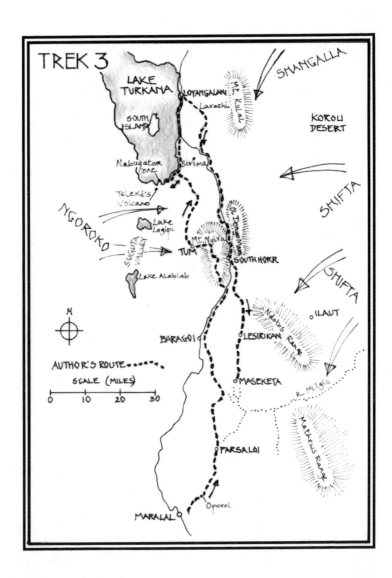

Matatus, Maralal and meeting Thesiger and his people

AFTER ENDURING the furnace of Turkana I had taken to wearing a light sweater in Nairobi, although it had felt so hot there when I had first arrived from London. I had been back there a few days, staying in Omar's generous guest wing while his house staff indulged me and I relaxed lazily in his beautiful garden. But soon I was itching to be underway again. I had bought the new maps I needed and one morning Omar's driver took me down to the place near River Road on the edge of the slums where the *matatus* set off north for Nyahururu. It was Tuesday 26th October 1982.

I had arrived early enough to reserve the comparative luxury of a seat in the cab next to the driver, and now watched it gradually load up as I sat nearby on my camera box. More and more people squeezed in and more and more luggage was pushed in through windows or thrown up to be strapped to the rickety but ample roof-rack which already held my own bags. It was a converted Peugeot 404 pick-up truck and by the time nineteen people had disappeared into its diminutive interior the leaf springs on the rear axle had not only flattened but actually formed a slight curve the wrong way round.

At 11am we were off, bouncing and vaulting over the broken road surface, scraping the vehicle's underside on every bump as the exhausted shock absorbers banged loudly. A breeze, sometimes cold and full of rain, blew onto me from the side window which would not wind up, and throughout the entire journey not a single dial on the dashboard made any attempt to flicker into life. In fact nothing really worked at all. Selecting reverse was a lengthy operation accompanied by startling grindings and bangs. Only one windscreen wiper functioned, or sometimes did, and I never discovered where the handbrake was. It was certainly never used. So we thundered off north-west by God's good grace, down the escarpment of the Rift Valley into the interior of Africa, and turned north at Gilgil towards Nyahururu.

At 2pm we pulled into the simple bus compound outside the town. Someone had recommended staying at the lodge overlooking Thomson's Falls and the *matatu* driver offered to drop me off there, a couple of miles away. It was only a century since Joseph Thomson had discovered this spectacular waterfall draining from the Aberdare Mountains to plunge 243 feet in white ribbons of foam. Much higher than Niagara. The discovery of Africa's marvels by the European was still so comparatively recent.

Although almost on the equator, it was cold at this altitude and every bedroom had a roaring fire as well as an en-suite bathroom, for a very modest fee. The lawn led almost to the brink of the falls and the thundering of the water was dramatic. Dinner was excellent despite the menu promising it would be rounded off with

'Assorted Cold Sweats'.

After I had slept for twelve blissful hours the manager kindly dropped me back at the bus station, where a *matatu* to Maralal was already loading, and again I had a place in the cab. Three hours later it was still loading, every new passenger somehow squeezing in. In Africa there is always room. When the tarmac gave way to a corrugated, potholed, dirt road, I was especially glad to have the remains of springs in my seat, while the cluttered passengers behind were shaken around like peas in a food blender. The country started rather like south Turkana, gradually rolling into low hills, and about halfway to Maralal we passed several large ranches stretching over scores of miles. When a helicopter flew over, the driver announced, 'That is carrying President Moi. He has spent a day in Maralal.' After the attempted coup he was touring outlying regions to reassert his authority, and now disgruntled air-force units were supposedly camped in the hills, formed into yet more bandit gangs.

As we approached, the bush thinned out to a wider landscape of open grazing and we passed a herd of over 400 zebra with a striking Thomson's gazelle (always known as tommies) posed stock-still on a small hummock, silhouetted against the sky. Once past the landing strip the road was adorned with flags and thronged with colourful Samburu warriors resplendent with beads, their faces and shoulders painted with red ochre mixed with animal fat in the Maasai style, and with spears in hand. A magnificent-looking race.

The small town of Maralal was quite spread out. Dusty streets, partly shaded by lines of small trees, formed a rectangle through its centre, flanked by the usual *dukas* and other businesses, cleaner and better organised than Turkana towns. There was even a garage workshop and a filling station, although this was regularly devoid of petrol. While more sophisticated than Turkana it was also much more expensive. Crowds of warriors milled about in their bright colours, undecided when to set off home after the festivities of the presidential visit.

The *matatu* finally stopped outside the Buffalo Boarding House, a bar with simple rooms behind, and I booked one for 115 shillings (£5.75) – quite expensive for somewhere so basic. I went for a drink and found a rather drunken group of white farmers from the ranches we had passed discussing the damage from elephant on their land. They invited me to share their supper and asked what I was doing. When I explained my plan to walk up to Lake Turkana from Maralal they were sure it would be impossible, but when I added that Thesiger was helping me they agreed I just might make it. Everyone knew of him. Among the Samburu he was universally known as *Mzee Juu*, meaning a wise and respected old man, the same term used for Jomo Kenyatta.

A bank in Nairobi had assured me they had a branch here, so in the morning I was shocked to find that was hopelessly wrong. I would have to go back to Nyahururu to draw money – seven or eight more excruciating hours in a *matatu*. But first I walked round to the garage whose owner, Sadiq Bhola, let Thesiger have a room, where he worked on his epic autobiography, *A Life of my Choice*.

Thesiger welcomed me warmly, and we sat and talked for over two hours. It was a small dusty room up some stairs, with just a table overlooking the street and a couple of hard chairs, but that was all he wanted; a few books and handwritten papers were spread around. I felt privileged to meet this great traveller on his home turf, where his permanent tan, deeply lined hide and sunken, sparkling eyes belonged more naturally than in London. He wore old flannel trousers and a well-worn sports jacket over a light jersey and open-necked shirt. At a much higher altitude than Kalokol, Maralal was comparatively cool, although I think Thesiger was impervious to heat anyway. I remembered someone telling me that the first time they saw him was on a meltingly hot day in Baghdad where everyone was wilting under a ferocious sun. Thesiger had stepped out of a bank dressed warmly in a suit, apparently unaware of the temperature.

Over a cup of tea he told me he had put out feelers via Lawi, his Samburu protégé, for donkeys and men to go with me, and we discussed different routes to the lake. 'As the crow flies it's about 100 miles but, d'you see, much further with the convolutions of a trek.' He filled in some details, 'Here we're not much affected by *ngoroko*, but as you go north they might be a nuisance, and you'll be going into an area at risk from Somali *shifta*. Ordinary tribal raiding shouldn't be a problem as the Samburu and Rendille tribes have a good relationship. But further north there's always a risk of attacks from Abyssinia.'

Down on the street he introduced me to some of 'his people', particularly his most constant companions, Lawi, Laputa and Kibriti, all in their 20s, with whom I was to become good friends. Thesiger's penchant for nicknames had produced the name Laputa from the character in John Buchan's *Prester John*. He was tall but casual and vague, which Thesiger considered due to an artistic temperament. Kibriti, from the Swahili word *kiberiti* for matchstick, had been nick-named by Bhola due to his sticklike physique. He was just as tall with a very deep voice and an attractive nature, quick to laugh and a fund of carefully remembered details. You knew where you were with Kibriti: a steady gaze and as straight as a die; a man to be trusted.

Only Lawi Leboyare retained his own tribal name, and was effectively Thesiger's 'adopted son' (*see photo 24*). He was in the warrior age-group with an athletic physique, good-looking and alert, and always quick to enjoy a joke. He had a well-proportioned face with wide-set, very steady eyes which remained calm and un-phased in any situation. It was easy to see why he and Thesiger had such mutual respect and affection, and why he was later to become mayor of Maralal. They had been together most of Lawi's life since Thesiger had once visited the primary school in Baragoi, north of Maralal. At the end of the day, when he climbed into his Land Rover, he found the twelve-year-old Lawi, who simply said 'Mzee Juu, I am coming with you'. And he did.

Next day I would have to go back to the bank in Nyahururu, but for now Thesiger invited me to come up to see his 'camp', and Lawi drove us the couple of miles cross-country in his Land Rover. It was still called the camp, as for many years Thesiger had insisted on remaining under canvas on the edge of the forest. Eventually he had decided to buy a substantial parcel of land on the side of a hill to build a house, as he believed it was important for Lawi to have a proper base to rear a family.

Now there were two small buildings constructed in the local style of town houses, with walls of vertical cedar logs, one end dipped in old engine oil against white ants and buried in the soil. The walls were roughly plastered inside, with concrete floors and corrugated-iron roofs, vital in this frequently wet area. Lawi and his wife lived in the larger of the two, around which she had planted an attractive garden highlighted with bougainvillea. The other was the guest house where Thesiger stayed, and also the general store for tools, foodstuffs, and assorted paraphernalia.

Lawi had divided his house into different rooms like a larger version of the wattle-and-daub huts of a Samburu *manyatta*, but Thesiger's house was as basic and ascetic as I had imagined it would be, a couple of simple wooden chairs by a small charcoal brazier on the floor, and his bed, an old iron frame with stretched springs like the ones I had known at school, on which a sheet of two-inch-thick foam rubber lay, with a sheet thrown over it and a blanket laid on top. Under the pillow was a Borana dagger in case of attack by night.

It seemed remarkable that a 72-year-old man of international esteem should spend nine months of every year living so uncomfortably, but it was clearly what he wanted, in accordance with his complete contempt for luxuries and comforts. At the other end of the single-room building, behind a partial screen, was the great heap of stores, above which a large platform had been constructed and where an ever-changing melange of local people slept under a chaotic pile of blankets.

Behind the houses was a cook house and a small grass-screened enclosure in which to have a wash from a bucket. A surrounding *boma* kept night-time animals at bay, mostly buffalo but occasionally elephant, lion or leopard, as well as assorted antelope, zebra, topi and so on. It was a short walk of about 50 yards outside the *boma* to the 'long-drop' loo, a tiny shed containing a deep narrow hole with wooden boards over the top leaving an opening for the obvious purpose. A torch was always necessary after dark, not only to illuminate your activity but also because long-drops were sometimes popular with snakes. At night the glowing eyes of dung beetles shone as they went about their work below. A torch was also important when venturing outside the *boma* into the realm of potential predators, and Thesiger had strung lengths of rough string across the vehicle entrances, from which hung tins containing a few small stones to make a noise and frighten off animals who knocked into them.

The ground inside the *boma* was tended into a very rough lawn in which he had planted some fleshy-leaved plants like aloes, collected in the forest. The perennial problem was lack of water, which had to be collected daily from streams or waterholes and ferried up to the camp in jerry cans by one of the vehicles. Thesiger was always worried that his plants might die from lack of watering while he was away in England each spring.

Lawi took me back to Maralal where he seemed to know everyone. He was always on the lookout for anyone selling *miraa* (known as *khat* in Arabia), a mild stimulant chewed extensively throughout this area. Bundles of the slender green shoots were constantly traded on the street, and people would keep a ball of chewed *miraa* tucked into their cheeks, frequently spitting out a stream of yellow saliva. While the Turkana were addicted to chewing tobacco the Samburu were inseparable from *miraa*, which had been used in the Horn of Africa for centuries, and Lawi invariably had a bundle of the leaves in the front of his Land Rover.

While we sat there a young Turkana man came up and Lawi introduced him as one of those he had in mind for my trek. His name was Netakwang. He sported a very thin, grizzled beard and close-cropped hair, and might have been good-looking but for a disconcertingly sour and resentful expression. However, Lawi had recommended him because he said he knew the area between Maralal and the lake well, and at this first acquaintance he seemed competent. Lawi arranged for the Nyahururu *matatu* to pick me up in the morning and dropped me back at the Buffalo.

I was up at 4.30am and ready when the *matatu* arrived at 5am, my bags left in Thesiger's writing room, so I carried only a toothbrush and sweater. It had rained in the night and was very cold as we rattled and banged down the rough road in the darkness. This time I was in the back, dreadfully cramped, yet we kept stopping to take on more and more people who waited at the side of the road, and they all squeezed in by some miracle, each taking the last conceivable pinch of space until yet another climbed in. There were many more traditionally dressed Turkana than on my way up, and the familiar smell of fire smoke and camel's milk that lingered in their clothes, and the goat fat rubbed into their skins, was curiously reassuring. Even when the dawn came up the *matatu* remained silent as everyone tried to sleep, not an easy task wedged so tightly between my neighbours that my legs and backside were completely numb and badly aching.

We arrived at 8am and I staggered off stiffly to withdraw 12,000 Kenyan shillings (£600) from the bank and find items like enamel mugs and plates, spoons, a tin opener, *panga*, and a 10-yard roll of strong polythene to use as a groundsheet. At 10.30 the *matatu* was waiting for me, already loaded to the gunnels, and my stuff was tied onto the roof. On the return journey the muscular agony was relieved by a puncture, giving me the chance to stretch my legs for 20 minutes and inspect the lethal state of our transport.

At home with Thesiger:
an explorer's anecdotes

THESIGER AND LAWI were waiting for me with my luggage already loaded and we set off at once. Thesiger pulled out a tent and told some of his people to erect it for me outside the *boma*. It struck me as strange hospitality to put your guest outside with the wild animals but I considered it a game to test my reaction. He also gave me a foam-rubber camping mattress, so I slept in great comfort, being used to only the hard ground, except that as they had erected the tent on a slope and, as in those days sewn-in groundsheets were unusual, I kept waking with my feet sticking out at the bottom; a tempting morsel for a hungry hyena.

After unrolling my bag I went up to Thesiger's house and we sat and talked while Laputa made us coffee. Thesiger liked to keep abreast of everything that was happening, constantly barking questions about who was coming and going. 'They're just like goats, you go and look for one and while your back's turned the others all disappear!' However, while he pretended to be a hard taskmaster, he cared deeply about them all. They had become his family.

Thesiger enjoyed stories of my last trek as he had not walked in Turkana for many years. The first time he had walked up to Lodwar with his camels it was still a restricted area due to the dangers, and he had to sign a special permission and a disclaimer in case of death. When he camped, some bullying young men came and started trying to push him around, demanding food and gifts, so in unmistakable terms he told them where to go. They sloped off sheepishly, to everyone else's astonishment. Afterwards someone whispered to him, '*Mzee Juu*, that is not a safe way to speak to the *ngoroko*!' Such was his extraordinary aura.

He talked about other walks in Kenya, drawing a sensitive finger across the map, criss-crossing the NFD to the Indian Ocean and back. He instinctively seemed to choose the most dangerous areas. In the camp he, like Lawi and me, usually wore a kikoi, the coastal equivalent of the Indonesian sarong, hanging to about mid calf. And what calves he had – like sides of beef – testament to a lifetime of trekking.

We talked about books by other authors. His attitude to writing was straightforward: 'Write the way you talk and never use a long word when a short one will do. That's a common fault of modern writers, who think it sounds clever.' He was almost universally scathing of modern travel books and his normal literary review was short: 'Bloody book, absolutely bloody!'

The afternoon passed pleasantly and when supper was due he announced grandly, 'Tonight we are having *la spécialité de la maison*', so I assumed that something special was on its way. It turned out to be goat stew with cabbage, onion and potato, seasoned with a variety of spices, and was what he ate every single evening of his life, with minor variations. It was indeed *la spécialité* – but the only one. We sat on the two hard wooden chairs beside the charcoal brazier, which Laputa had lit outside and carried in for us, as the nights were very cold, and after supper we drank Earl Grey tea and continued our talk, ranging over a wide variety of subjects.

Surprisingly, it turned out that Thesiger had an acute and devilish sense of humour, thoroughly enjoying doing rather good and very funny impersonations of public figures, many of whom he knew personally. When he was in this mood he became very relaxed and his eyes sparkled with the fun of it all. I was enjoying being there.

As I had known him for several years, he had for some time used my Christian name, but only now did I feel the time was appropriate to return the familiarity, and from now on I always knew him as Wilfred. He became almost like a second father to me over the course of these treks, even admitting to having been very unnerved when, in his youth, he addressed the RGS after his crossing of the unknown and very dangerous Danakil desert of Ethiopia. 'In those days the Society was very different from today, very formal and intimidating, and, d'you see, I was a very young man.' There grew a very comfortable relationship between us.

He particularly liked the fact that I preferred to travel hard in the way that he had chosen, and never reserved any special privileges for myself among my tribal companions, eating what they ate, and sleeping on the same rocky ground that they slept on. He thought for a moment, 'I remember when a young man asked for my help to make a safari so I sent him off with some of my people. But after a few days they arrived back without him, saying he had been insufferable, insisting on special treatment over everything, reserving the best food for himself, doing no work and ordering them about like slaves. So they had stealthily got up during the night in some desolate spot, silently loaded the donkeys and left.

I asked what had become of him and they had no idea, they never heard of him again.' Wilfred played the scene over in his mind for a moment and then chuckled. 'Can you imagine his shock when he woke up? Bloody man!'

He recounted a recent incident at a dinner party in London society when a lady beside him had asked, 'Mr Thesiger, have you ever eaten anyone?' Quick as flash he had answered, 'Oh yes, just the other day we cooked up a young boy...he tasted particularly good!'

I mentioned that I should like to visit Teleki's volcano en route to the lake, having failed to reach it on my last trip. He reminded me that it was close to the Suguta Valley which could be perilous because of the *ngoroko*, and that it was also unnaturally hot. He suggested it would be much safer to head directly for Loyangalani on the lakeside. But I sensed him warm to the sniff of danger.

He talked of lions and his friendship with George Adamson whose wife Joy had written *Born Free* about keeping Elsa, a lion cub. He used to visit George at his home in the Kora National Park, but he profoundly disagreed with him about keeping lions in close contact with human beings. Wilfred said that George's lions had mauled, maimed and even killed several people, about which George had kept very hush-hush. Even 'Boy', George's favourite, had mauled the son of a friend and later, after he had killed his assistant, George had to shoot him. George himself was later killed by Somali *shifta* and was buried next to Boy.

Wilfred had had a great deal of experience with lions, hunting them extensively when in the Sudan political service, and at one stage had reared a pair of cubs himself. Unlike George, he understood the likelihood of their becoming man-eaters once their natural fear of mankind was gone and they had learned how defenceless we really are. So when they became adults he took the difficult decision to shoot them both before the day came when they might kill someone. He was adamant that it is foolish and dangerous to form sentimental attachments to wild animals who do not understand the concept of being a pet.

He remembered one of his own close shaves when hunting at Kutum in Sudan. 'In that area there were a lot of marauding lions who attacked the villagers whom it was my responsibility to protect. One day, tracking a lion on foot through long dense grass, I had a quick glimpse of its coat extremely close and, thinking it was the shoulder, I fired at point-blank range. But I was wrong and it was the rump, making it spin in fury and attack. With limited visibility through the long grass it missed me, but knocked me back into a thorn bush as it flew past and landed instead on my three assistants and began to maul them. I pulled myself out of the bush and it was so close that I just pushed the gun into its ear and pulled the trigger.'

Over the years his ideas about hunting had changed with the diminishing numbers of animals, and he spoke with distaste of the unrestrained killing by early hunters like Richard Meinertzhagen and Theodore Roosevelt. 'It would give me no pleasure to hunt now. I prefer to take photographs. Africa is very different these days.'

His conversation drifted from Darfur to Abyssinia, Haile Selassie, and so to the Bedu of Arabia. By the time I crept into the tent my brain was ringing with the momentous stories I had heard that evening. It was hard to sleep with the excitement of it all, and the wild noises of the bush at night further increased my thrill to be there on that lonely hillside at the camp of the last of the great explorers.

Lawi introduced me to a young Samburu called Ayoko as a colleague for my trek. He was a very slim 19-year-old with almost European facial features, golden black skin, and hair worn longer than the usual close crop. He obviously fancied himself as a stylish dresser and was always spotless in a different pair of long trousers and tee-shirt. He lived in a *manyatta* close behind the camp.

I wondered if there might be problems having a Samburu and the Turkana Netakwang on the trip, since these tribes traditionally dislike each other. In this area, however, there was a lot of overlap between them, and although Lawi lived as a Samburu, had been circumcised as such and was now one of their *morans*, he was actually born a Turkana.

Along with good blankets for Netakwang and Ayoko, I gradually assembled the now familiar provisions needed for my trip: 24 kilos of maize flour (*posho*); 10 kilos of rice; 5 kilos of dried beans; 10 kilos of sugar; 2 packets of salt; 2 large packets of tealeaves; 1 bag of boiled sweets (for children); 2 tins of Kimbo cooking fat and an assortment of cooking pans etc. One of the Maralal street tailors had made me a lot of small cotton sacks with drawstring tops, and I decanted the foodstuffs into them to make it easier to balance the weight between the donkeys' loads. Together with the jerry cans of water it seemed an enormous weight and I was sure that three donkeys were not enough.

I stacked it all in a corner of Wilfred's writing room. Far from being distracted by my coming and going he loved all the activity and was happily reminded of his own journeys, always stopping me to have a quick word to make sure that I had not forgotten this or that, which I never had, as I prided myself on having become a proficient quartermaster. In fact I never found myself lacking something important, and my medical kit was now also comprehensive.

At the end of his day's writing Wilfred always sat outside his house overlooking the enchanting view across the valley, and when I was there he would bring up another chair for me to sit beside him. I loved the quiet and comfortable emptiness, dappled with trees in the evening light, sizzling with the myriad sounds of insects, and the movement of game passing through just as they had for millennia: black groups of buffalo or scatterings of antelope and zebra. And not another building in sight.

He had gazed over this view many thousands of times and never tired of it. Laputa made us coffee and Wilfred told me about the direction I would be following towards the lake. 'You used to see twelve or fifteen rhino a day up there, but now you'll be lucky if you see one'. He talked about a time when he could look over a landscape teeming with tens of thousands of animals, since shot by white hunters or poached by a rapidly increasing population. Wilfred was bitterly disappointed to see the world he had known irrevocably passing for ever, and I knew I was honoured to be catching these final glimpses of an earlier time; an era that would soon vanish completely.

He advised me to take one of his tents, not only against the weather, now that the rainy season was starting, but also as protection against lion and hyena. 'There are some bad lions around South Horr.' He mentioned elephant but said that they never stand on tents, even stepping nimbly over the guy ropes. I hoped that I would not have to put that to the test! He said that on the slopes of Mount Elgon he had woken one night and heard a deep and disturbing rumbling directly above the tent. He had quietly prodded Lawi awake and whispered to ask him what the noise was. Lawi whispered back, '*Mzee Juu*, it is the stomach of an elephant.'

Lawi at last agreed that I needed another two donkeys and should take another man. He chose another Samburu called Abdilahi (pronounced Abdilai) and I bought another blanket and a few last additions. When Wilfred gave me the tent he had recommended I found it to be peppered with holes, so sat on the grass for a couple of hours and cut up the bag it was kept in to patch them. Wilfred showed me how to mend a hole on safari by pushing a small pebble against it from inside and binding it round tightly with string so it stood out like a wart. That's fine for one or two holes, but we would have needed an extra donkey just to carry all the pebbles! As usual there was no sewn-in groundsheet.

Just when I felt I had covered every eventuality I found that the donkeys were not being supplied with the necessary skins and sacks to protect their backs from the loads, so I gave someone 60 shillings to go and find a sufficient number for five donkeys. But more importantly no one had any of the Turkana-style panniers. What had people used in the past? No one seemed to know. Chaos. A great debate started and at last they told me that the tradition here was to tie the sacks together in pairs and hang them across the donkeys' backs. I did not like this at all, but there was nothing else to be done. The Turkana knew much more about travelling with donkeys.

Next morning at 6am I was already up as the camp began to stir. We drank coffee as someone went to fetch the animals from the *boma* and the heap of sacks was brought out. A crowd assembled to watch the preparations and offer advice. You could cut the excitement with a knife. Wilfred loved it. The donkeys were full of energy and very frisky with good grazing since the rains arrived; something our animals in Turkana would not have recognised. They were loaded and the moment had arrived. I said goodbye to Wilfred and Lawi and thanked them for all their help and advice.

As I was about to start Wilfred asked, 'What do you want me to do if you're killed on this trek?'

I grinned and said, 'I think the best thing would be to put my body out in the bush for the hyenas.'

His eyes sparkled with delight and he said, 'D'you know, that's exactly what I would have said.'

Welcomed into the wilds
with a Samburu wedding

SETTING OFF ON ANY trek is rather similar: a little nervousness not knowing your colleagues or exactly what the route will be like with its attendant risks, and of course the thrill of curiosity. It was Monday, 1st November 1982. We set off down the hill past the occasional small 'poison arrow tree' and turned right onto a track leading up into the Karisia hills north of Maralal. Abdilahi gave me confidence from the word go, an able chap with a long, quick stride and a decisive, intelligent attitude. Like several in this area his very black skin belied curiously European facial proportions, with the quick, searching eyes of someone who misses nothing, and would prove to be conscientious and eager to work. I had a long chat with Ayoko, who told me of his ambition to go to a seminary and become a priest. Yet, curiously, he never expressed any interest whatsoever in Christianity and I became convinced that he had noticed how the African assistants of missionaries had a pretty easy time and lived well compared with their tribal cousins. Although a nice lad, he not surprisingly turned out to be lazy. I was not sure about Netakwang; I doubted his commitment or loyalty but could not exactly put my finger on it.

The hills were forested with East African cedar (correctly *Juniperus procera*), attractive, tall trees decorated with long swags of hanging lichen called Spanish moss, and we passed through dense clouds of white butterflies mixed with swallowtails and orange tips, drinking from the damp ground. Sunlight streaming through the leaf canopy made me feel jubilant, and there seemed something sublimely English about it all, until I was brought back to reality by numerous piles of elephant dung! A muddy pool was deeply pockmarked by their enormous footprints and the smell of elephant made the already skittish donkeys very nervous. Already their loads were slipping.

A Samburu *mzee* caught up and helped us retie them, then invited us to stay at his *manyatta* just north of the hills. He wore a red blanket flamboyantly thrown over one shoulder and a pair of spectacular ear decorations pierced through the tops of the ears and protruding about three inches from each side of his head. They were made of curved pink plastic rods, ending in green beads. His ear lobes had large holes to house ivory plugs and his face was also of European proportions, with a short moustache, more common here than in Turkana. I guessed he was in his early 30s, some years older than the *moran* age group.

Samburu society is strictly divided into age groupings. The most prestigious, the *moran* or warrior group, begins in their mid to late teens and usually lasts about seven years. Consequently, to be a *mzee* or elder did not necessarily imply any great age, and at the age of 31 I was always referred to as '*mzee*'. During their time as *morans* the responsibility of being a warrior dominated their lives, almost exclusively in all-male company and never ever seen by women while eating. They maintained constant alertness, even when asleep, as I was to find out on my next trek. At times of risk they hyperventilated to sharpen their reactions and pump up their bravery to formidable levels, completely insensitive to pain; the perfect fighting machine. Good-looking *morans* were idolised by the girls although no contact was allowed until after their days as warriors.

During the initiation into the warrior class the men were circumcised in an elaborate and painful way unique to the tribe, and during the operation would sit upright with eyes wide in a fixed stare, not showing any reaction. Reacting to pain would disgrace their family. The women were also circumcised by the older women prior to their marriage, despite the fact that officially clitoridectomy and other female genital mutilation (FGM) was now outlawed in Kenya.

A steep, rocky stream-bed led us down the hill, the donkeys lurching and skidding, with the loads constantly slipping onto the backs of their necks. This was hopeless; why did we not have proper Turkana panniers? As soon as we left the hills the forest thinned and died back to acacia scrub, the heat escalated, and we immediately arrived at the *mzee's manyatta* at a place called Opiroi.

His hut was of the typical rectangular Samburu design, with a very low opening and a couple of rooms, one with a lit hearth which kept the air chokingly thick and hot. The women repeatedly plastered the outside walls with fresh cow dung against the heavy downpours of the rainy season, and over time the thickness and weight must have become immense, but it worked. It was a sizeable homestead with a large thorn *boma* containing separate areas for the different species to be penned in for the night. Our donkeys were safe here.

Years later, when I lived on Dartmoor, I was intrigued that the layout of the ancient Bronze Age settlement of Grimspound was exactly the same, with a perimeter wall containing a random arrangement of homes, and walled enclosures adjoining the outer wall to hold the livestock – obviously a system which worked irrespective of the differing terrain, culture, building materials, or climate. We put up the tent behind the *mzee*'s house, and after our meal he brought us the rest of the evening milking, as a line of 'patients' queued up for my medical attention.

Next day was to be a wedding in a *manyatta* close by, but the unhappy bride was to be circumcised during the festivities, so the marriage would not be consummated for 20 days. A bull had been slaughtered by the time we got up, and was about to be roasted on a huge fire, and *morans* were expected to come from a wide area to dance. It was going to be a big occasion, so I was lucky to be able to do a deal with the elders of the *manyatta* that if I paid for all the *pombe* I would be allowed to take as many pictures as I liked. Some of the visiting *morans* were not too pleased but they knew the arrangement. I was excited as this was a proper traditional wedding with no outsiders except us.

The groom was superbly attired, his hair ornately dressed for the occasion, plastered with red ochre mixed with animal fat and decorated with several lines of threaded beads which criss-crossed his head, buttons sewn at their centres. His ears were full of decorations, large rings of aluminium, brass and copper hanging from the lobes, and with more beadwork punched through their tops. Despite being a handsome young man he looked decidedly gloomy and was slightly hunched, his head slumped into stiffly raised shoulders. Perhaps he was not a willing husband? His friend, a sort of best man, was decidedly more cheerful, with a lopsided buck-toothed grin and also a fine head decoration, but without the intricate beadwork.

After a couple of hours we were invited to eat roast meat from the bull. The younger *mzees* began dancing in a circle, with singing and high-jumping, but everyone was awaiting the *morans*. I climbed to the top of a nearby hill to watch out for them and gradually they appeared in groups on adjacent hilltops, dramatically poppy-red against the green landscape in their colourful costumes, with hair, faces and shoulders all painted with red ochre in animal fat. Eventually they started towards us, small crimson streams winding down the hillsides and meeting up to become larger rivers of exotic colours until at last flooding onto the clearing where they were to perform. They were a proud and fine-looking collection of young men, riding high on a tidal wave of testosterone as they began their dance (*see photo 26*).

They stayed together in a tight group, and then in twos or threes would walk forward from the rest and begin to jump, rigidly upright with hollowed backs and heads pulled backwards with pride, higher and higher as if bouncing on springs. After a time they would venture further from the others, jumping or hopping, before returning to the back of the group (*see photo 27*). As they jumped they hyperventilated, so that from time to time one of them would be consumed by a fit and throw himself to the ground to lie shaking uncontrollably, or perhaps flinging himself into a thorn bush, and being carried away by his friends until the fit passed. I could easily see how, in times of battle, these young warriors would be beyond the limitations of normal physical endurance.

At the same time the unmarried girls formed their own circle and began singing, taking it in turns to move to the centre of the circle two at a time to make short shaking dances face to face, letting the whole of their upper bodies gyrate frenetically, then being replaced by another pair. One of them particularly caught my eye with an enormous pile of beaded necklaces starting below the chin and forming a brightly coloured pyramid to almost the top of her breasts. The upper edge of each ear was pierced and hung with such an elaborate decoration of beadwork, buttons and chains that the ear was pulled over to hang down vertically. Her arms were heavy with bracelets and around her waist she wore a red cotton *shuka* (*see photo 25*).

The *morans*, who continued to dance throughout the glorious occasion were the stars of the show, and they knew it, pushing themselves to ever greater heights and increased demonstrations of physical prowess as they jumped. Although most wore red, some wore *shukas* of white, yellow or pink, many with lengthy red fringes which twisted and flailed dramatically as they leapt into the air. Some had the long tresses of traditional warriors, but sadly most had given way to the modern practice of wearing their hair cut fairly short. They were magnificent, with their shoulders, foreheads, and jaws painted with red ochre, and thin lines drawn across their cheeks (*see photo 28*). Many of their spears were transformed into banners with red or white flags dancing below the blades.

The dancing continued for a long time and I was beginning to wonder how it would end when, at 5pm, a violent rain storm suddenly had everyone fleeing for cover to protect their fine costumes and make-up. I could not resist a smile as I watched these proud, indomitable warriors scurrying off to avoid getting wet.

During this joviality the bride waited inside a dark hut into which the older women ducked to carry out their secret and grotesque operation. How they could see what they were doing I could not imagine, and did not wish to. But, without undergoing this mutilation, tradition dictated that no Samburu girl could marry.

Abdilahi, who was already distinguishing himself as the hardest worker of my team, cooked up rice and vegetables, and immediately afterwards we made our way to our beds. Like the Welsh, the Turkana tribe were renowned for their singing and Netakwang

173

never missed an opportunity, although frankly I had heard more musical sounds. Irritatingly, as we dozed off, he burst into loud song and would not stop until at last I got angry and told him to shut up. His voice was replaced by the much lovelier rising notes of hyena in the night, their eerie calls soaring like wolf songs in the darkness.

Crazy camels and the thorny path to a rich man's *boma*

ABDILAHI WOKE US ALL with tea and at 8.45 we were underway, with our genial host walking with us to bid farewell. Picking up a little track from an outlying police post, we followed it between unremitting curtains of dense bush. At our lunch halt a sharp shower made us huddle round the base of an acacia tree, cowering under a layer of goatskins. When it had passed I put my head out to check the donkeys but they had gone. A moment later they dramatically reappeared around the shoulder of the hill at full gallop, closely pursued by a lion, and we leapt to our feet, shouting and waving anything we could grab. Luckily the lion made a run for it.

The donkeys had naturally taken violent defensive action, bucking and lashing out with their back hooves, and this had thrown off my personal bags, which now dragged behind in the mud, getting a ferocious kicking. Strangely, nothing was broken but, more importantly, we were lucky still to have five serviceable donkeys, although they were demons to catch after their shock, and very jumpy as we readjusted the loads. I could hardly blame them.

We spent the night close to a *manyatta* at a tiny village called Parsaloi, where there was a camp of mining surveyors and, as a full moon rose, the *morans* began to sing; first a song to call the girls, and once they arrived they also began to sing in another group a little further off. It was lovely to listen to as I sank into sleep, and I tingled with pleasure in the wildness of my tribal surroundings.

Next day we killed a goat and spent a lazy day feasting. It was a blessing that Wilfred had lent us the tent, as a violent rain storm flooded even the groundsheet inside it, and although it only lasted half an hour, a nearby dry *lugga* was soon a rampaging, thundering torrent of foaming brown water, carrying all before it. I walked over to watch it and was amazed at how quickly the surging force rushed past; within another hour there was just damp sand to show where it had been.

The next morning I was irritated that the others all went to drink *pombe*, so I started out with the young man from the dispensary, who showed me a way cross-country to make a shortcut with the donkeys, which saved a mile and reached the vehicle piste northwards, leading towards the lake via Baragoi. There the others caught up with me and we stayed on the track, making good speed. When we camped that night I was disappointed to find that the remains of the goat were already covered with fly eggs and would soon be crawling. After turning in Netakwang started up again; truly he would not have won an Eisteddfod.

In the early morning I crept out of the tent before anyone stirred and sat watching the first fingers of light creep over the horizon, tinting the eastern sky with the palest silver aquamarine, which alchemically warmed to a thin gold and finally resolved into the endless blue of the implacable tropical sky. I felt deeply content. Within moments my flesh began to warm as the throbbing heat surged to regain centre-stage of the heavens. Sunrise and sun-fall happen swiftly in the tropics, the sun leaping vertically from the long shadows of earth or diving steeply back to sleep.

At a tributary of the Milgis River we dug for water so that the donkeys could drink their fill. The Milgis, fed by scores of seasonal *luggas*, rises in the hills north of Maralal and is the largest of the seasonal rivers that finally vanish in the deserts of the Rendille tribal country south of Marsabit. In fact not a drop of rainwater in Turkana or Samburu ever reaches the sea, most rivers sinking without trace into the sand, while the few lucky survivors drain into Lake Turkana, only to evaporate there.

The lush green country now changed to a dry landscape of short scrub and scattered rocks between low, flat-topped hills. Here a Samburu *mzee* joined us with disturbing news: 'On the road in front, *shifta* are killing travellers. Very dangerous.'

'The bastards,' I muttered, sounding confident, but I felt a hollow pit in my stomach.

'We leave the road before that place and make new path through the hills.'

As he spoke, the thought came to me: 'If I was a *shifta* I wouldn't hang about on the road for the GSU to come and shoot me, I'd hide in the hills.' The same hills we were heading for now? (*see photo 29*) I felt unnerved and vulnerable and the familiar old fear quietly started to gnaw at the sinews of my being again. What the hell was I doing here?

We pushed on, passing a suspicious group of Grant's gazelle and soon afterwards some ostrich, close to the track. Their bulky plumage always struck me as more upholstered than feathered and they ran off with enormous strides, displaying an extraordinary delicacy while shooting us accusing glances. One even made a few impotent flaps as if it might fly, but I believe this helps the birds to steer.

Our self-appointed *mzee* guide said, 'We must go now, up the hill,' and we turned right towards a large, white rock and carried on through the low hills till we came to a *lugga*, where we stopped at midday in the shade of a majestic, spreading acacia (*see photo 30*). I always found something noble in these trees, prospering from this hostile land to spread their limbs and provide shade for man and beast alike, the fine filigree of attractive leaflets – and sometimes even delicate flowers – making an exotic canopy. Their discarded timber was good for our cooking fires, but such generosity was balanced by a need for caution, as the ground was frequently littered with fallen twigs, whose long thorns were arranged so that however they fell some would be pointing vertically to drive into an unwary foot.

On this occasion I had one, thick as a matchstick, push straight through the sole of my shoe, deep into my foot. I was nailed into my shoe until it could be prised out, a painfully awkward and very bloody operation. Our *mzee* friend now decided, 'It is too hot for footing, so we stay and walk to Baragoi in the night'.

My throbbing foot was happy with that decision, but the charm and frustration of tribal Africa was that nothing was ever predictable, so no one except me found it strange when, within a couple of hours, we were reloading and ready to continue.

The *mzee* now said firmly, 'We keep footing now till Baragoi', so I was no longer surprised when a little later, on reaching a Samburu *manyatta* near a waterhole called Iltepesaare, we immediately stopped to camp for the night. My foot was increasingly painful and I did not object.

Inside the large *boma* it was subdivided as usual into various compartments for goats and camels, and in one corner was a small hut occupied by only a young boy and girl to look after the animals, and a couple of *totos*. This was quite usual as children often had the task of staying away from the family with the livestock, subsisting on milk and blood for long periods and very rarely killing a goat.

Our young hosts offered us one of the small goat enclosures and we laid out a carpet of our skins and sacking on the deep, soft litter of goat droppings, which made a comfortable mattress. Our water was in very short supply but they generously gave us milk from the evening and morning milkings. This goat pen was immediately adjacent to the camels and, as we were lying down to sleep, we were treated to an extraordinary percussion concert of rumblings, belches and farts. The strangest were the gurglings of a couple of bull camels, who constantly blew out large membranous bubbles from the side of their mouths, showing that they were in season or *musth*, a time when they can be highly unpredictable – and sometimes lethal.

They were clearly not enamoured of their new neighbours, and soon after dozing off we were startled awake by an enormous roaring sound as if we were on a flight path, which in a sense we were. I was halfway to my feet almost before I had opened my eyes, and looked up to see one of these bulls in full and furious charge straight at me. The thorn barrier between us looked extremely fragile in the face of this onslaught, but at the very last minute the camel decided that he had more faith in its strength than I did and shied away with inches to spare. With a pounding heart I lay down again to try to sleep, but moments later looked up to see the monstrous head of this brute leaning over the thorn fence and leering down directly at me in the moonlight, with an ugly glint in his eye, his inflated cheek pouch swinging over my face. I prayed he would move away as I was not keen to be splattered by his revolting saliva. Fortunately he soon decided I was unworthy of his ministrations.

The next morning I spent time talking with our guide. Such was the mutual dislike between Samburu and Turkana that it amused me hugely when he said, with curdling disdain, 'The Turkana are not human beings. We are neighbours to baboons.' Certainly I appreciated the enormous difference between the sophistication of these cousins of the Maasai and my more primitive hosts on the other side of the lake.

We set off while the young people of the *manyatta* were still moving among the dense flock of goats and fat-tailed sheep, a lovely dapple of whites, browns and blacks, like pebbles on a beach, their backs gently rimmed with the first light of day. They milked a little here, a little there, always leaving enough so that when the kids were released to their mothers, they would still have sufficient. The sun was just peering over the horizon, warming already, as we began the last leg of our walk to Baragoi. The donkeys were tired, and slow to build up to the rhythm of the march.

We soon came onto the El Barta Plains, a plateau of parched grass and low scrub almost as far as the eye could see, with very little sign of life. In this drought only an occasional distant group of trees marked where there must have been some underground water. Away to our right the far horizon was dominated by the long chain of the Ndoto Mountains, darkened by its covering of forest, and dimly ahead of us lay the smaller massif of Nyiru, which is where the Samburu god 'Nkai' lives. The Karisia hills around Maralal were now almost lost to sight behind us.

Our legs were scratched practically raw by the constant scouring of the dry stems which helped to keep us alert in the monotony of our march, as from time to time someone would leap aside with a cry as a snake slithered past, hurrying out of our way. Butterflies sometimes landed on us in large numbers to drink our sweat. As we swept the yellow scum off a small pool I spotted the spoor of a pride of lions who had recently been here to drink. I was thrilled by the frisson of crouching to drink on the very same spot and of the very same water that these great beasts had so lately lapped.

Ayoko knew a Samburu sub-chief who had a very large *manyatta* outside Baragoi and we crossed a *lugga* and climbed a low hill to reach it. The homestead was immense, the home of a very wealthy man, and we discovered that he had 700 cows, 200 goats, 70 camels and 20 donkeys, all of whom were brought in each night to sleep inside the *boma* of the *manyatta* in different fenced compounds. The chief showed us around his home, introducing his four wives, each of whom had her own wattle-and-daub house, and some of his 40 children, who milled about everywhere in one extraordinarily large and happy family. He was a kindly man in his 40s with wide-set eyes and a broad smile. We watched his animals being driven into the *boma* for the night and I was fascinated to see that he did not count them, simply knowing them so well that he would notice if, for instance, the mottled one with the curly horn was missing. Extraordinary instinct.

Abdilahi and Netakwang went to sleep in the town while Ayoko and I were installed, with all our gear, in the house of one of the wives. This hut, although of the traditional design, was much larger than others I had seen, about fourteen feet by ten, rectangular with rounded corners. The main doorway was four-feet high, giving access to a small vestibule which led into the cooking area, where a fire still burned in an earthen hearth, filling the whole house with dense, choking smoke.

Two bedrooms contained sleeping platforms of brush nine inches high, covered with cow skins, and also an iron bedstead for the chief when he stayed here. A powerful smell of the cow dung used for re-plastering filled the house, and the thick smoke made my eyes stream so I tried not to cough with each breath. It was like a sauna and we ran with sweat. I was honoured with the chief's bed but it was two hours before I could sleep due to the intensity of the heat, and yet by 3.15am I was shivering with cold. The wives and children loved having me as a guest and everyone wanted their photos taken, including the chief – in a uniform of khaki with a beret and cap badge of the King's African Rifles.

After a couple of nights we continued through the town – little more than a line of shops each side of the road together with a medical clinic and a small primary school – and staying on this level track we had an easy day, covering virtually 20 miles with hardly a single passing vehicle. The rough road glowed golden as it wound its sinuous path across this flat landscape of bone-dry scrub. The Kowop Mountain on our left was capped by impressive rock formations almost like a medieval fortress, but more imposing was the range of Nyiru ahead, growing steadily closer.

We passed no *manyattas* all day, due to frequent *ngoroko* attacks, and began to wonder where to camp. Abdilahi commented, 'This not safe here, very dangerous, we continue footing.'

'It will soon be completely dark, as the moon is not rising until four hours after sunset, and Wilfred said the lions here are dangerous,' I pointed out.

A dilemma. But just then Ayoko heard the sound of cattle being rounded up for the night, and we found them half a mile to our left, where a little *boma* stood on the brow of a hill containing some animals and two huts. We asked to camp with them and erected the tent quickly before the darkness engulfed us. It was comforting inside the comparative security of the *boma*.

Mount Nyiru: from nightmare to nirvana

TWO OF THE MEN in the *boma* were Home Guard and carried rifles because of the *ngoroko* threat. I negotiated with them to act as our guides to take us over Mount Nyiru to Tum. They agreed – for 30 shillings each. They were unhappy about taking Netakwang, a Turkana, and thus forbidden to climb the sacred mountain. Only recently a group of Samburu *morans* had had to race to drive off a gang of *ngoroko* who were climbing the mountain. Somehow I made a case for him, although he did not deserve it, having now proved himself bone idle.

A lovely series of rock pools in a *lugga* close by allowed us to bathe in the morning, while baboons and a statuesque dik-dik watched us from a cliff top, and the donkeys grazed happily. Abdilahi had a wonderful way of roasting meat so we bought a goat to have meat for the journey ahead, and once it was cooked we set off, climbing round the southernmost peak of the mountains (*see photo 31*).

This was going to be a hard slog, the loads constantly scraping against rocks or trees and threatening to be shredded by thorns, most dangerous of which was a species of acacia the Samburu called 'Wait', which the early settlers had adapted to 'The Wait-a-Bit thorn'. If it caught you, you had to wait while you painfully unpicked its fish-hook thorns from your skin. This happened frequently.

Around the spur of a hill we came at last to a group of buildings glowing with the evening light caressing their red mud render. Above them a large, spreading tree was festooned with the spherical nests of weaver birds. Our guides told us this had been a Foresters' Post, large enough to include its own school and with outlying *manyattas*, until earlier in the year a huge and particularly vicious *ngoroko* attack had left many people dead, and the remainder had fled, never to return. An eerie, hollow feeling remained like in a ghost town; the floor of the schoolroom was littered with paper and torn books half-eaten by termites and cockroaches, and scattered pieces of chalk showed where the teacher had stood. The only life now were the large numbers of lizards darting across the floors and up the walls. We made a fire to smoke out any snakes and swept it with leafy sprigs before eating the remains of the goat with beans and *posho*. It was an unsettling feeling that where we lay to sleep children had so recently been gunned down in an inhuman act of savagery. I wondered how close those *ngoroko* might be now.

After an early mug of tea we turned to face the mountain, first crossing a stream of very pure, icy water. Our guides were uncertain whether the donkeys could reach the top of the mountain as seasonal torrents might have torn away the tracks, but we hoped for the best. Recent rain meant that many plants were flowering and we had to bend double to worm our way through their lush growth, and under overhanging branches so dense that we were only aware of where the ground rose or fell. There were no obvious paths and we just pushed through where we could and thanked God for these guides, without whom we would have become hopelessly lost, walking up blind side valleys or even to the vertiginous cliff edges of hidden ravines.

The air was full of the scent of wild mint crushed by the donkey's hooves, and the sun streamed through the dappled leaf cover of the tree canopy above, speckling the flowers below, which glowed and sparkled in reply. We came into a clearing, the home of a large and ancient baobab tree at the base of one of the formidable buttresses of rock we had seen from below. Here we rested, before following the narrow bed of what must recently have been a raging torrent.

Sometimes the rocky sides were so narrow that the donkeys became completely wedged with their loads and we had to fight to free them, putting our shoulders against their rumps like a rugby scrum to push them through. Loads constantly shifted or were thrown completely, and our stops to reload were more and more frequent. As Abdilahi said, 'This is not a place for donkeys, this is crazy.' When three loads were thrown at the same moment in a very narrow defile we decided to stop to rest and eat the last of the meat. The donkeys just waited where they were, wedged firmly between the rocks.

Reloading them was extremely difficult as there was no room to pass a donkey to reach the next without climbing over the large boulders which hemmed them in. There was also insufficient space to squeeze in between the head of one and the rump of the next where they stood in a crocodile line, in order to shove one or pull another forward. The day had become a serious challenge.

Once we were finally on the move again the terrain rewarded us unkindly by becoming steeper still and the stream bed we were following became even more tortuous, with huge granite slabs scattered about, between which we tried to pick a route. The donkeys started to shy at each new obstacle, and, if there was room, would sometimes turn round and start back down the slope, becoming trapped against the donkey below, who was still facing uphill, and fights started between the panicking animals, with loads slipping and bags tearing open. They were having a terrible day, and we too were utterly exhausted. It was mayhem.

I decided to initiate a new strategy. 'One man must go ahead of each donkey to keep them apart. That way he can push the one in front or pull the one behind.'

We were following the course of frequent past torrents, under the forest's low, dense canopy. In this new configuration, we nursed the donkeys slowly up the treacherous gradient of steep, water-polished rock, which they somehow had to jump their way up. After a sharp shower of rain the rock became even more slippery and the donkeys started to fall sideways to add to their problems, sometimes ending up trapped and unable to move. I worried that one had broken a hind leg as it lay helpless and floundering, its leg at an extraordinary angle beneath it. But after it had rested for a little while it summoned a superhuman (or super-donkey) effort and struggled desperately to its feet. I was increasingly overwhelmed with respect for them, driving themselves so hard to do what we were asking of them, quite against their natural instincts. They are such tough little creatures.

Hour after excruciating hour, we continued to force ourselves upwards, until at last, when I was wondering if this battle with the mountain would ever end, we unexpectedly and suddenly emerged from the forest and found ourselves at the top. The delight at having conquered the climb, finally to be able to gaze out into the infinity of a breathtaking vista, was extreme. Mount Kenya was clear, even close, a mere 150 miles away, and far beyond it a tiny pimple on the horizon must surely have been Kilimanjaro, 350 miles distant.

This was truly a view across the whole of Kenya, a worthy throne for the Samburu god. I was stupefied by the immensity of it all and thought instinctively of Kipling's Kim when he 'threw his soul after his eyes across the deep blue gulfs between range and range'. The gruelling climb had taken six hours but it had all been worthwhile to have gained entry to this nirvana (*see photo 32*).

We spent two days on the mountain top, wandering through moist green meadows with burbling ice-cold streams, and although we saw enormous amounts of buffalo dung we never saw the animals. How they had got up here I could not imagine. Our donkeys pulled at the lush grass in delight. This was a fairytale oasis in its harsh surroundings of dry stone and dust, Spanish moss streaming from the branches of cedar trees in pale grey-green festoons and exotic large-leaved single-stemmed plants clustered wherever there was water, like gigantic Asplenium ferns.

There was no shortage of firewood to make a roaring blaze in the evening, as the nights were wickedly cold at this altitude, even inside the tent where all six of us crowded like sardines. Extraordinary that it can be so cold only 150 miles from the equator. The first German missionaries to see the snowy cap of Kilimanjaro were derided as frauds when they reported their findings to the wise men of science in 1848.

At last the foliage parted like a theatre curtain to reveal a breathtaking view to the west. We had crossed the top of the mountain and now gazed onto a new land, the country stretching endlessly until it faded into a distant haze, perhaps in Uganda. Under towering cumulonimbus clouds with flat slate-grey bases, Lakes Logipi and Alablab shone silver like sheets of glass in the late afternoon sunshine, way down in the sweltering Suguta Valley, almost 8,000 feet below us, lower than Lake Turkana itself. Beyond them in a haze of heat lay the mountain rubble of the Loriu Plateau.

Beyond another meadow our guides took us to a shoulder of

rock which offered another commanding spectacle of the whole landscape, even allowing the southern tip of Lake Turkana to peep round the corner of the next bluff to our right. On its western shore I could just pick out the shape of Mugurr, which had so recently threatened to take my life, now just a harmless grey dot in the vastness. The side of Nyiru fell away below us at about 60 degrees, with several curtains of rock faces emerging from the scrubby vegetation which clung fiercely to the tumbling slopes. It was glorious to soak up such a panorama, seen by few from a foreign land. Of course Wilfred Thesiger had already witnessed it about a decade before me.

The National Museum in Nairobi had asked me to collect seashells from this mountain top, almost twice the height of Mount Snowdon in Wales, and our friends took me to a place among the trees where I was able to gather some. The convulsions of the earth's crust which had caused this tall mountain to erupt from the seabed were hard to contemplate.

Before arriving at the place where our path headed downwards we had one last glimpse of the lake to our north. Below us was the small town of Tum, laid out like a haphazard scattering of matchboxes threaded on a tracery of dusty tracks. The way down was easier and shorter than the way we had climbed up, although it was still difficult and slow enough, with the loads continually slipping forwards onto the necks of the donkeys and our bags ripped to shreds against rocks and bushes.

Netakwang followed 50 yards behind us in a sour sulk, having had a row with Abdilahi, and refusing point-blank to do any work whatsoever. The heat increased as we dropped lower, and we found a welcoming stream to drink from and wash in before entering the tiny town – just an overgrown village. We must have looked a strange apparition following behind our battle-scarred donkeys with their shredded loads. Everyone turned out of their houses or stopped what they were doing to stand and stare at us.

I had a curious feeling that we might have been a bunch of well-known gangsters riding into some shanty town in a spaghetti western, and almost expected the appropriate Morricone music to strike up. Then the 'sheriff' came forward in the shape of the chief, impeccably dressed in a spotless uniform, his smartness making us feel even more ragged. In flawless English with a cheerful smile and a warm handshake, he asked, 'Where do you come from?'

'We've walked from Maralal and are on our way to the lake.'

He gave a little whoop of surprise, 'That is a very long way. You are very welcome to our town and I hope you will find a comfortable place to camp.'

They certainly did not often have visitors like this; 'deus ex machina'. After a brief chat with the chief we carried on past the little hillock on which the Kenyan flag fluttered, and down to the handful of *dukas* beside the road from Baragoi, where we pitched our tent in the shade of a pair of spreading acacia trees. The buildings shimmered with roofs of unpainted corrugated iron and walls rendered with an attractive honey-brown mud.

We deserved a treat after our struggles on the mountain and went off to the little 'hotel' tea house. Unhappily our treat was strictly limited by what was available, so we drank some tea and shared one antique chapatti with the consistency of very old leather.

Ngoroko nerves, desiccation and an elusive volcano

NEXT DAY WAS A rest day and we caught up with chores. Netakwang was holding forth to an audience of admiring and astonished Turkana about the dramas of our journey and I asked him to come and talk. 'You're not doing any work, so if you leave now I will give you 250 shillings, but if you stay you must start to work hard.'

He complained, 'Abdilahi is too quick to work and there is nothing for me to do!'

So I made a list of jobs for each member of the team: Abdilahi loading and unloading the donkeys and looking after the loads; Ayoko to be the cook and to be responsible for the tent; and Netakwang to pack and unpack all our provisions and help Ayoko with cooking. Everyone agreed and said they would work well.

But soon afterwards, when Netakwang left to eat a goat with his brother I reminded him of his duties and he said, 'I cannot refuse my brother'. That was it. I gave him the promised sum and told him to go. I found out soon afterwards that he had stolen the chewing tobacco, so loved by the Turkana, and also that a large sum of money had disappeared. I demanded he return the tobacco, but could not prove the theft of money, which left our coffer very short. The man was rotten to the core. He sloped off disgruntled to the Turkana *manyatta*.

I got hold of some hessian sacks and some Turkana women did a fine job of stitching them into useful saddle bags. But the damage had been done, particularly by the climb of Nyiru, and one poor donkey had a deep and ugly sore on its back. I would just have to try to protect it as best I could. More importantly, rumours began to circulate during the day about *ngoroko* massing into a huge raiding party in the Suguta Valley, preparing for an attack.

An armed stock-theft patrol had just returned from Parkat, a little village north-north-west of Tum, and had brought back this news. What they told us was very worrying.

'We have seen 200 *ngoroko* 50 miles west and coming this way. It is very bad. We expect an attack in Tum or Marti or Nachola. Even all three. We do not know if 200 is all of them or part of a larger group'.

'That's an enormous raiding party,' I said.

'They used to come like this and kill many people, but it is now long time with no big attacks,' they answered.

This was scary news. I had planned to walk from Tum to Parkat en route to Teleki's volcano next day and so, perhaps absurdly, I asked them if they thought that was dangerous.

'Yes, very much.'

'What would happen if we ran into these *ngoroko*?'

'They will not just rob you. They will shoot you dead. No chance.'

Everyone was quoting an incident the previous year when the *ngoroko* had even shot dead a white Catholic father in his vehicle, as he was driving from Parkat to Tum. Things were looking desperate, and my chances of ever reaching Teleki's volcano seemed minuscule. In fact, was survival itself looking dicey?

Our only chance was to go due north, hugging the foothills of Nyiru, and then turn west to Teleki's volcano along the southern shore of the lake, just praying that we stayed out of the way of the brigands. Either way, there was no safe place to be; staying here offered no more security, perhaps even less. My brain was reeling.

In the evening more and more people were carrying rifles over their shoulders. So an attack was expected imminently. Yet there was an extraordinary sense of calm. Perhaps they had been through it so often in the past that it held few new terrors. But it certainly did for me. I was desperate to leave at first light next day, but astonishingly the others had arranged to kill a goat and spend the day feasting with Abdilahi's sister, who, I was suddenly informed, lived in a *manyatta* on the mountainside above Tum.

In those days the population of the western NFD was sufficiently small that people's relatives might be found in the most remote places, and, it turned out Abdilahi's sister was married to a teacher at the primary school here. I have no idea how or when she and Abdilahi had made contact regarding this feast, without phone or post, but the 'bush telegraph' spread information very rapidly and I was often surprised how people we had never met knew exactly who we were, and where we had come from.

And that meant the *ngoroko* might also know, so it struck me as quite crazy to delay our departure on account of a family get-together! Without donkeys the *ngoroko* could cover 50 miles in a day, and as they got closer I could feel our chances of slipping away unnoticed were evaporating. But this was not a place where Western logic was appreciated or appropriate.

So next day was spent eating roast meat and drinking too much *pombe*. Perhaps our last meal in this world? However, we used the time profitably by putting out a rumour that we would continue to Parkat, certain that the Turkana community would pass this on to the *ngoroko*, and we planned to set off in the night before anyone was awake.

Unfortunately the donkeys had other ideas, and as we prepared to leave they set off on a boisterous stampede round the town while we tried to catch them in the darkness. Did we deserve this? But despite their antics we were packed up and loaded and had melted into the night before the first long fingers of dawn crept over Nyiru and stealthily swept the sleep from Tum. No one seemed to have noticed our departure.

We hugged the bottom of a *lugga* to stay well out of sight until coming to a place which translates as Black River, with a couple of very brackish waterholes where we filled the jerry cans, and here met a Samburu *moran* called Letipile. I liked him immediately. He was cheerful and humorous, with great energy and keen to please. He claimed to know the area between there and the lake well and said he could guide us.

That was perfect and I immediately took him on. He was probably in his late 20s, a faded orange *shuka* tied round his waist with a short Samburu broadsword hanging at his right hip. Before setting off, Letipile climbed into one of the waterholes and had a bath – the next travellers' drinking water!

We followed what I assumed were a couple of evenly spaced goat tracks until it dawned on me that we were on a vehicle trail of sorts. 'These tracks are police and army patrols chasing *ngoroko*,' Letipile explained. Even here? So we were still in the heart of bandit country. I did not like this at all.

Eventually we dropped down into the steep-sided valley of the dry Sonyabor River, which we followed for the rest of the day. Only when we were deep in this valley, surrounded by high, rocky cliffs and committed to this route, did Letipile point out many prints in the sand. 'This is *ngoroko* after raiding animals. These marks are fresh'. Oh, great! He added, 'The *ngoroko* like this valley very much. There is good grazing and they look down from the cliff, where they can hide and shoot when police come.'

Almost immediately, to prove his story, we came to a lot of deep troughs made by the wheels of police Land Rovers and trucks which had sunk into the soft sand. Everyone now felt jittery. Why the hell had Letipile brought us this way?

Naturally I wanted to get out of this place as quickly as possible, so why did it surprise me when everyone decided it was time to make tea? There we were, sitting ducks in the epicentre of this bandit hideout and now putting up a thin column of smoke to make it even more clear where we were. Incredible! But once on the move again I noticed my companions' eyes continually scanning the tops of the cliffs, or scouring the valley behind us.

At the end of the valley was a small *manyatta*; a Turkana family with 200 goats. They must know the reputation of this place. So whose goats were they – theirs or *ngoroko*? It seemed very suspicious, and I wanted to move on fast. But naturally, being in such a vulnerable situation, the others all decided this was the perfect place to camp. Unbelievable.

We were very short of water so our host half-filled a jerry can for us before starting to beg for everything we had. My companions were suddenly overcome with illogical generosity and cooked supper not only for us but for our host's whole family too, and as a final flourish of profligate water wastage then made another round of tea. How desperately we were to need it the next day.

Despite my impassioned remonstrating, they made more tea before we set off. I had seen on the map that we were about to enter an area of volcanic rubble which, being so close to the Suguta

Valley, would be blisteringly hot, but they were unconcerned. We had only one and a half litres of water left. I could no longer be surprised when at 10.30 they decided, 'We are thirsty now so we drink the rest of the water.' What madness! There were only 12 miles to the lake across low hills and *luggas*, but I knew it would be desperate. Strangely, I had already discovered that I could tolerate heat and thirst better than they could, and I was damned sure that I, at least, would get there.

This was the hottest place in Kenya, and with the reflected heat from the petrified lava it became a cauldron. I felt bitterly sorry for the donkeys, who had still drunk nothing since Black River. And the dreadful sores on the back of one donkey from the climb up Nyiru were now oozing copious pus down its flank. Thesiger had passed this way in 1960 and described in *My Kenya Days* that, 'On the last two [days], it was hard-going, for the surrounding country was one vast lava field of boulders, red or black in colour, and we had to push on for there was no water anywhere except for what we carried.' Thanks to my profligate companions we carried none. The cruel sun drummed down on us unrelentingly, hour after hour, and the earth below gasped for breath.

Thirst began to take its toll on us as I had forecast, and Ayoko soon became almost demented by his craving for water. 'I cannot continue, I am going to die. This thirst is too terrible, I am dying.' He collapsed weeping, resigned to die. Luckily a breeze from the lake sprang up, which was a godsend, but when we were shielded from it in the lee of hills or gullies, the throbbing, thick, airless furnace was torture. Abdilahi said to me afterwards that it was like sitting too close to the fire without being able to move away; he believed his flesh was starting to cook, all over his body. He had never known such heat. It was an accurate description.

When we reached the last line of red lava hills overlooking the lake we could finally see our way clear for the last couple of miles, no more hills or *luggas* to cross, just the twinkling, beckoning water. Thesiger wrote of this glorious view, 'Few other sights have made a greater impact on me.' Abdilahi and I selfishly pressed ahead and on reaching it sank into its coolness, drinking, splashing, drinking, washing off the salt and sweat which had crusted on our skins, and drinking again. When Count Teleki's expedition had first arrived here several men were taken by crocodiles, but we had no thought for that. My shirt, rigid with salt, floated away into the lake and was not seen again.

An hour later Ayoko arrived with the donkeys, and when they smelled the water they broke into an ecstatic canter for the last yards to wade into its shallows and drink and drink and drink (*see photo* 33). Letipile was not with them. We waited and waited, and after a couple more hours he at last appeared, broken and staggering. He told me afterwards, 'I knew I was going to die so I climbed down into the shade of a deep *lugga* to wait for it'. He slipped into a coma of collapse and exhaustion for well over an hour. He had not drunk water for seven hours in this brutal heat. Now, feeling cool by the lake after that hellish griddle, my thermometer still registered 43°C (110°F). God knows what it had been earlier. I wondered if they had learned their lesson about managing our water supplies sensibly. Probably not.

When everyone, men and animals alike, had drunk as much as they could hold, we filled two jerry cans and I washed the back of the wounded donkey. Nearby were the remains of a Turkana graveyard. We decided to camp there, a poetic union of the dead and the almost dead. A strong wind blew up and we lay exhausted in the light of our cooking fire, aching with every movement. Deep into the night we kept returning to drink, over and over again. It was taking a long time to rehydrate our wasted bodies. Never was sleep more embracing or soothing, the rough uneven rocks on which I lay were like a feather bed. It was so good not to be walking.

Next day was 18th November and we had so far covered over 130 miles. Our noble donkeys had earned a well-deserved rest, so I decided to leave them in camp today as there was some scant grazing and a lake full of water for them to enjoy. This was the closest I would ever get to Teleki's volcano so I thought I would try to make a final attempt to cover the 18-mile round trip. But at that moment some fishermen came past who said they had just been chased away from exactly that spot by a gang of *ngoroko*. I finally admitted to myself that it was not to be. The volcano had defeated me in the end.

But refusing to be completely beaten I decided to walk along the lakeshore to the Nabuyatom cone which projects into the waters of the lake, six miles from where we were camped. Frustratingly, Teleki's volcano was only four miles south of it. I planned to go on my own and leave the others to rest but, despite his anguish of the previous day, Letipile bravely insisted on coming too. We spent the morning in camp, still drinking constantly with insatiable thirsts, and after some dried beans and *posho* we set off. Without the donkeys we could cover the ground quickly, which was heartening, although my feet and ankles ached badly after the jumble of volcanic rubble the day before. A powerful wind still blew, now from the south-east, bringing with it the heat of the Rendille deserts.

After more than two hours we reached a large tongue of water stretching south from the lake, with the cone of Nabuyatom reaching upwards on its other side. I had noted this from my maps but had hoped that, with the falling level of the lake, it might have been crossable. It was not, and must have been very deep. In fact, even if it had been dry we could not have crossed it as we were now on a rocky cliff that dropped vertically into it. The map showed it extending a mile and half south and there simply was not time to walk further, and anyway that would have taken us perilously close to the *ngoroko*.

My consolation prize was that Nabuyatom is actually much more impressive than Teleki's volcano and is a fine-looking cone, and from here I had a splendid view. After resting for half an hour we reluctantly turned back, arriving as the sun was kissing the tops of the mountains in the west. Everyone was keen to leave this awful place so we quickly loaded and walked for an hour close to the lakeshore, still drinking all we could hold. We found a deserted *manyatta*, ate and prepared for sleep immediately. I was desperately tired of walking in this unforgiving heat.

From dehydration to drowning

WE HAD BEEN DANGEROUSLY dehydrated and for the next two days we, and the donkeys, went on drinking and drinking. We slept like babes on an uneven drift of cobbles, such was our exhaustion. It was not far to Loyangalani, our furthest destination, so we relaxed and ambled (*see photo 34*).

When we arrived I chose a place to camp surrounded by wind-bent palms, which turned out to be where Thesiger, too, liked to camp. When he had first visited Loyangalani in 1960 he had found it 'a surprisingly beautiful place' but he had told me what an awful place it was now due to its expansion from a little oasis village into a small town. He used to say, 'All change is for the worse.' Personally I found it rather attractive, with its groves of doum palms, but there was now a tourist campsite (although infrequently used) and I sensed the beginning of the end.

A young Turkana turned up at the tent and introduced himself as Chukuna, another of Wilfred's protégés. He was a remarkable chap, only 21 years old yet highly articulate, with remarkable fluency in English and widely read of both Shakespeare and Kipling (under Wilfred's guidance), yet living traditionally in a grass hut with his mother. It turned out that his uncle Laroi was one of the two who had accompanied Stephen Pern on his circumnavigation of the lake, sadly now a hopeless alcoholic, chanting an inarticulate never-ending catechism about his achievements with Pern. Booze was a serious problem that affected many, usually a local illegal spirit, rather like the old Irish poteen, called *changaa*, meaning 'kill me quickly', which it more or less does. Wilfred had told Chukuna that we would be arriving and he said he would love to come with us to Maralal. So, as Letipile was really just a stopgap, he was quite happy to be laid off here and replaced by Chukuna.

Later that night Abdilahi came back from the town worse for wear from *changaa* and saying that a Turkana woman was going to treat the pains in his stomach (which I put down to the *changaa*). Next day he came back with dozens of little vertical razor cuts across his stomach in three rows about 16 inches wide. They were not a pretty sight, with rivulets of dried blood down his body, each cut now swollen open and showing puffy pink flesh inside. I assumed that before long they would be hopelessly infected and gave him some antiseptic cream to rub over them.

This style of scarring was commonplace among the Turkana especially, and most adults in the bush had similar lines of scars across their stomachs, backs or sometimes arms. I gave him the money to pay his 'surgeon' but I was concerned about our dwindling funds since the theft at Tum, now having only 700 shillings (£35) for four men over the remaining 175 miles. I also needed to have my shoes repaired, as they were finally giving up the unequal struggle in these conditions.

I was wondering when we should start off again, but the next evening Abdilahi was once more wrecked on *changaa* and, in a fight with some Luo fishermen, was badly beaten up, with long cuts down the side of a leg and deep wounds to his forehead as well as several gory weals across his back. I treated his wounds and he looked very sorry for himself. When we set off for a spring called Larachi, on the west flank of Mount Kulal, he must have had a thundering head in the mounting heat.

My ambition was to cut through a pass in the middle of Kulal and then circle the Ndoto mountains to our south through a village called Ilaut in Rendille tribal country; Dr Schuyler Jones, the eminent ethnologist, had eulogised about the tribe when I met him at Oxford, where he was Director of the Pitt Rivers Museum.

At a delightful waterhole, Mawingaten Spring, we met a Samburu *moran* and his sister with their goats, so we made our midday break, hiding from the aggressive sun under a spreading acacia. Our friend told us, 'The track to Larachi is too very hot and too hard for the donkeys. It will be one whole day to get there.' That did not worry me too much after what we had survived already, but he continued, 'To walk behind the Ndotos will be five days and no water. The donkeys will die.'

With only two leaky jerry cans, that would be suicidal for us too. It was clearly impossible. I was deeply disappointed but I re-routed us onto a seldom-used motor piste leading south to a waterhole called Sirima, imagining it to be a boringly easy stretch.

After our break, we continued across difficult rocky ground until we found a disused *manyatta* to spend the night in. Rainwater was lying in a *lugga* so we turned the donkeys loose to graze. The sky was clear so we did not bother with the tent, despite a great heap of louring cumulonimbus clouds climbing over the top of Kulal and decorated by the crowning arc of a rainbow. That was a mistake. I woke with some large splats of rain and woke the others, but we decided it was a passing shower. It had been so hot that we simply could not believe the weather might suddenly change so dramatically. An even bigger mistake...

... An instant later the heavens opened with a vengeance and we ran to pull out the tent, just to cover ourselves, and huddled under it as we were lashed by a full-scale tropical storm. When it had passed everything we owned was saturated, so for the rest of the night we turned the wet tent over to use as a groundsheet while we covered ourselves with the plastic sheet.

This was not a success, as the cotton tent let the groundwater through, and we found ourselves sleeping in puddles. This was bearable as long as I did not move, allowing the water around me to warm up like the water in a wetsuit, but if in my sleep I turned over, the new cold water woke me with a start. It was a ghastly night. This was the risk of trekking during the season of the 'short rains,' and although average annual rainfall here was only 10 inches, when it did fall it could be apocalyptic.

The morning groaned under a cold leaden sky as we laid out all our soaking things on rocks in the vain hope that they might dry. A miserable beginning to a day which only became worse. When we loaded the dripping donkeys the bags had doubled in weight with the water they carried. Fortunately I had been keeping my spare clothes in plastic bags, which had kept out the worst of the deluge, so I was able to change and also give Chukuna a pair of dry trousers.

The track had been transformed from dry dust and rock into a continuous canal of huge, deep puddles lying on thick, clinging clay. The donkeys repeatedly sank into it almost up to their stomachs, sliding and kicking, falling sideways and slipping their loads, until we, the animals and our luggage were all thickly plastered. The donkeys hated every moment of it, and so did we.

When everyone was at their most dejected the heavens opened

yet again with enormous force and the water which they threw at us was witheringly cold. I had read that during the rains many animals in these northern districts die of pneumonia, which I had found hard to believe in the tropics. I believed it now. It was freezing and absolutely miserable. We felt positively victimised.

We sat out the storm under a group of small thorn trees which gave no protection whatsoever, and emerged dripping and shivering. Soon after we set off again, a steady drizzle began in which we gallantly tried to force our way, dragging the donkeys through the mud and often having to leave the track to take them one by one across fields of rock and mud into which they sank repeatedly. Sometimes they sank so deeply into the morass that their hind legs completely disappeared and they could no longer fight their way forwards, meaning we had to lift them back to ground level by hauling on their tails.

Just when it could get no worse the rain suddenly restarted in even greater anger, so heavy that visibility was reduced to only a few yards, blowing in from Mount Kulal and agonisingly cold from the altitude at which it had left its clouds. We shuffled on in dejected silence, the water literally cascading down us, and our feet great heavy clods of oozing clay on the end of our mud-encased legs. We shivered uncontrollably as we trudged along, but there was nothing we could do, nowhere to hide on this wide exposed plain. To have unpacked my old and leaky plastic raincoat now to wear in preference over my companions would have been disgraceful. Driving the donkeys forward became almost impossible and I took to splashing ahead, feeling for the firmest path rather than just sinking mud. I called the donkeys along with the falsetto melodic 'cooh' used by the Samburus and very effective at giving animals a direction to follow.

The vicious rain was unremitting in its violence and the cold penetrated right through me. Finally I turned, and was shocked to find no one within sight through the falling columns of rain. Not even the donkeys. Shaking so violently with cold that I found it hard to keep a grip on my stick I crouched under a skeletal thorn tree to wait for them. And there I waited, and waited, and waited.

The track beside me gradually turned from a bouncing mud bath of small interconnecting lakes into a brown river, flowing forcefully down the hill. I felt as if I would shake to pieces, and considered the possibility of dying of exposure, wearing only the thinnest cotton tee-shirt and shorts, without thermal or waterproof protection. My face ached and my brain was becoming sluggish.

It must be better to keep moving, so I crawled out from under my scarecrow tree into the ankle-deep brown torrent and turned to retrace my steps. Now I was facing the full force of the storm, which knocked me about and bucketed into me. I had never heard of rain like this. I tried to jog to get my circulation moving, but as all the rocks were now under water, I kept stumbling and floundering about. I did not even know where the track was any more and just plugged on in what I hoped was the right direction.

After several hundred yards, having found no sign of them, I began to fear that I had inadvertently wandered off across the surrounding plain. I had begun seriously considering my chances of survival when I spotted, hidden among a stack of large boulders, the forlorn, dejected and hopeless silhouettes of the donkeys, standing stock-still in complete and utter misery. Their heads were turned away from the storm in vain and they still carried their loads, from which water cascaded.

But it was the direction of their accusing eyes which drew me to what I had taken to be another of the large rocks, and which I now reinterpreted as the uneven shape of the tent canvas under which the others cowered. I had not heard anyone try to alert me that they were stopping. I was angry and shocked. I felt hopelessly betrayed, yet perhaps they had tried and I just had not heard through the deluge. Anyway I knew that I must bite my tongue, as recrimination would shatter our working relationship. After all, I was the stranger in this land and needed their help more than they needed mine.

I dropped my stick, pulled up the canvas and crawled in. Compared with the cold outside, the huddle of bodies was warm and snug. The rain hammered on the crumpled tent which rested on our soaking heads and shivering backs, pouring through it and running down our bodies, but it was a blissful hovel to shelter in. Gradually my shaking diminished and, crouched on one of the cold wet rocks with my head on my arms, I sank into exhausted sleep.

Perhaps it was the quieter slapping of the rain that woke me but slowly the storm moved on and we tentatively peered out. The icy wind caught us with a shock and at first we winced and retreated under our warm shroud. Gradually the sky brightened, and eventually we emerged, bowed over with aching backs and stiff from head to toe, saturated and dripping. It was over.

The longed-for sun was trying to fight its way through, and a little warmth crept into our aching muscles. Abdilahi took the *panga* and cut into the heart of a dead tree, splitting and re-splitting the slivers of wood. After 40 minutes a timid flame was tickling a tiny wisp of smoke and we coaxed it lovingly into a small fire. Never had a mug of tea been so welcome, and soon afterwards we managed a meal as well.

Everything in our bags was sodden, cold and heavy. Even my camera inside its 'waterproof' box was wet. Fearful that it might rain again, we reloaded the weary, cold and destitute donkeys and I teased them into a fast walk to try to warm them and ourselves. We slowly started to feel a little human again. There was no chance of reaching Sirima now, but despite the dreadful condition of the ground we pressed on closer than we had expected, stopping less than two miles from where our track joined the main South Horr to Loyangalani road.

We put the tent up quickly to start it drying in the breeze, and sat round a sad, smoky fire, constantly nursing it back to life on a diet of wet twigs and damp grass. After a long time it gave us a round of tea and a panful of maize-flour porridge. The dried goat skins which covered the donkeys' backs were as wet as everything else and now just slimy, very smelly parts of dead animals, and would soon be distorted and unusable. The only place we could think of to lay them flat was under the plastic groundsheet of the tent, with all of us sleeping on top of it. We crawled in, surrounded by our soaking things, and lay under wet blankets, content that the day was over. I had not expected to spend one of the coldest days of my life so close to the equator.

But when we woke in the morning we were horrified to find the footprints of a hyena who had followed the enticing scent of these stinking skins, and had managed to push its huge head far enough under the groundsheet to get its teeth into a corner of one, which it had dragged out from under us as we slept, to eat at leisure. Its monstrously powerful jaws had been within inches of our feet, but mercifully it had not sniffed out the donkeys, who must have been downwind. None of us had noticed a thing in our exhaustion.

The donkeys were in an appalling state, three of them with dreadful sores from the bags, the worst with an open hole about two inches by four. Chukuna gasped, 'Good God, this is very bad, I can see a piece of rib!' I dressed them with Fucidin and was furious that we had not had Turkana panniers from the beginning. Now I just wanted to get them back to Maralal alive.

For two days we walked south on the South Horr road, just another impassable mud bath, buying a goat to eat en route. Gradually the surface dried out and Chukuna built an enormous fire, which he gleefully called an 'empire fire'. On the third day we were following some lion tracks when a shot rang out as a bullet ricocheted off a rock beside me. Stupidly, my reaction was outrage: 'You bastard, how dare you!' We had been through enough already without this. I scoured the hillside with my binoculars, but saw nothing. I had no idea who or why, but that was all. Perhaps my reaction had unnerved him? Perhaps if I had turned and run I might have had another shot in the back? It was all rather strange.

Feasting, fasting and fleeing from bandits (again)

As usual we were soon desperately short of water – absurd so soon having been almost drowned! The sun was now fierce and we were parched again. We checked roadside *luggas* for puddles, but they had all drained away. So when we were joined by a couple of Turkana it was good to hear them say they knew a waterhole close by. They beckoned to Abdilahi and me to follow them up the hillside into a jumble of huge rocks. Almost at the top, set into a vertical rock face, was a small crevice inside which was a hidden pool of beautifully cool, clear, sweet water. This was undoubtedly the very last place anyone would look, and so well hidden that you might die of thirst just a few yards away. We filled a jerry can and soon had tea brewing. They only knew of this secret place because their *manyatta* was nearby, and they led us from the road along a substantial dry riverbed past a strange hill that was a rock face on one side and a sand dune on the other, without a single mark on it. I tried to imagine how it had formed. Chukuna told me, 'This is one of Wilfred's favourites places because it's so strange.'

A rainstorm briefly chased us along the *lugga*, but happily relented and went off looking for someone else to curse. Soon we were walking through chest-high scrub for a mile or so to a low rocky crest, but great black storm clouds were building yet again (*see cover photo*). Where was all this rain coming from? Why were we being so victimised? The next day we would find out.

In the valley beyond the rocky crest were several Turkana *manyattas* where a wedding was in progress, filling the air with the joyous sounds of dancing and singing. The valley was dominated by an impressive wall of immense rock slabs, which Nature had assembled like courses of bricks, each roughly 10 feet tall and 30 feet long, crowning a low, sheer cliff. Cresting this edifice, silhouetted against the sky, sat an imperious group of old *mzees*.

There was something particularly fine about the elegance of these dignified tribesmen, perched high on this remarkable viewpoint, where their forefathers must have sat for generations. A dramatic setting, where they so rightly belonged. Further along the crag sat another endangered species, a lone white-headed vulture, which ignored us contemptuously as it gazed over its vast domain of rocky outcrops, flat topped acacias and the high ridges of Ol Donyo Mara, which walled in the other side of the valley.

We erected the tent under a thorn tree close to one of the homesteads, and sat watching a theatrical display of lightning crackling and flashing over Mount Kulal 25 miles away. I felt whacked and headed for bed, leaving the others chatting and dozing outside, but they were suddenly driven in to join me by the arrival of the storm, which was another monster of bucketing rain with unceasing lightning flashes overhead and the explosion of thunderclaps rolling around us.

For over an hour it was trapped in our valley and we were at its epicentre, the lightning directly above us while the ferocity of the thunder hammered against the surrounding hills. The rain was awesome, pounding the tent so hard that inside we had a constant spray. The ground water poured in under the walls, soon leaving our things saturated again. My sleeping bag, still uncomfortably damp after its last dousing, was once more a sopping heap of feathers. Another unpleasant, shivering night.

Our neighbours coped much better than we did, their huts being covered with skins which shed these violent torrents. In the morning I discovered the reason for the rainstorms. After a lengthy drought, the women had been dancing for many days to plead with 'Akuj', the god of the skies, for the arrival of the rains. It seemed to me that they had overdone it. Now that yesterday's wedding was over they were continuing to sing as a celebration and thanksgiving for the arrival of the rains. I just hoped that Akuj did not misunderstand the message and send yet more. To celebrate the rain there was to be a great feast of goats from all the families in the *manyattas* to thank the rain-dancers. The poor goats always got the rough end of these deals.

We stayed there three nights, and survived further dousing by digging a small moat round the tent. Throughout this time an endless stream of 'patients' came for medical attention, many of them bringing small children or babies with burns from falling in fires. Sometimes extensive. The local remedy was to cover the burn with raw meat or *posho*, which seemed to work, but I hoped that my antibiotic gel and bandages were more effective. At one 'surgery' they numbered over 20.

Our last evening was the feast to thank the rain-dancers, and in return for my doctoring we were invited too. Unfairly, the women who had danced for Akuj were not! Seven goats had been slaughtered and the feasting was underway when we arrived. A 'table' of cut twigs and leaves had been laid on the ground in a semicircle, about six inches deep, behind which sat about 20 of the older men in a line. On a much larger pile of leaves and stems the roast meat was cut up and divided into individual portions, each containing some meat, some ribs, and some fat. From this 'serving table' a team of half a dozen young men were taking portions to the elders while others kept bringing more meat from the fire to be jointed up. Nearby, small groups of younger men, like ourselves, sat at other twig tables and were served, the meat simply dropped onto the vegetation to keep it off the ground. As soon as someone had finished their portion another pile of meat was brought over.

It was very well-organised and I was aware how special was this invitation. In the middle of it all one of the senior elders whom I had treated in the morning picked up a piece of his own meat and carried it over and gave it to me. This was indeed an honour and I was deeply touched. It was clear that the Turkana of this area were quite unlike their cousins on the west side of the lake; much more sophisticated and generous. I would never be in a social environment like this again and now, almost 40 years later, I wonder whether Turkana women still make rain dances to their ancient gods? I would very much like to think so, but fear that an era may have passed.

When we could eat no more Abdilahi sharpened a stick and spiked onto it our remaining meat, ready for our journey. We slept early and by 5am next day were striking camp. We stayed on the same piste as before, keeping up a good speed after our rest, the massif of Nyiru on our right and the Ol Donyo Mara range on our left. Only two vehicles passed, tourist trucks called 'The Turkana Bus', heading for Loyangalani full of white people who scrabbled for cameras to snap our dusty progress as they roared by. It was strange being a tourist curiosity and I disliked it, fully understanding why tribal people do not like to be gawped at and photographed. I had long since forgotten that I was a different colour from my companions, and to me it was unnatural to see these white faces.

We happened on a small tourist lodge at which we indulged ourselves with a cup of tea and a piece of cake for the ungodly sum of five shillings each. I felt cheated, but we had the last laugh. As we entered, Chukuna had driven the tail of our spear into the ground in the way that tribesmen always do, and on leaving I pulled it out to find that it had gone clean through the underground water pipe, leaving a thin arcing fountain in our wake. We left giggling irresponsibly.

An hour and a half later we arrived at South Horr, and there found Letipile who, as usual, was full of stories and jokes. He gave me a little tobacco container carved from buffalo horn. South Horr was a slightly overgrown village with just four *dukas* which were all empty, but Abdilahi managed to track down some fiercely hot chillies which brightened up our meals for the rest of the trek. Despite my allocation of cooking duties to Ayoko, Abdilahi was still doing everything and I had noticed that he and Chukuna were sick of Ayoko's laziness. I sensed some tension developing.

I still wanted to get to Ilaut in Rendille country if possible, so I planned to take a track to the east of the Ndoto Mountains. We set off in that direction, but stopping at a small *manyatta* they greeted us nervously, 'There is very bad news, three men have just been shot dead by *shifta* on the road ahead to Ilaut; one even an armed Home Guard soldier.'

They implored us not to go that way, as five loaded donkeys and a *msungu* was a target no *shifta* would be able to resist and our days would be numbered. At first I was not deterred, but so insistent were they that my resolve weakened and I realised it would be irresponsible to risk our lives. In this area *shifta* were considered a greater threat than the *ngoroko*. I was bitterly disappointed; it seemed that all my plans were scuppered by bandits.

Passing another Samburu *manyatta*, the others went in to ask for some milk to make tea, while Ayoko and I stayed with the donkeys in the wide, sandy-floored *lugga* below. Nearby, in the shade of a large, spreading tree, four Samburu *morans* were sleeping. Like all *morans* they slept on their backs, straight as rods, with their brightly coloured *shukas* pulled tightly over them so that they were completely covered from head to toe as protection from flies and mosquitoes. Even in their sleep it is the duty of warriors to be always alert and ready for anything. Beside each sleeping figure his spear was driven into the ground by its tail shaft as was normal, to be immediately to hand.

After a while I heard Chukuna calling from the *manyatta* 50 yards away to bring the donkeys to unload the tea things. I shouted back, 'OK', and immediately, like four coiled springs, the *morans* were on their feet, snatching up their spears almost before their eyes were open, and charging me with weapons levelled at the shoulder ready to throw. After a few paces their eyes must have focused on the extraordinary apparition of a displaced white man and realised that I offered no threat. They slowed to a halt, gradually lowering the spears. I was very impressed by the incredible speed of their reactions, but strangely did not feel in any way threatened as they faced me with the fixed, staring eyes that *morans* adopt to summon courage and ignore pain, their shoulders shaking violently with adrenalin as they hyperventilated, ready for action. They gave aggressive grunts and hooping noises, and quite illogically I just said cheerily in English, 'Oh did I wake you? I'm frightfully sorry', and smiled apologetically at them as I turned away. They continued to stand stock-still, shaking and grunting as they slowly wound down from the brink of attack.

It was only afterwards in the *manyatta* that I understood the gravity of the situation. The others told me that every year several people are speared to death in exactly this sort of situation by *morans*, whose automatic reaction to attack is triggered by mistake when unexpectedly woken. It had only been the shock of seeing my white skin which had made them pause for a moment before hurling their spears. Chukuna said, 'You're very lucky indeed to be alive! That was close.'

The Samburu, like the Maasai, are the people of the cows, and used the milk in different ways. Now they gave us bowlfuls of sour milk to drink, which was both delicious and refreshing, particularly as I had learned to drink it through clenched teeth like a portcullis to filter all the dead flies. I commented to Chukuna that it was a nuisance that these *manyattas* were so overrun by flies and he answered sagely, 'A *manyatta* without flies is a poor *manyatta*'. Naively I asked why and he incredulously retorted, 'Because if they have no flies they have no cows, and without cows they starve'. How stupid I had been. We must never let Western values interfere with our understanding of another culture.

I mentioned the road to Ilaut again here, and they too were adamant that it was out of the question, a certain death sentence. So after leaving them we continued to follow the same *lugga*, and coming to some vague tyre marks in the sand which crossed our path (and were in fact the main road to Ilaut), we ignored them and carried on south through the open scrubby bush. For the rest of the day we followed animal tracks and little rocky *luggas*, passing the peak of Sartim and finally climbing onto a peaceful grassy plateau, on the far side of which stood a lovely, solitary thorn tree, for which we headed to make camp. It was an exquisite spot and commanded a spreading panorama overlooking the Ndotos to our south-east with the El Barta Plain stretching emptily to their west. As we followed our eyes northwards they passed the mountain of Kowop, arriving at the massif of the Nyiru Range which we had crossed three weeks before. Looking north along the South Horr valley, Mount Kulal was still visible in the distance.

We cooked and then sat watching the sinking sun gild the plains with its dying fire as a full moon swung into the eastern sky from behind the clouds which hugged the Rendille deserts. The magic touched us all. I wanted it to continue forever. Soon those same deserts were sending us their bitter cold on a piercing wind, which sprang up and drove us early to our beds. The very last of the sun's radiance seeped gently from the huge night sky and the vast continuum of impossibly bright stars now held court; but we were already fast asleep.

We went thirsty again for the first seven or eight miles in the morning, crossing low scrub now green from the rains, until we came to a solitary *manyatta*, where we bought a gourd of refreshing sour milk. With our fast-diminishing budget, we also bought a goat, which complainingly accompanied us for the rest of the day to Lesirikan, a tiny village tucked into the flank of the Ndotos. We had not eaten all day so went straight to a little mud-plastered single-room tea house, grandly named, 'New Hill Side Hotel'. They had only one very stale mandazi, a sort of sweet fried bun lightly flavoured with cardamom, very popular with the Samburu. The one *duka* was completely empty.

A new rainstorm was blowing in and we hurriedly unloaded the donkeys and had the tent erected with our possessions stowed inside in exactly four minutes, which astonished the inevitable audience, and even surprised us. The owner of the *manyatta* close to the tent invited us in for the evening and we gratefully expected something to eat. A quarter of a mandazi does not go far after a 13-mile walk. But nothing, except endless tea.

We were heading for the Milgis River so I was disappointed when our host told us, 'The rains have made the river into a big flood, very dangerous and nowhere to cross. Many herds of cows and goats have been drowned already.' This was a blow as I had intended to cross it to reach the Matthews mountain range, which I wanted to walk around, but more importantly, they all now said that the Milgis had become a notorious *shifta* stronghold. So much so that one man even called it, 'the home of the *shifta*'.

My treks in the NFD had turned out to be less 'footing', as Thomas had described it in those early days, and more 'tip-toeing' between each band of bloodthirsty outlaws and the next. That was to continue even more poignantly on my next trek. So I set a new course for Maseketa, a tiny one-shop village on a river of the same name, in the direction of Parsaloi once more.

By now friction was developing between Ayoko and the others due to his laziness, but I tried to remain impartial. We only had a few days of the safari left. In the morning we were blessed with boiled eggs at the New Hill Side Hotel before starting off again. It was a pleasant day of blue sky, warm and sunny, and even the goat trotted along with less struggling. We stopped at a *manyatta* and they filled one of our flasks with milk, and at another I watched circling eagles picking up scraps in their talons and transferring them to their bills as they flew, wheeling and diving in the happy sky. We were exhausted from the trek and resigned now to be heading home to Maralal; and pleased that it should be so. We were on the edge of the El Barta Plains again, now magically transformed by the rains from the dry brittle scrub we had walked through before to rich verdant grazing, and consequently we saw herds of antelope and groups of camels.

When we arrived at the dry Maseketa riverbed, which we planned to follow for our last few miles that day, we discovered that there were two villages of the same name. The first had been deserted after a ferocious *shifta* attack less than four months before, and we stopped at this empty village to make tea. As we entered the larger, second village, we were shown a building where missionaries had taught religious studies, now riddled with bullet holes through the walls and the corrugated-iron roof. The windows had rough wooden shutters, and one of these had been smashed in by one of the *shifta* using his rifle butt. As he broke through, a Home Guard soldier inside had shot him, and we were shown the dark blood stains on the ground and surrounding rocks where he had fallen and died. The remaining *shifta* had run off to the other village where we had just drunk tea, which they then sacked and looted in revenge, killing anyone they could find. No one would live there now. Maseketa had a curse of death hanging over it, just like the dark clouds which had gathered again above us. That curse still harboured its menace.

We cowered in the shelter of the shop, where its owner was battling to save his roof from being blown away in the fierce squalls; it was torrential. Abdilahi gallantly dashed into the storm and hastily unloaded the donkeys before all our things were spoilt yet again. For a little over half an hour the rain hammered down without mercy or relief, and then suddenly stopped, as quickly as it had started. A pale sun shimmered through its dripping aftermath, misty in the rising steam of the gathering warmth.

A few minutes later we heard an extraordinary, eerie roaring from the *lugga*, and the next moment a wall of water 18 inches high and 40 feet wide surged round the corner of the valley in this bone-dry watercourse, tearing up everything in its path. I ran to its edge to photograph it, and within 45 seconds there were crashing waves six or seven feet high ripping trees from the bank and leaping over boulders in wild Valkyrine rage. Where it was forced round bends by rocky outcrops it could not tear down, it vented its fury by circling into massive, hollow-centred whirlpools which might have swallowed a house. The savage brown water carried a milky white scum of froth as it hurtled round the chicanes of the *lugga*. I had never seen anything so violent, and for the first time could easily understand how so many people and animals drown in flash floods without any hope of escape. I never slept in a dry riverbed again.

Within fifteen minutes the frenzy of the water relaxed but continued to rush past as excitedly as any mountain torrent. The sun had been strengthening and the day was again becoming pleasantly warm, so we put up our tent and drove the donkeys out to graze. I decided to kill the goat next morning before leaving for Parsaloi, with a further two days to Maralal and the end of our trip.

By sundown the river was sedate. After dark we heard the singing of women in a nearby *manyatta* as, in the morning, they were going to circumcise a girl. It was tempting to consider staying for another day to watch the dancing of the *morans*, but everyone was now tired and keen to reach home after 32 days on this trek, having covered almost 350 miles.

Fighting for life

By the time I woke, the goat was already dead and a local *mzee* was skilfully dismembering it with a very sharp Samburu dagger. As usual, Ayoko had managed to absent himself from the process of the goat. Abdilahi said to me, 'If Ayoko is now the cook he must prepare the offal for lunch.'

I told Ayoko to do so.

'It will be better to eat the meat now and take the offal with us,' he replied.

'That's impossible, it would not survive a day in this heat, as you know perfectly well,' I told him.

He started to become disgruntled. At last he began cutting it up begrudgingly with the *mzee*'s Samburu knife and throwing the pieces into a pan. His resentful attitude annoyed me, and I think the other two had started to deride him for his laziness, but as the conversation was not in English I could only guess. Certainly, he had done no work at all that morning while no one else had stopped, not even the helpful *mzee*.

Ayoko started to complain to me that Chukuna and Abdilahi were accusing him of being 'a bad boy'.

'They have said nothing of the sort,' I told him.

He argued more and more and became angrier and angrier, which struck me as strange for someone intent on going to a seminary. Probably he was exhausted, never before having spent over a month away from home in harsh conditions. He certainly did not have what it took to be a *moran*.

Soon his fury boiled up to such intensity that, although the argument was almost entirely in Swahili, Abdilahi and Chukuna independently told me afterwards that he had threatened he was going to kill one of them. They did not take him too seriously, and I was quite unaware at the time that things were reaching such a fever pitch. Abdilahi went off to pay for some milk we had bought earlier in the morning and while he was gone the situation became increasingly brittle.

Chukuna suddenly turned to Ayoko, and said in English, 'OK, we're sorry, it's not worth fighting about. Do what you want,' and other similar remarks to try to defuse the tension. By this time I was watching intently to see what would happen, sitting on my camera box some yards away. Chukuna had been using my Buck hunting knife to cut up the meat and now, having finished, had put it down on the ground. Ayoko still continued to argue furiously, working himself into a tantrum.

Suddenly, he threw down the knife he was using and charged at Chukuna with fists flailing wildly. For a moment he took Chukuna by surprise and knocked him backwards into the tent, which partially collapsed as he fell heavily against it.

At this stage I was not unduly concerned, knowing that Chukuna could easily look after himself in a fist fight, and as he scrambled to his feet he soon forced Ayoko backwards. Not only had Chukuna been taught to box by Wilfred, but in his turn had taught boxing at Loyangalani, so he knew how to look after himself. I thought that if Ayoko got a punch on the nose it would serve him right.

Just then Ayoko tripped over backwards and fell into the thorn *boma*. For a moment he was rendered helpless. Chukuna assumed it was all over and, turning his back, began to walk away. But as Ayoko scrabbled to his feet he seized the Samburu dagger and rushed at Chukuna again, looking much more dangerous.

I leapt to my feet. 'Put that knife down!'

I moved in to separate them, but what happened next happened very quickly.

There was a brief struggle, with Ayoko slashing wildly at Chukuna, who parried the blade with his bare hands and managed to push him backwards again, so that he fell next to the fire. He was on his feet in a flash and charging to attack, knife in hand. This time, in self defence, Chukuna had picked up my hunting knife and was ready for him. There was another momentary struggle, too quick even to see what happened, and a couple of seconds later Ayoko stepped back.

At that moment I reached them and grabbed Ayoko from behind before he could attack again, and I threw down his knife. He immediately relaxed and I saw blood on his tee-shirt under his left armpit. Assuming he had received a graze, I unclipped his belt and began to pull off his tee-shirt to see the wound. At first he resisted, but Abdilahi had just arrived back and he helped me pull the shirt over Ayoko's head.

As it pulled up I jumped sideways to avoid a great spurt of blood which arced well clear of his body, pumping over and over again with every heartbeat. In my diary I likened it to holding a wine bottle on its side and shaking it sideways. Abdilahi and I laid him down quickly on the ground and I ran for a bandage from my medical kit, my brain reeling with the gravity of the situation. Already his eyes were rolling backwards, showing the whites. Abdilahi shocked me by callously saying, 'This one is dead. Leave him', as he turned and walked away.

I bandaged Ayoko tightly and Chukuna and I carried him into the shade of a tree. The blood soon saturated the bandages, and my arms and legs were covered as well. I wondered desperately if it would be possible to keep him alive until we could get him to a hospital, where they might be able to stitch the internal wound. After a while the bleeding seemed to stop and I told him he was going to be all right, which I tried to believe myself, but guessed he was still bleeding internally.

I wrote a quick letter of explanation to the District Officer in Baragoi, and sent Abdilahi and two *morans* to run for help. That was a distance of 17 miles as the crow flies across a multitude of *luggas*, any of which might have been in flood. By the rough vehicle track it was about 25 miles. It was going to take a long time and I wondered if he had even the remotest chance.

Ayoko had become delirious, the bleeding had stopped but already his pulse was almost too faint to feel. He was breathing heavily and complained of being cold and that the bandage was too tight. I was reluctant to loosen it in case the bleeding started again, and covered him with a blanket. Soon he slipped into unconsciousness. I hoped that he would stay asleep for a long time as it kept him still, but after 20 minutes he woke complaining of thirst, sometimes cold, sometimes hot. He was frightened and asked me to sit with him and hold his hand, which I did, but he kept saying the bandage was too tight and started trying to wrestle it loose.

He repeatedly asked to be carried to the tent, which I kept refusing, as I believed the movement would restart the bleeding.

He became increasingly agitated, turning this way and that as if in a nightmare, which must have been exactly where he was. Eventually I relented, probably wrongly, and with the help of a *moran*, Chukuna and I carried him back to the tent, but my instinct had been correct and the bleeding started again profusely.

He asked for another blanket, despite the inside of the tent being an oven in the sunshine. Although he felt very cold he then complained of being hot and threw off the blankets. He was desperate for water, but our jerry cans were empty so I hurried down into the *lugga*, and when I returned he wanted it poured on his liver and his legs to cool them. I also wet his head and left a cold compress on his brow. He repeatedly tore at his bandages which continually restarted the bleeding. I eventually cut the bandage, which quietened him, but then the only way to stem the blood was to keep the dressing pressed over the wound by hand, and Chukuna sat by him doing this. I was impressed by the way Chukuna cared for him considering that he could easily have been the one now in this condition, victim of Ayoko's knife. Alternatively, he could have made a run for it.

By this time almost the entire groundsheet was under a thick pool of blood, now congealing in the heat like raw liver, and its rich, strangely sweet stench was sickening and shocking. I had never before understood the expression 'sweet smell of death' but I did now. The tent walls and somehow even the flysheet was splattered with blood, and of course Chukuna and I were smeared from head to foot. All our luggage was also covered with blood and my sleeping bag had absorbed it like a sponge and would never be useable again.

Soon Ayoko was too hot again and asking to be carried out of the tent, but this I refused as I was sure that would be the last of him. Instead I dragged him as gently as possible by his feet until just his head and shoulders remained inside on the groundsheet with the entrance to the tent tied open. Naturally the flies were repulsive, swarming over the blood in their thousands and the air buzzed loudly. His restlessness continued, turning this way and that, but his bleeding had lessened which I feared was only because he could not have had much blood left. His skin was looking grey, and paler by the minute. I was forcing myself to face the blatant reality that there was absolutely no hope of survival. We all knew it.

At last he became quiet and I went outside, feeling helpless. There was nothing more I could do. A couple of minutes later Chukuna came out to say that he was dead. I went to see, but in fact he was still breathing very slowly and faintly, and with immense difficulty, just hanging on to the last hint of life; but as good as dead. His head was tilted back with eyes wide open in a terrible unseeing stare, the pupils almost hidden, rolled back under the upper lids, and his mouth wide open in a silent scream, trying to suck in the last few breaths. The small of his back was arched with the effort of gasping for air as if he was suffocating, his stomach pulled into a concave pit as his diaphragm was taut against his lungs. He must have been completely unconscious by now, and I just crouched beside him and watched as he drew three or four last breaths, several seconds apart. And then he was still. I considered looking for a pulse, but knew that it was hopeless. He was dead.

He looked terrifying like this and I tried to close his eyes but they just sprang open again each time I tried, so I covered him with his blanket. The life of this 19-year-old boy was over. Our safari was over. We had all walked our last mile. My mind was numb. For a while I felt that everything was over. It had been two and a half hours since the fight. I was only surprised that he had stayed alive so long.

The curse that hung over Maseketa was palpable.

Now it was time to turn my attention to the living. First

Chukuna's hands needed dressing where Ayoko had slashed them. Looking at them closely I could see one hand was cut deeply across the fingers where he had parried the sharp Samburu knife; one finger even showing the movement of the flexor tendon. I washed and bandaged them. We left everything in the tent the way it was in case the police wanted to inspect it and collect evidence, but in the event nothing forensic was done at all.

Chukuna and I closed up the tent and went to sit by the empty administrative police house above the village at the top of the hill. I wrote out a detailed report of everything that had occurred as a statement for the court, having been the only witness who was present throughout. It was a clear case of self defence, ending tragically for the attacker. The local tribal chief arrived and asked for a report also, although I suspected that was just bureaucratic posturing.

It began to get chilly and I went to the tent for another shirt. Inside it was a scene from hell, and the smell was unspeakable. I closed it again quickly. Back at the police house I asked a *moran* for water so that Chukuna and I could wash off the blood. Then we sat and talked. I tried to consider Chukuna's options. Here was a young man of 21 in a terrible position, through no fault of his own, where innocence might be harder to prove than in my own country.

I said, 'Chukuna, if you want to try to reach the Sudan border I will not do anything to stop you. But if you're caught the assumption of guilt will be automatic. And it would also mean that you could never enter Kenya to see your mother or friends again. If, on the other hand, you stay to face justice I'll do everything I possibly can to help defend you.'

I trusted that in the end he would be a free man again, with his life once more before him. He opted for justice and we continued to sit and wait. I felt proud of his decision but very afraid for him.

Would he get justice?

As I churned over the events of the day I increasingly felt emotions of bewildered helplessness and fear for Chukuna's safety. I am ashamed to say I even felt a little fearful for myself, as this was a horror I had never dreamed of facing. Guiltily, despite the wastage of Ayoko's absurdly premature death, I felt no particular sadness for him.

The price of justice

Just before sunset an open lorry rattled and banged over the hill towards us carrying Abdilahi and a mixture of soldiers and policemen. Chukuna was immediately handcuffed, absurdly melodramatic after he had sat and waited half the day for them. No inspection of the 'crime scene' was undertaken at all, and all our things were just thrown headlong onto the flat back of the truck, and the donkeys were left behind to graze, which must have been their dreams come true. Ayoko's body was cooling down and already stiffening up. I wrapped it in some of my black polythene and we loaded it too. Then the rest of us scrambled aboard, Chukuna having great trouble with his handcuffs and damaged hands.

In no time we were off, bouncing and slewing down the rough dirt track to Baragoi, bucking and heaving in and out of *luggas*, with everything sliding about in the back of the truck, including the corpse, which kept skating across and crashing into us in the most sinister way. It was dark almost immediately and becoming very, very cold. We were still wearing only our safari clothes, thin shirts and shorts for the midday heat.

The police were strangely nervous of touching the body so Abdilahi and I carried Ayoko into the temporary mortuary at Baragoi, a small concrete block room just big enough for one table, which I was relieved to find had no other occupants. His body was still slightly warm, which surprised me, but now much less flexible.

Then on to the police station, where they began to interrogate Chukuna roughly. I tried to stay with him, as I was the only person who could provide any evidence, as well as for his protection, fearing that he would be at the mercy of meaningless brutality. However, Abdilahi and I were politely pushed out and told by the senior police officer to find somewhere in the town to sleep. Before leaving I stressed to him that Chukuna was innocent, having fought for his life in self defence, and pleaded for him not to be mistreated. It did not make any difference.

My mind was dazed and someone took us to Moh'd Jama's shop where his cousin Hussein welcomed us with a meal and a room to sleep in. But just as we were lying down, exhausted at the end of this nightmare day, a Land Rover arrived to take us all to Maralal, the Samburu police headquarters. So, back to the police station and the mortuary to collect the body, still wrapped in polythene, which we loaded down the middle of the truck-back Land Rover. Our luggage was left in the police station but I grabbed my small personal bag.

Each side of Ayoko were freezing metal bench seats under a canvas hood with an open back. The night was desperately cold as we thumped our way across the plain and climbed over the Maralal hills through the forest. Ayoko lay down the middle of the Land Rover while the three of us and a couple of armed policemen sat each side of him, but with nowhere to put our feet we finally had to rest them on his body. Appalling.

Our lightweight clothes gave us no protection and we shook with cold. Despite strong objections from the policemen I insisted on getting a spare tee-shirt from my bag for Chukuna to wear as a vest although I would have loved it myself as my teeth were chattering. We were all in shock. We sat in silence, lost in the hollowness of our individual thoughts and miseries. The nightmare continued.

We arrived in Maralal at 1.30am and drove straight up to the hospital, looking for the watchman with keys to the mortuary. We were dog-tired, cramped and frozen. Again, the police would not touch the body so Abdilahi and I carried it. Compared with Baragoi this was a large, well-lit room with several tables and stainless-steel racks against the walls to take cadavers. It already had several occupants, some of whom must have been lying in the bush for a long time, partly eaten by wild animals or in the first stages of decomposition. Carrying Ayoko through the chaotically arranged room to where he was to be left we passed a body with one arm hanging limply across the walkway, against which it was impossible not to brush. The arm and hand were old and withered like parchment and slightly transparent; it must have been in the bush for days. There was no refrigeration system and I was suddenly glad of the cold, as the stench was horribly ripe. We put Ayoko onto a stainless-steel rack and left quickly.

At the police station I pulled off my lightweight sweater and gave it to Chukuna, as the cells were obviously going to be icy, but I did not see him wearing it again. I made my ineffective speech to the officer in charge about Chukuna's innocence and begged for his safe treatment as he was taken away, but the next time I saw him he had been badly knocked about.

The police took Abdilahi and me up to Thesiger's camp, where we woke Lawi and then Wilfred, and we all sat up for a long time going through the facts. Wilfred's immediate concern was naturally for Chukuna's welfare, and his reaction to Ayoko, 'Bloody man! Got what he deserved!' Exhausted, we finally went to bed, and despite my somersaulting brain I vanished quickly into unconsciousness.

The police had told us to be there at 8am and we all went down together. Lawi's increasing importance in Maralal carried some authority and they listened to him respectfully, and naturally they treated Thesiger with great deference. But I do not think any of it helped Chukuna. I bought a blanket and took it in for him but rather doubted whether he received it. Police stations did not reckon to feed their prisoners so I also arranged for one of the Maralal cafés to send up two meals a day for him. Again, whether he got all, or indeed any, of it I had no way of knowing.

After paying for Ayoko's burial I gave his family a futile sum to soften the financial loss of a future breadwinner. I stayed in Maralal for several days doing what I could to further enquiries, and several times went uninvited to the home of the senior policeman to discuss the case and the condition of his prisoner. He was charming and a perfect host, but repeatedly referred to Chukuna as 'the criminal' and every time I pointed out that he had not been convicted, and in fact would not be as he was as innocent as we were. He profusely agreed and then continued calling him the criminal.

It slowly dawned on me that the police were not interested whether Chukuna was guilty or not, but wanted him convicted of murder and hanged. This would be a feather in their cap for apprehending such a dangerous man. It all seemed hopeless.

I went back up to Baragoi to retrieve our possessions, which had been meticulously guarded by the police with nothing pilfered, and arranged for a man to collect our five donkeys and return them to their owners. I hoped that they would never again have to make such a gruelling trek. At Wilfred's camp the tent and all our blood-encrusted things were taken to a nearby dam and washed by some

Turkana women. I cut the zip from my sleeping bag and threw the rest of it away.

Lawi told me that shortly after I set off on my trip a couple of British walkers had arrived wanting to make a similar journey to the lake, setting about it as someone might walk in the Lake District with a rucksack and walking boots. They were back in a few days, crippled by heat and exhaustion. Perhaps they were lucky to have survived on their own in such an alien world. It was absurd not to take local advice and travel with pack animals in the company of local people.

During those awful days waiting for the summons to the magistrates' court, Lawi and I became close friends and we used to sit to watch his animals being watered, and talk for hours. There were still moments of the old humour, and I remember one evening, sitting in Lawi's house with Wilfred, Lawi picked up a very large conch shell he had found on the beach at Lamu and asked me whether it reminded me of anything. I could not think of anything until Lawi held it next to Wilfred's head and said, 'Don't you think it looks like one of Wilfred's ears?' We all collapsed into peals of helpless giggles. Thesiger did indeed have very large ears.

Feeling a burden to the housekeeping at Wilfred's camp, I decided to go and stay with Omar in Nairobi while I waited, and he immediately welcomed me with exemplary hospitality as a long-stay house guest. Having given away or worn through almost all my clothes, I went shopping to make myself presentable in court, but after hearing nothing for several weeks I decided to relieve Omar of my constant presence and went down to Mombasa to stay with his father Moh'd Abeid.

After only two days a policeman in Maralal rang to break the sudden news that the court case was to be in three days' time. It was a desperate rush to get across the country in that time, but Chukuna's defence depended on me. The case was to be heard in

Nyahururu. Thankfully, the various *matatu* connections all worked, so I reached Maralal the night before the trial.

Early next morning I went down to Nyahururu in a police Land Rover together with Chukuna. I was immediately shocked by his gaunt appearance, with no spark in his eyes and seemingly little hope left. He had been through hell and was completely broken, initially showing barely any recognition of me. The case was heard about mid-morning after a series of petty felonies which received hard canings and short prison sentences from the presiding magistrate.

I was aware that a contingent of the press would be there for a murder trial, especially with a white man involved, and was determined to present Chukuna as an honest, respectable, and likeable character. I winced as my well-prepared statement was read very badly by a court official, who stumbled over and mispronounced my carefully considered words, and I worried in case it weakened the defence case. I was only there to verify that the statement read was indeed mine and to answer a few 'yes' and 'no' questions.

However, at the end of it all the magistrate seemed extremely compassionate towards Chukuna and summed up in court, 'It sounds to me as if the dead boy got what he deserved.' Then it was over, referred to the High Court in Nukuru, and Chukuna would continue in detention. I left details of how I could be contacted in England and stressed that I would return as a witness to the High Court trial at my own expense, but never heard from them again.

Outside the courthouse I managed to speak with Chukuna for a couple of minutes and gave him a few packets of cigarettes. He was very lethargic, aimless and dejected. He had been through a nightmare and treated savagely. I later discovered that after this magistrate's hearing he was again held for weeks in solitary confinement before being allowed to mix with other prisoners in a high-security camp. At last, after more initial beatings, his treatment improved.

I stayed a few more days with Wilfred but there was nothing more I could do, so I returned to London. Wilfred and Lawi kept me up to date with how Chukuna's case was progressing. There were several hearings in the High Court, which seemed monstrous, as the only witnessed evidence was mine, clearly proving his innocence. But it was equally clear that the police were pressing hard for a capital sentence.

Eventually, months later, Wilfred invited me up to Tite Street to say he had heard from Lawi that a final hearing of the High Court had been arranged but that things were looking bad. However, Lawi had discovered a new angle of approach to the public prosecutor, and with financial support from Wilfred and me, he hoped to have the case looked at in a new light. A couple of weeks later, when it came back to court, the case was once more presented to the judge, who studied the charge and the evidence once more, and immediately threw it out with no case to answer. Chukuna was released immediately.

Justice had at last prevailed, but how badly had he been damaged psychologically? A ghastly ordeal for an innocent man. When I was planning my next safari I hesitated to ask him if he would like to make another journey with me; would he want to, be able to, or willing to do so? I would be surprised if he was physically or mentally strong enough to face another gruelling trek. I would be honoured if he agreed. We would see…

'We shall not cease from exploration
And the end of all our exploring
Will be to arrive where we started
And know the place for the first time.'

TS Eliot (1888-1965)
***Quartet* No. 4 'Little Gidding'**

Trek 4

North to Stir up a Hornets' Nest

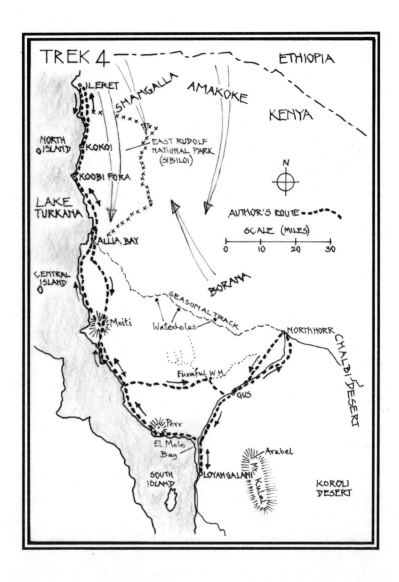

Once more into the heat

AFTER FIVE MONTHS in Kenya I arrived back at Pinewood Studios as they were still putting the finishing touches to shooting *Krull*, which was perfect timing to rejoin the Special Effects team now moving onto a new project, *Supergirl*, followed by *Santa Claus: The Movie*, still inclined to haunt TV screens at Christmas. So it was almost two years later that I was free to make another trek. Meanwhile, for much of this time, Chukuna had been rotting behind bars for having committed no crime. I felt awful about it.

Soon after I had returned to the UK, the Explorers and Travellers Club at Cambridge University had invited me to deliver an illustrated talk on my expedition with camels in the Sahara. It was a crowded lecture hall of perhaps 300 students and I would sooner have faced a band of *ngoroko*! Giving the same talk to a similar number at my old school was less daunting, with less risk of there being people out there who knew more about the subject than I did.

During this time I was, of course, in continual touch with Wilfred, Lawi and Chukuna, once he was released from his savage ordeal. After a lecture Thesiger gave at the RGS I queued up with people wanting him to sign copies of his books. Rather embarrassingly, with still half a dozen people in front of me, he suddenly looked up, caught sight of me, and promptly put down his pen to walk round the queue and come with outstretched hand. 'Oh John, how good to see you. We must get together for some lunch and talk trips. Give me a ring and we'll choose a date.'

I certainly did have a trip to talk to him about: my intended walk from Loyangalani to the Ethiopian border along the east side of Lake Turkana, an area under constant attack by the Shangalla tribe from Ethiopia. I was curious to see how this side varied from the Turkana tribal side, and was intrigued by the dangerous reputation of the Shangalla, curious to see more of them, perhaps even to reach their base at Ileret. I was also eager to see something of the Chalbi desert, having heard that some of it is salt flats, so I greatly wanted to include a visit to North Horr.

As my proposed route would take me through the East Rudolf National Park (Sibiloi) at Allia Bay it was courteous to seek the permission and advice of Richard Leakey, the famous East African palaeontologist and Kenyan wildlife campaigner. In 1984 I wrote to him from England to explain my plans. As Director of the National Museums of Kenya, he effectively controlled the park, especially as it contained his productive Koobi Fora archaeological site. That very year the 1.6-million-year-old skeleton of 'Turkana Boy' had been discovered by his team near Lake Turkana – the most important evidence of early man found to that date.

Later on in Nairobi I had a lengthy talk with Leakey over the phone and he gave me an authorisation letter to say that I should be 'given passage through the National Park at his [my] own risk'. He advised me that, 'there are lions, and you would run some risk of losing donkeys, but if you have several, perhaps this will not be critical.' I made a note to take extra donkeys for the lions.

He added, 'Other wild animals should not be a problem and the people are unlikely to trouble you.' I would remember those words with a wry smile.

Like the west side of the lake this was an area of largely volcanic desert, and would often be very physically demanding. Thesiger later recorded in *My Kenya Days* that 'Even the redoubtable Lord Delamere on his expedition to the lake in 1896-98 was so disheartened and tired by the experience that instead of continuing north up the [east side of the] lake…as he had intended, turned back south'. Fortunately, I felt ready for a challenge.

So, once *Santa Claus* had been laid to rest, I was on my way back to Kenya, landing in Nairobi on 24th November 1984. Within four days of arriving I was in a *matatu* to Nyahururu and found an ongoing bus leaving almost immediately for Maralal. I went straight to the Buffalo Hotel and soon Wilfred and Lawi came with Kibriti to take me up to the camp.

I was no longer expected to sleep in a tent outside the *boma* but was added to the confusion of African bodies on the large sleeping platform above the stores at the other end of Wilfred's room. Now I at least knew some of its transitory occupants, especially Lawi's younger brother Lotterewa.

The routine of life at the camp had not changed, Wilfred going into Maralal each day to work on the final edit of his autobiography, *The Life of My Choice*. Once again I assembled the equipment necessary for my trek and stored it in Wilfred's writing room, now much easier as there really was a bank in Maralal at last. In the evenings we sat, as usual, side by side outside his little house overlooking the wonderful view to the west, and watched the game moving about between the lengthening shadows of the trees. I felt that the numbers of buffalo had increased and after dark it was wise to be extremely vigilant as they are intelligent, aggressive and often wilful animals. We talked until food was ready, the never-changing *spécialité de la maison* of goat stew, cabbage and potato.

People came and went while Wilfred barked questions at them. If he doubted someone's answer his tongue-in-cheek response was, 'Don't stand there lying like Ananias!' Lawi would pop in and sit to discuss 'affairs of Maralal state'. Wilfred tried to help fund some of his business ventures, although he confided to me that in truth his own financial resources were starting to wear very thin at this stage of his life. He was now 74.

I was absolutely delighted when Chukuna said he was keen to come on this safari, and I arranged to meet him at his home in Loyangalani, from where we would walk up to the Ethiopian border. I really looked forward to seeing him again.

Lawi introduced me to a Samburu man called Lopus, a guest at his house, and recommended I take him on this trip. I immediately had huge faith in Lopus, a very knowledgeable, hard-working and courageous man of 32, with great experience of life in this desolate landscape. His own home was on the edge of the Rendille country, where he kept camels, and he turned out to be a veritable aristocrat of Samburu traditional life.

Chukuna had also recommended a friend, Barnaba, a local Turkana at Loyangalani who had worked as a shepherd and a fisherman and knew a lot of the area we hoped to cross. For the first time everyone would be able to speak English well, so communication was going to be easy and direct.

Wilfred told me I should have learned Swahili. 'It's such an easy language. If you'd opened a grammar book when the plane took off in London you'd have been fluent by the time you landed in Nairobi'. I mentioned this afterwards to Lawi, who roared with laughter and whispered to me that Wilfred's Swahili was awful!

As preparations continued, Lawi drove Wilfred and me up into the forest to visit his cows. He had about 70 grazing among the trees, guarded by a couple of finely dressed Samburu *morans*, one wrapped decoratively in a green, yellow and red striped blanket, as the nights were cold. Keeping cows in the forest was illegal, but as Lawi became increasingly influential no one dared challenge him. On the way back we stopped at dusk to watch a large herd of over 30 Beisa oryx in a clearing on the forest edge. A fine and rare sight.

Once I had amassed the large stock of provisions, on Friday 7th December Lawi drove Lopus and me up to Loyangalani. As invariably happened when any kind of journey was arranged, a large number of people suddenly had a pressing need to come too, including Lotterewa and Lawi's new Kikuyu wife Francesca, who had never been to the lake. I gave Lawi 1,400 shillings to cover the petrol for the return trip of almost 300 miles and once all my luggage had been loaded everyone scrambled aboard. Even a couple of Samburu *morans*, finely caparisoned in full tribal regalia, perched on top of my kit on the roof, spears in hand. They made a handsome sight.

We set off along the Baragoi road which I had travelled at night in the police Land Rover with Ayoko's body, but this time I was able to admire the astonishing views, plunging over 2,000 feet into the Rift Valley. This vast landscape stretched away across lava fields populated by occasional stumps of old volcanic plugs to the mountains of the Pokot people, formerly known as the Suk. A very few tiny *manyattas* were barely discernible in the immensity of it all (*see photo 35*).

The Land Cruiser was decidedly top-heavy, and I was glad of Lawi's remarkable driving skills in conditions of often treacherous sand. At one stage he invited me to drive, but after a few miles I passed the steering wheel back to him as I found the vehicle uncontrollable, slewing about dangerously on the loose sand, the poor *morans* on top riding a four-wheeled rodeo.

After weeks reaching the same destination on foot it was peculiar to be soaking up the miles so rapidly this time. This was exactly why Thesiger so hated travelling by car. It was all too quick and superficial, with no chance to experience the terrain, meet the people and engage in their lives; merely a passing view framed by the car window like a television screen. A virtual journey rather than the real thing.

Once at Loyangalani we made camp under some doum palms by a fresh-water source and I went off to find Chukuna. He was buoyant, almost as if all his suffering had never happened, and we swam and talked together as old friends, continuing after dark in his mother's hut. His uncle Laroi came and went in a state of permanent alcoholic stupor. How long could he live like this? With Chukuna's help I hired three donkeys for the duration of the trek at 150 shillings each, but we decided that we needed another three, both for the luggage and perhaps for the lions.

It was viciously hot and, having left the English winter just 13 days ago, I found myself suffering with headaches, deeply burned and covered with water blisters. I had forgotten the savagery of this heat. On previous trips I had often walked all day in nothing but shorts and without a hat under this merciless sun. That seemed impossible now. Even the Samburus who had come up from Maralal were suffering from the heat. In the evening we killed a goat, ate half of it and were quickly asleep.

I kept returning to dip in the lake, the only way to cool down, but each time I was back in the sunshine the brutality of it shocked me anew and it hurt like holding an arm above the flame of a gas cooker. I simply could not remember this degree of cruelty in the heat. That evening I sat for a long time talking with Lawi in his Land Cruiser while we listened to the BBC World Service news, absurdly surreal in this far-off little town surrounded by wilderness and desert. When he had introduced the World Service in 1932, King George V had said that it was for people 'so cut off…that only voices out of the air can reach them.' That was clearly still appropriate.

Chukuna introduced me to Barnaba, a tall, jet-black Turkana who looked tough and resilient. He had an intelligent, well-proportioned face, strongly set, with a cheery expression and the hint of a moustache. I liked him immediately. Lopus was a little shorter and more broadly set, with a thoughtful, serious expression underpinned by a humorous nature. He also had a moustache which turned down at the sides giving him a slight touch of the Mexican bandit. With Chukuna they made a magnificent team.

Sharing clothes and stories
– and the odd drenching

WE SET OFF AT 9.30AM on Monday 10th December 1984, following our six loaded donkeys. Lawi left a few minutes earlier, his car reeking with the rancid smell of a bulging load of sun-dried tilapia to sell in his *duka*. I was glad to be in the fresh air and thankfully the day began cloudy, as I was burning badly. We followed the road north, heading uphill from the town. However, it was not long before the dreaded heat built up, despite the clouds, making me regret my shorts, my legs glowing with a painful luminescence.

Almost at once the adoption of my clothes was underway – Barnaba in a still-white tee-shirt while Lopus had settled on a red and grey striped one, often topped by my safari hat. He also liked his own, strangely inappropriate, silver-framed sunglasses. Chukuna was more demure, in a short-sleeved khaki shirt. I had bought three bright-red check *shukas* and initially everyone wore these wrapped round their waists like cheerful French tablecloths.

Thankfully we had Turkana panniers this time, and each donkey already had a rope threaded through its nose, the length of which was wound round its ears like a cleat. It looked uncomfortable and undignified, but no doubt they were used to it.

The miles passed quickly with the wealth of stories from my companions, and due to the remarkable memories of people in cultures with an ingrained oral tradition I suspected that they were pretty accurate. The person with the most constant supply of good tales was Chukuna, and on this occasion he told me about the total eclipse of the sun in 1973, when Loyangalani had been the best place on earth in which to record it; scientists had flocked from all over the world by plane and vehicle.

He said the eclipse was on the 30th June at 4.30pm, and after the scientists had spent several days setting up complex technical equipment, which astonished and intimidated the tribal people, the sun duly disappeared on cue. Chukuna said that as a boy he was as confused and frightened as everyone else, but later, of course, learned the reasons behind it. However – and he chuckled to himself – the local Turkana still say, 'That was the year that the white men came and made the sun disappear'. Chukuna now enjoyed the similarities to the lunar eclipse in Rider Haggard's *King Solomon's Mines*, one of the many African adventures Thesiger had loved as a boy.

We made a happy group, strolling along behind our six laden donkeys across the grey, baking gravel plain, flecked by tufts of dry grass, while low, sombre hills always clung to the horizon. Chukuna was as relaxed as ever, and great company. Sometimes it was impossible to believe what he had been through since our last trek together and I felt honoured that he had chosen to be here. They were all experienced, tough and unshakeably courageous. I could not have asked for three better companions.

From the top of the hill we gazed down into El Molo Bay, home to the tiny El Molo tribe, whose proud traditions of hunting hippo and crocs with spears while in the water with them astonished me. We went down to take water and let the donkeys drink, then climbed the rocky hillside once more and erected the tent Lawi had loaned me. It had been a short first day, and I sensed that the others were taking pity on the painful condition of my burned skin. After eating some goat meat I hid away in the tent. It was over 38°C (101°F).

Lopus took our donkeys to join the other 100 or so enjoying the plentiful grazing at the water's edge together with many cows and goats. He had already memorised their individual scarring to identify them in the morning. Looking down on their village from our position above, the very round grass huts looked exactly like a collection of smooth pebbles thrown down on the beach. They did not lay siege to our camp, begging and staring as the Turkana would have done, but largely ignored us. Looking across the sparkling lake towards the evening sun, the mountains of the western shore where I had walked in the past were silhouetted black and menacing.

I walked down for a cooling swim and bought four tilapia, but due to the lack of nearby trees we also had to buy firewood. As we started to prepare them for a delicious supper Lopus looked at them with complete disgust and said, 'Am I to eat a lizard?' reflecting his traditional Samburu prejudice. Living well away from the lake, its harvest was beyond his interest or curiosity to try, so we had great difficulty ever persuading him to experiment with these cold-blooded, glassy-eyed creatures from the unimaginable depths of this other, watery world. When there was no fresh meat he contented himself with our stock of corned beef. After dark a curiously loud, high-pitched whine, rising and falling, turned out to be innumerable thousands of mosquitoes swarming above our heads, yet, very strangely, none of us was bitten and a breeze soon carried them off.

Next morning we walked through the landscape of Chukuna's childhood and he pointed out several landmarks familiar to him, including the tree under which he was born. He also showed us some rocks on which he used to sit and fish as a boy, now at least 50 yards from the receding water. I was touched to hear these familial details of this engaging young man who had so narrowly escaped the hangman's noose.

Black rain clouds bore down on us, with lightning stabbing at the tops of the mountains and thunder rolling around menacingly. We discussed erecting the tent, but decided the storm was going to miss us. Oh how wrong we were, soon drenched to the skin, and unloading the donkeys in a panic to make camp as quickly as possible. The rain rapidly moved on, but not before everything was sodden, cold and heavy, and as soon as the sky had cleared we all changed into dry clothes (mine) and cooked up a meal before continuing on our route.

We swung out of El Molo bay along its northern shoreline up towards the perfect volcanic cone of Porr, a landmark visible for many miles around the southern end of the lake. There we stopped for the night. It was a great position, although it turned out to be a bit of a haven for dangerous creatures. Lurking in the hollow centre of a rotten log we were breaking up for firewood, we found a coiled puff adder as well as two very large grey spiders, which I was told were very poisonous. They were quickly dispatched with the flat side of the *panga*, together with a harmless lizard whose only crime was to be in the wrong place at the wrong time.

We began the night in the open to enjoy the cooling breeze, but were soon chased into the tent by more rain. As Chukuna sat up from where he had been dozing he found a scorpion had crept in under his head assuming it to be a nice, warm, furry rock! We all thought it hilarious. The poor scorpion quickly entered paradise to join our other poisonous guests. Heavy rain in the night once more flooded our ground sheet and reduced my sleeping bag to a sodden lump. I was getting a bit sick of this 'desert' weather, and despite the cloud cover, I continued to burn the next morning as the UV penetrated.

The shoreline going north was a series of small, shallow bays and stretches of soft, sticky mud. A Nile perch we bought from a fisherman provided lunch and, as its flesh is much meatier than tilapia, Lopus made an exception to risk it, without enthusiasm. The ground here was littered with clues that it must have been an El Molo camping ground; scattered crocodile vertebrae and patches of crocodile scales still mounted on a grisly layer of dried sinew like plates of medieval armour.

Barnaba told me, 'When I was a boy a huge crocodile was shot at Loyangalani. It measured more than 23 feet in length, and when they cut it open they found bones of an antelope, a giraffe and a man. All the children at the school were taken out of class to go down to the shore to see it before it was taken away by aeroplane.' Presumably to a museum? A crocodile of that size would have been truly Jurassic, even compared with the large Pacific estuarine crocs. Wilfred later observed, 'It must have had a head five feet long!' An awesome prospect.

We walked through a flat wasteland of basalt gravel littered with small rocks, and camped as a glorious sunset over the Kerio delta shimmered across the lake. We slept under the stars, but after our previous soakings we had put up the tent as an insurance policy, and when I woke later, bitterly cold, I shuffled into it. When we set off the next morning, I noticed that Barnaba and Chukuna had swapped clothes – clothing was definitely considered as communal.

Despite a three-hour lunch break, we covered 18 miles and the donkeys kept up a good speed. Gradually a haze of young grass was appearing through the gravel after the rain, and the grey landscape began to take on a softer, green hue. Good news for the donkeys, and it had also attracted a herd of Grant's gazelle. Stephen Pern's description of this side of the lake had been of plentiful grass and wild flowers bringing in game from further afield. This hungry land was clearly rich in dormant seed waiting to burst into life.

The night started very dark as the moon was rising late, and when it did appear it had waned to only half the full orb we had seen at Loyangalani. We slept open to the sky throughout an unpleasant night, pestered by mosquitoes and dampened by a heavy dew which made us very cold. However, the mood was lifted by the conversation, and Lopus told us of his fascinating family heritage. I was particularly interested to learn what was happening here in the early days of the white man's 'discovery' of Africa, in parallel with the lives of my own immediate ancestors.

Lopus' paternal grandfather had been a famous Maasai warrior, having been circumcised as a *moran* in 1873, so about ten years older than my own grandfather. Being a legendary fighter he carried two spears, a bow and a quiver of 60 arrows, and made himself a shield which he claimed was from a whole buffalo skin. Lopus' father was born to this warrior's fourth wife in 1910, four years after my father and the same year as Thesiger, and was one of those who moved north to what is now Samburu District and Lake Turkana.

Lopus told us that a century ago there had been great wars between the Maasai and the Shangalla from the north, but as the Shangalla had firearms (perhaps from the Sudanese conflicts with General Gordon?), they relentlessly drove the Maasai southwards down the east side of the lake, even as far as Nanyuki near Mount Kenya, killing them every time they stopped to rest.

It was a privilege hearing these stories of the past, which may never have been recorded and would soon fade into the mists of forgotten history. Lopus told me that in the old days the Maasai and Samburu described all the tribes of southern Sudan and Ethiopia as the Reshiat. Perhaps that was why people now were still vague about the exact differences between the Shangalla and the Merille.

On the move early the next morning, heading for the small mountain of Moiti (across the lake from Eliye Spring), we found a large group of Tukana nomads starting to build a new *manyatta*. We had only walked five miles, but as there was a good clean spring here we decided to have a rest day doing chores and drying out our things.

We also bought a very large he-goat, who was killed immediately. Lopus skinned and prepared it at astonishing speed, as well as making a new wooden shaft for our spear, which he said was badly weighted. Nearby, the Turkana were busy stretching animal skins over light structures of small branches which were the framework for their new huts.

Building a house was a simple affair for nomadic people moving from one area of grazing to another, and once the construction of the huts was finished they cut down young acacia trees to make a thorn *boma* to protect the goats at night. Their jobs complete, in true Turkana spirit they came straight over to us, begging for chewing tobacco, but as this was their tradition we were ready for them. I also dished out boiled sweets for the children, but they remained terrified of me as a white alien.

Soon my 'surgery' was open as half a dozen came for treatment, mostly eye diseases, coughs and headaches. Someone even brought us a gourd of milk in appreciation, unthinkable in north Turkana. Then a lazy day of eating the fried offal from the goat and relaxing. 'Full, fat and happy,' as Chukuna put it.

As night settled, a terrific rumpus from the donkeys had us running with spear, *panga*, and fighting sticks, and the dogs of the *manyatta* also dashed out to join the attack, but the lion or hyena had gone. In our torchlight we just saw bright eyes looking back from higher up the hill. So we settled for sleep to the enchanting sound of singing from our Turkana neighbours.

Next day was another rest day for us, enjoying meat from the goat while Lopus prepared it for the journey. My skin was finally getting used to the heat, but the sunburn had been a painful and worrying start to the trip. As we rested, the donkeys grazed. Like the herd of Grant's gazelle and impala that had come down from the hills, they loved the new grass, refreshing their spirits as well as their stomachs. They were not keen to leave the following morning, causing Lopus and Barnaba to chase them far and wide, but by 6am they were tethered, and we were off soon after.

Into the killing fields

Moiti is separated from the chain of mountains to its north by a pass leading to the lake, scattered with huge red-brown rocks, reminiscent of old-fashioned leather rugby balls. On many of these were piled little cairns of sticks and stones in tribute to the large numbers who had been killed in this pass by raiders from Ethiopia. The latest ones very recently. We added our offerings of respect to seek favour with the gods for our own safe passage. This little pass was the gateway to the lands scourged by the Shangalla, and north of it the risks increased exponentially. Throughout this trek we had seen few *manyattas* due to the risks from *ngoroko* and *shifta*, but from now on we saw none – only isolated police posts, hopelessly out-gunned. Although this was the territory of the Borana tribe they had mostly fled south, and even the feared *ngoroko* and *shifta* had made themselves scarce. All in terror of the bloodthirsty

Shangalla. I wondered who was left for them to kill. Perhaps us?

Looking back now this seems idiotic, suicidal. Was I really hoping we could throw ourselves on their unlikely hospitality in their feared stronghold of Ileret? Even at the time, my resolve faced increasing moments of uncertainty. But my curiosity got the better of me. It would be fascinating to meet these terrible killers face to face; were they not, after all, just human beings like us? A pair of sinister marabou storks balanced precariously on the unsteady umbrella crown of a small tree nearby, like morbid funeral directors fixing us with a sanctimonious and disdainful air while they measured us up. Perhaps they also knew that this area was ravaged by the Shangalla.

Large numbers of crocodiles eyed us coldly from the shallow waters; in one group we counted over a dozen. The others were naturally expert at spotting them and would be astonished when I could not pick out a dark eyelid just below the surface that was perfectly clear to them. Pelican were plentiful, with other shoreline birds, the water constantly flickering with silver flashes of fish just below its surface. This area was alive with game compared with the other side of the lake, and in patches of sand between the black rocks were innumerable prints of gazelle, hippo, crocodile and a solitary hyena. It was a meltingly hot day but we covered 17 miles as the donkeys were on fine form.

Next day we found an escarpment of mountains tumbling dangerously into the lake and we had to pick our way carefully, sometimes through rocky defiles so narrow that the donkey's loads jammed tight and had to be wriggled free (*see photo 36*). It was exhausting work. All day long the numbers of crocodiles floating close by increased, and we decided to water the donkeys from our cooking pots rather than allow them to drink at the water's edge, for fear of losing one. On one occasion we rounded a rocky bluff to find a particularly large specimen sound asleep on the sand, his mouth open while a plover picked between his teeth. He was quite oblivious to us, and like naughty schoolboys we crept as close to him as we could before he suddenly awoke with a start and, giving a great thrash of his prehistoric tail, flew into the lake with a spectacular explosion of water.

Our rocky path gave way to a land thickly strewn with volcanic shards, through which grew a haze of small spiny shrubs leading down to the lakeshore, where the view of a wide, shallow bay bewitched us. The vitality of the new grass among these black rocks dissolved into the pale gold of the beach, fading imperceptibly to silver, before submerging in the thin bottle green of the shallows, glorious against the beauty of its sapphire blue depths. All crowned by the limitless expanse of an unblemished blue sky bleaching to a merest hint of pink where it kissed the horizon of land and sea. In this magical scene we could almost forget the unforgiving drum of the African sun, the cruel debris of shattered basalt, the sinister unblinking eyelids hidden in the sparkling surface of the water, and the brooding knowledge that the Shangalla frequently painted this beautiful landscape with blood (*see photo* 37).

Lakeside birds were plentiful, including pelican, marabou stork, heron and various duck, and we found many pieces of hippo skulls and teeth, presumably the work of the El Molo. More gazelle watched us from the hillsides, and their numerous tracks continued to decorate the sand of the beach together with those of hippo, crocodile, hyena and the ubiquitous, strutting, black and white, spur-winged plovers which paraded constantly along the water's edge. In a thorn tree on the beach a fish eagle watched us critically, surrounded by the evidence of his craft: a dozen or more fish tucked and wedged between the twigs to keep them safe from scavengers 15 feet below – these aerial fish stirring crazy memories of Dalí and Magritte.

We camped high up the slope in an attempt to evade the

ministrations of clouds of mosquitoes. I was more and more aware that none of us had washed since we had left Loyangalani, and the time was ripe – in more ways than one. So after unloading we went down to the water, drove off a couple of crocs and bathed one by one while the others kept up a constant volley of pebbles into the water on all sides as a deterrent. This became our normal bathtime routine and successfully overcame the appetites of any peckish crocs. We did not want the same casualties that Count Teleki had encountered on this lakeshore. As a result of our wash we were nicer to know, and our clothes were no longer stiff with the caked salt of dried sweat.

The donkeys had been pestered by dog fly and tsetse fly all day, and once unloaded had gratefully galloped off, bucking and rolling in the dust to shake off these pests. Lopus said to me, from experience, 'Tsetse flies can save a man's life as, if they settle on a lion, his only thought is to get rid of them and he'll run and run until they've gone.'

After sundown it was hard to find the donkeys in the darkness as they had covered an enormous distance, but once they were all safely grazing close to our camp we cooked up rice and a goat *mboga* stew. Lopus killed a huge hunting spider with a leg span of five and a half inches and, like the one I killed in north Turkana, big enough to push a pencil between its mandibles. This propelled the conversation into the realm of dangerous creatures, and Lopus told us that in October, less than two months earlier, he had speared a large lion which had killed five of his camels.

'The lion charged me, and when it was just ten feet away I threw my spear as hard as I could. It went through the left shoulder and came out through the right side of its stomach, breaking some ribs. I thought I had killed it but the lion jumped up with a furious roar and came at me again. So I grabbed my short Samburu sword and threw that straight into the lion's mouth and it stuck through its lower jaw. But still it came forward. It was very frightening. All I had close to me was a *panga* so I threw that, but it just bounced off the lion's head. I knew I was dead. But when it charged me again it suddenly dropped down and died, almost touching my feet.' Despite Lopus' extraordinary bravery, I couldn't help noticing that looking at the size of this hunting spider had put a shiver down his spine. It certainly put one down mine.

Although we succeeded in avoiding the mosquitoes that night, we found them replaced by other pests. Apart from the hunting spider, lots of soldier ants were rummaging through our bags, and while waging war on them I killed another of the grey poisonous spiders and then a scorpion by my feet. At last, contentedly ready for sleep, I spotted a little tick plodding doggedly across the groundsheet towards me, determined to succeed where his larger comrades had failed. He quickly joined them all beyond the grave.

I had long since learned that, before going to sleep, an intimate inspection for ticks was time well spent, as I often found one with its mouthparts happily buried in the flesh of my groin. I suspected these usually came from our own donkeys so I would sometimes spend ages working through their coats picking them off, which improved our own lives too.

On this particular evening, before finally giving ourselves over to sleep, a last sweep of the surrounding mountainside with the torch revealed a couple of pairs of glowing eyes in the darkness above us. Determined not to have another hyena attack, we collected the donkeys and tied them to the tree next to where we were camped. I was never quite sure if this improved the safety of the donkeys or would just attract the hyenas to us as well, but I hoped that the scent of Man was offputting. Eventually, a little cautiously, we were asleep.

Next morning we climbed into the hills and picked up one of the tracks of the Sibiloi Reserve which led us to Allia Bay. We looked down on vast numbers of flamingo, with sunlight dazzling from the corrugated-iron roofs of the Game Department, and we branched off to walk along the dry, cracked mudflats near the water's edge, ploughed deeply with furrows left by hippo dragging themselves through the collapsing surface of the dried mud like great earth-moving machines. Among a tangle of zebra tracks we spotted those of several lions; Richard Leakey's warning had been apposite.

At the park office I showed them Leakey's letter giving me safe passage, but they took no notice and charged us all a fee for camping as if we were tourists. Well, perhaps I was, but surely not my friends, in their own homeland? At least the money would go towards the preservation of wildlife. We topped up our supplies from the Game Department shop and filled our jerry cans from their lorry, which was returning from a fresh spring. This was a luxury, as we found that the administrators and soldiers from down-country tribes were incapable of drinking the lake water which we lived on.

The sand and mudflats around us danced and rippled in the midday heat haze while oasis mirages trembled in the distance. The donkeys, unimpressed by these atmospheric tricks, got their heads down to some serious grazing while they had the chance. They had walked about 100 miles so far and still had more than 300 to cover. Despite a thick mist of mosquitoes we laid out our bedding under the stars and my Autan mosquito repellant impressed everyone enormously when it did exactly what it promised. No one was bitten and we did not even hear another whine.

As usual we had put out feelers for the latest information about Shangalla raiders on our way north towards Ileret. The danger posed both by them and by Borana raiding parties had been a frequent topic of conversation, and as we moved north the threat was mounting with each day's walk. I understood that the Borana people were usually quite friendly, did not normally use firearms, and had a unique way of throwing a spear with both hands. I was puzzled by this but fortunately never saw it used in anger.

The Shangalla on the other hand were quite a different kettle of fish, moving freely across the porous and unprotected border from Ethiopia. They had settled openly in the northern strip of Kenya, from where they raided their southern neighbours, and they were heavily armed with AK-47s. Physically they were indistinguishable from the Turkana and even used Turkana names, but apparently spoke a different language. I assumed they were a closely related Nilotic tribe and yet they were sworn enemies, missing no opportunity to attack one another.

The Borana tribe, originally from Ethiopia themselves, were their closest Kenyan neighbours, so suffered the brunt of their raids, frequently having livestock pillaged, often with considerable casualties. The carnage was worse due to the Shangalla custom of social rank being dependent on the number of men a warrior had killed; a man could not marry until he had killed at least one person, and the more the better. Sadly they were not a tribe of bachelors!

We heard that only a few days earlier a group of four Shangalla had stolen three goats from the Game Department camp but the Rangers had given chase and managed to shoot one of them dead. Unnervingly, the area I had chosen to walk through to Ileret was exactly where they were now most active. The Game Rangers repeated to me, 'It is crazy to go to Ileret. That is the home of the Shangalla, and they will kill you.' But when I insisted on going they advised, 'If you go then come back quickly to the protection of the armed Rangers here at Allia Bay.' They were totally against my plans to continue from Ileret south-east to North Horr: 'That will be a certain death sentence.'

I had noticed on the map, however, that there was a seasonal track from Allia Bay to North Horr with three water holes along the way, so I suggested we could go that way instead. This started a great debate that lasted into the next day, some saying it might be possible, some that it would be lethal: 'These water holes are used all the time by Shangalla going north or south to raid. If they find you they will kill you.'

I had wanted to visit North Horr, as it was on the edge of the Chalbi desert, parts of which were salt desert, an unusual feature in sub-Saharan Africa. But they stressed again that from now on our route would become increasingly dangerous as we went further north, including dire warnings that we would definitely be killed. 'You don't even have a gun.'

I was getting the message and beginning to lose confidence, but to have to retrace our steps along the lake to Loyangalani would be to admit defeat. From today's perspective it all seems completely irresponsible, extraordinarily dangerous; survival unlikely. But we were young and full of adventure.

Surrounded by game
and tales of tribal wars

As we continued north the heat increased even more, and it became particularly gruelling following the lakeshore, as we got into trouble in the mudflats. The donkeys were breaking through the crust into deeper, softer mud beneath, floundering badly, and sometimes giving up completely and refusing to move. Occasionally one of them would panic and lurch round in circles, becoming more and more bogged down. A couple fell over sideways and we had to lift them back onto their feet, so before long, we, the donkeys, and everything we owned, were all thickly plastered. To get further from the water onto firmer ground we dragged the animals out of this glutinous quagmire one by one.

On our way we passed an impressive group of over 100 marabou stork, birds often standing over four feet high. I never overcame my revulsion for these sinister creatures, morose and solemn as a public execution, their funerary shoulders hunched with hands clasping their tailcoats behind their backs. Why had they not been created with pince-nez perched on those improbable Gerald Scarfe noses? As we approached they took off and landed further ahead, mighty wingspans claimed to rival those of condor and even albatross, one unverified measurement allegedly 13.3 feet.

The bones of hippo and crocodile were scattered everywhere and we passed tracks of very many lion, antelope, Grant's gazelle and both Grevy's and Burchell's zebra. Ever-vigilant topi stood sentinel on old ant heaps. A one-horned gazelle stopped to stare suspiciously from only 50 yards. The ground here was just firm sand, with no rocks, so we were forced to dig narrow trenches in which to light our cooking fires, the pots spanning the flames astride the side walls. Many scattered groups of thorn scrub obscured what lay behind – a little disconcerting with so many lion tracks criss-crossing everywhere – and in one place we followed the very fresh tracks of an entire pride heading to a small pool of yellow-scummed water, where we too stopped to drink. We kept a wary lookout behind us.

Some Grevy's zebra put on a wonderful display, galloping round and round us in a circle of frenzied excitement, no doubt considering our donkeys to be their unadorned cousins. The feeling was reciprocated and the donkeys wanted to break into a canter and join them. It was a long time before they quietened down. I wondered what would happen if we lost control of them and they carried away all our worldly possessions, leaving us destitute in this unforgiving, empty landscape.

Closer to the lake we found a large herd of 150 topi mixed with 80 zebra and the same number of gazelle. I had never seen such a gathering of topi before (and believe it to be a rare sight). They are more often seen as solitary sentries, forever on watch for predators.

As we approached, the three species separated, the gazelle keeping the whites of their rumps towards us with just the occasional large male turning a fine profile as he studied us. The topi stayed in front for two or three miles, stopping to stare for a minute or two, then breaking into their stiff-legged canter before halting to scrutinise us once more. The zebra were less nervous, and repeatedly crossed our path, alternately trotting and pausing to graze, but always under the watchful eye of a few larger animals who made sure that the herd kept a respectful distance of about 100 yards. Eventually all three species wheeled round en masse to head back to where we had first seen them. It was a thrilling experience to be on foot so close to these wild creatures of the plains.

We saw more groups of gazelle as the sun slid towards the lake, turning its surface into a bed of diamonds which silhouetted the curious dark shapes of pelicans at the water's edge. We repeatedly crossed the tracks of hippo where they had left the water at night to graze, great clear prints where the surface was firm, and gouged trenches a foot deep where it was soft.

Approaching Koobi Fora, where Leakey's team had been finding so much of archaeological interest, we began to notice more and more fossils on the beach. There were vertebrae of Nile perch, occasional large ribs, the thigh bone of a hippo, a complete hippo jaw cracked into two pieces, and even the undamaged pelvis of an antelope. How old they were I had no idea, but in this birthplace of mankind fossils were well-preserved and might be very ancient. I picked up a couple of black, fossilised Nile perch vertebrae, one of which I gave to Thesiger after the safari. A couple of years later, in his London flat, I was amused when he picked it up from his writing table and showed it to me as something he had collected. I kept quiet.

It had been a long walk of 22 miles in over 40°C (104°F), but with all the interest of the day it had passed unnoticed. I was amazed how the donkeys had kept up the pace – twice their comfortable range – but they had grazed well at Allia Bay. However, unlike them, such a wave of exhaustion suddenly flooded over me that even within a couple of hundred yards of the simple buildings of the Koobi Fora Museum, I had to sit for a long time to rest. My legs were on fire with bursting muscles, and my back was aching badly. For a while I was unsure whether I could even reach the park rangers' camp less than a mile away and wondered about bedding down there and then. So we sat and watched as the great red sun settled on the water for an instant and then slipped quickly into it, leaving a golden wash across the sky. We staggered to the camp as the dusk settled in around us, and I found it hard even to unload the donkeys before sinking down onto the sand to rest again. We ate a simple meal, laid out our bedding and plunged instantly into the blessed depths of a dreamless sleep.

It was a well-earned rest day at Koobi Fora. When I finally woke up after the others, at 6.45am, I found a kind mug of coffee beside me. We relaxed, ate two large meals and walked back to the little museum. Here they wanted to charge us 500 shillings to enter (in the NFD of 1984 £25 was an enormous sum), so instead we walked round the outside, noses glued to the windows, and saw almost as much. We learned that 10,000 years ago the lake had extended over six miles further east and had a western outlet to the Nile. Evidence had been found of three different forms of early man in this area, living contemporaneously with three species of crocodile, two of hippo, sabre-toothed cats and an early elephant with downward-curving tusks.

After sundown I spent another fascinating evening talking with Lopus about memories of his father and grandfather and recent Samburu tribal history. He explained to me that in the Maasai language the word 'Samburu' means 'those who roam around' because of their constant raiding of other tribes in the north. He told me about another sizeable tribe, also a branch of the Maasai, called the Laikipia, who had settled in the area between Naivasha and Maralal, separating the Maasai and Samburu homelands. Because of the fine quality of the farming land there they had been mostly driven off or shot by the early white settlers who claimed it for themselves. (So much for their evangelising spirit!) So, finding themselves homeless, some had rejoined the Maasai to the south, some the Samburu to the north, while the white farmers dominated the central ground, which became known as the White Highlands. This was how the Maasai homelands of the Mara and the Samburu region had become separate entities.

These days, Laikipia simply refers to a small area around Rumuruti. I asked about the Kikuyu, now the most politically powerful tribe in Kenya, and Lopus enjoyed telling me that at that time they were a small tribe in the forests around Mount Kenya, 'living like baboons in the trees and eating leaves.' A version of history no doubt open to debate...

He went on to list the great fighting tribes of the past as the Maasai, Laikipia, Samburu, Turkana, Borana, Rendille and Shangalla. 'Those were the tribes who traditionally kept animals and therefore raided from each other to increase their wealth.' Most were tribes of the NFD, which is no doubt why the area still maintained its wild charm, its dangers, and its fascination.

'At the end of the 19th century the Turkana were mainly north of the Kerio River, and they raided in all directions, attacking the Samburu, Rendille, Borana and Shangalla. The Rendille and Borana fought against each other as they were both keepers of camels, and the Shangalla controlled most of the east side of the lake, sometimes driven back to what is now the Ethiopian border by the Maasai and Samburu. This was the time my grandfather joined the Samburu, when they separated from the Maasai in the 1880s.'

As I had discovered, Shangalla still raided along this side of the lake, stealing stock from the Borana and wild animals from the national park. They also regularly pushed further south, as evidenced by the recent killings in the mountain pass by Moiti where we had added our tributes. Lopus warmed to his theme. 'The Borana also fight the Rendille and Samburu as well as the Shangalla'. He finished by saying proudly, with a flourish, 'The Samburu raid everyone except the Rendille!'

My four treks had all clearly been at the epicentre of volatile and dangerous areas. I wondered what the reaction of people on wildlife safaris in their zebra-striped jeeps in the Maasai Mara would be if they knew that only a few hundred miles to the north there was still so much savage and unbridled blood-letting!

It was no coincidence that the stories were increasingly about deeds of tribal fighting and heroism as we came closer to Ileret. Naturally the Shangalla were a constant fireside topic and the apprehension mounted palpably. These stories buoyed up everyone's courage; an astonishing courage to be sharing my foolhardy journey into this hornets' nest. Truly heroic.

Chukuna also loved to tell me about his own Turkana tribe, and explained that the following year, 1985, would almost certainly be chosen by the elders as the year for the moving up of age groups, assuming that the 'long rains' of the spring did not fail, as the animals must be fat for all the feasting this would entail. As with the Samburu, the creation of *morans*, and their subsequent progression to *mzees* or elders, was rigorously prescribed in distinct age groupings.

'The most senior *mzees* will choose a date and a place for all the clans of the south Turkana tribe, as far north as the Kerio river, to come for a huge ceremony lasting almost three months. During this time they will move together over a large area, feasting wherever they go at the hospitality of the *manyattas* they pass. There will be lots of mock fights using shields and whips made of acacia canes, or sometimes hippo-hide whips which are even more brutal. But things easily get out of hand and turn into more serious battles'. Chukuna told me that the last time this feasting throng passed through Loyangalani, about six years before, the elders asked the police for the names of all the local trouble-makers, 'and they beat them rudely so their backs looked like zebras.'

Turkana fighting would begin with a man singing, or in reality chanting aggressively, in praise of his bull, or if he had no bull he might praise his largest he-goat. He would sometimes call it by the name of a wild animal, so if he chanted the name for a 'kudu' people would understand that his animal's horns grew in that particular shape.

At this last feast-time the elders summoned Chukuna and announced that they knew who he was and who his father was, and wanted an explanation why he had not put himself forward to become a *moran*, as he was in that age group. He explained, 'I can't become a *moran* before my older brother, and he is away in the administrative police, so I have to wait.' The elders unfairly fined him three goats, but his animals were away grazing on Mount Kulal so he could not produce them. Instead, one of the elders threw him a shield and a pair of whips and told him he must fight a large and very aggressive man sitting nearby, who immediately started to praise his bull.

Chukuna, who had been involved in more than his fair share of fights and was not lacking in courage, admitted to me that he had been terrified. He did not dare run and did not dare fight. He had no idea what to do, and was more and more scared, but at that moment his sister came past and asked what was happening. She defused the impasse by giving the elders 30 shillings. Fortunately, they accepted this instead of forcing Chukuna to undergo a savage whipping.

The moving up of the age groups was different for different tribes. Lopus told me it would be another three years before the next big Samburu ceremony when Lawi's age group would move on to become *mzees*. Lopus himself had become *mzee* in the previous age group progression.

The social complexities of tribal life were often a mystery to me. Now, with the influence of the missions, new schools and the government trying to break down tribal rivalries, the days of these ancient traditions were bound to be numbered. I was lucky to be witnessing some of them before they vanished.

We left Koobi Fora at 7am and reached Kokoi at noon. There was a strong, fresh wind with a smattering of clouds, which gave us welcome relief, and at the small Kokoi game rangers' camp I was told that, due to recent rains, the game had all moved into the hills further from the lake to find fresh grazing.

Lopus told me a story of the coming of Count Teleki before he discovered the lake. 'In the area of the Koroli Desert, east of Mount Kulal, a group of Maasai *moran* saw him talking with the Africans he employed and, never having seen or heard of a white man before, they were puzzled about who or what he was. They guessed he was a god or an angel and were nervous about approaching him. But one of them, a *moran* named Lelerouk, was determined to discover the truth and went forward. From a distance Teleki told him to put down his spear and his bow and arrows, which he did. Then Teleki shook his hand and had food prepared for him. Afterwards Lelerouk told the other *morans* they must not fight this white man because he had given him food; yet still they believed him to be some sort of god. Puzzled by what they had seen they went to the Laibon (the tribal seer) near the Aberdares. The Laibon decided that Teleki must be a man, as he had heard of another like him who had travelled through Maasai country without doing any harm'. This was Thomson, after whom the waterfall at Nyahururu (and the gazelle) were named. As a result, Teleki was not attacked by the Maasai. A remarkable fact considering their usual aggression towards outsiders. All this, less than 100 years before me!

As we were preparing for sleep at Kokoi a shooting star tore out of the heavens and plunged to earth the other side of a low hill to the north of us, giving a great flash and a momentary pyrotechnic display. I imagined that next day we might pass a blackened crater where it had struck, but in fact we found no sign of it at all. However, my compass readings went haywire which was worrying and the electronic shutter of my Nikon camera also stopped working; a great nuisance. I wondered whether the meteorite had created some confusion of the electromagnetic field, as these disturbances continued until we were well away from the site.

The game rangers' camp at Kokoi lay on stony volcanic ground overlooking a particularly attractive sandy beach. They assured us that there were no crocodile there, so in the afternoon we all went down for a delightful, leisurely bath in the lake without taking any of our usual precautions. Next morning, however, we found that the shoreline for two miles north of Kokoi was infested by the largest population of crocodiles that any of us had ever seen, including Barnaba, who was a fisherman.

Their numbers were legion, and they floated, half a dozen at a time, close to the beach, or lay in prehistoric heaps on the sand, flopping lazily back into the water as we approached. Our blood ran cold at the risk we had unknowingly taken. One particularly large crocodile lay asleep on the beach with mouth wide open to allow the plovers to pick his teeth. Just as before, we crept up on him naughtily with handfuls of stones and, once within very close range of less than 15 yards, we launched a hail of missiles. He woke up with a start but then, like an experienced schoolmaster bored by the tedious pranks of his delinquent pupils, slunk off to the water slowly and rather grudgingly, clearly unimpressed by our frivolous game. We were most disappointed.

A little further on, a small spit of sand and rocks projected into the lake which evidently served as a nursery for two or three dozen debutant crocs. A few very large adults were on guard, basking in the sun and sprawled across each other. The water boiled on our approach as they all raced back in, slithering over the rocks and sliding down into the dangerous depths.

Into Ileret:
a night inside the hornets' nest

HALFWAY ROUND A large bay full of gazelle, zebra, topi and a pair of oryx, we left the lakeshore to continue due north towards Ileret itself. Adrenalin began to flutter. As we came closer to the shallow hill on which it stood we entered dense bush, for which we were grateful in order to hide our approach to this murderous village. If we were spotted I was not certain what sort of reaction to expect, although once we reached it I assumed they would not kill us right under the nose of the village police post. We crossed a well-defined *lugga* through thick bush of fleshy, cactus-like plants which I did not recognise. There was something rather eerie about the place, or was it just my trembling spirit?

I noticed that my friends were keeping a close lookout in all directions, conversation had almost dried up and anything necessary was almost whispered. Our increasing nervousness showed in the lack of patience with the donkeys, who received many an undeserved whack for the slightest misdemeanour. Our pace was slow due to the density of the bush, and the frustration of our restricted movement raised the tension further. At least I was confident that our approach was invisible from the village.

After almost two hours we caught sight of open ground to our left which we made for, as our progress had ground almost to a halt. Once clear of the dense bush we could see the corrugated-iron roofs of the police post shimmering in the sunlight, and we soon picked up tyre tracks in the sand leading towards it, which we followed. As we started to climb the low hill we began to see the huts of the Shangalla, and our disquiet mounted further. Even Lopus' nerves were frayed, and he remarked to me with a sneer of inter-tribal disgust, 'Those brown things are what they live in.' In fact they looked perfectly serviceable to me, covered with skins and the tin sheeting of flattened paraffin cans – not the quality of Samburu houses but far more spacious than Turkana huts.

On the slopes several flocks of goats were being tended, no doubt stolen from the tribes further south. I was surprised by the extreme edginess of my brave companions, and although I felt shaky and vulnerable, I was probably the least anxious – perhaps only because I had no experience of what these people were capable of, never having witnessed the brutalities of tribal conflict in action as they had. Barnaba had told me of a 22-year-old woman, still living in Loyangalani, who had been a child in Ileret when the Shangalla first attacked it. They had broken her skull for the sheer fun of it.

We entered the village without mishap as I had expected, and it unsurprisingly turned out to be nothing more than a scattering of *manyattas* on the side of the low hill on top of which stood the very sleepy police barracks and beside it what was proudly, but euphemistically, called a health centre. One house in the village had recently started to serve as a shop, although the woman who ran it was not there. Another was a butchery but without any scales, so the weight and price of meat was sheer guesswork and open to endless argument.

At the police post I reported our arrival to a bored-looking man who turned out to be the chief of police, although he wore no uniform. As he also spoke no English he called over one of his very smartly turned-out men to translate. He asked my name, but did not make a note of it, and told me to report again on departure. It was clear that the police made as few ripples as possible, being completely outnumbered and surrounded by this lawless tribe, who had reinforcements only a short day's walk away, north of the border.

We chose a tree by the health centre under which to make our camp, and were immediately surrounded by the usual large crowd of fascinated, naked, young children. They, at least, were friendly enough. Close by I noticed a couple of young men putting the finishing touches to intricately coloured mudpack hairdos of the same style as the northern Turkana, each surmounted by an ostrich plume. One in particular was preening himself lavishly while several young men fawned over him admiringly, crowding round or even lying down and resting their heads on his knee. I could not help being a little amused by this, assuming it was effeminate. How wrong I was! We discovered that a raiding party had just returned from attacking the Borana, and these two men were being lauded for each having killed a man. The one who held himself in the attitude of most haughty pride was an illustrious assassin. His name was Kiko.

We later discovered that Kiko was a remarkably good sniper and if, during a raid, one of the enemy was proving deadly Kiko would be called on to kill him. During the evening, in the *manyatta*, Chukuna talked to Kiko, who told him he had been watching our approach down the sights of his rifle. So much for me thinking we were unseen! He said the only reason that he had not shot us all was that he was curious as to why there was a *msungu*. He could not care less about the feeble authority of the police post. In fact we discovered that Ileret was the main source of Shangalla raids and the police did not dare raise a finger.

Because of the social requirement to kill men, raiders not only wanted to steal livestock but also to increase their tally of victims. This was a fairly common trait among Ethiopian tribes, and Thesiger had experienced the same when he explored the desert of the Danakil Depression. Dervla Murphy, in her book *In Ethiopia with a Mule*, quotes a popular Amharic poem: 'Kill a man! Kill a man! It is good to kill a man! One who has not killed a man moves around sleepily.' I did not notice any sleepy Shangalla, and the way they looked at us made me feel like an intended trophy for their collection. This was an extraordinarily dangerous place to be.

I decided on a little defensive diplomacy to try to curry favour by buying a goat to share with these leading warriors. But when the poor creature had its throat slashed and the blood spurted from the jugular, the men took it in turn to crouch and drink directly from the vein while the animal died. We all found it a shocking spectacle. Then, despite the fact that there was a strict rule of no fires after dark for fear of attack by the Borana, they continued cooking with us long into the night. These were men with contempt for all rules or ethics, consideration or pity.

Very surprisingly, the warriors of Ileret seemed to fear the raids of the Borana almost as much as others feared the Shangalla. At night all the old men, women and children slept in the inadequate security of the police post compound, leaving only the *morans* and some of the girls in the *manyattas*; a bizarre scenario in which foreign armed terrorists sought police protection from the nation they came to attack!

A young man, who spoke remarkably good English, asked me to take his picture. He was pleasant-looking, affable and chatty, and seemed keen to present me with a reassuring image of the Shangalla, saying that these ones in Ileret were not the ones who raided, which we had seen was patently untrue. However, his friendly manner won me over, and so when he casually asked where we were going when we left I gullibly told him that we would return to Allia Bay and then head east to North Horr.

To my horror Chukuna told me soon afterwards that he had heard in the *manyatta* that this man was one of their leaders and a distinguished raider. I had just put us all at enormous risk. What an idiot! I felt like a Judas. Chukuna also said that he had seen large numbers of AK-47s stacked inside the walls of their huts, ready for immediate action. Kalashnikov had designed this famous assault rifle at the end of WWII, partly inspired by the American M1 Garand, which Chukuna told me the administrative police still used. Its name comes from Avtomat Kalashnikova, 1947, easily pressed out of steel and cheaply produced in vast numbers. And responsible for unimaginable amounts of death and misery around the world.

A huge worry was that during the night our donkeys had gone missing. That seemed more than coincidence. What the hell would we do, isolated in this hornets' nest? So it was an immense relief when they were discovered happily grazing on fresh grass in a verdant *lugga*. It was time to get out while we could. After signing out with the police chief and smoothing the outraged feathers of an assistant chief, to whom I should apparently also have reported and was now clearly after a bribe (which he did not get), we were underway.

Lopus had very cleverly put out false information that we were intending to spend four days at the lakeshore before heading south, so we set off in that direction, sure that many pairs of eyes would be watching us. Lopus was certain that once we were away from the village a raiding party would quickly come after us, as the prize of six donkeys and whatever good things a white man must be carrying would be impossible to resist; not to mention the added perks of killing a couple of Turkanas, a Samburu, and even a *msungu*. I felt like a pheasant, released to be shot for sport, and equally unarmed! Once out of sight we switched direction and started towards Kokoi as fast as we could go.

When we had put a good distance between us and the village I felt the tension ebbing away from my companions and the chatter gradually resumed with more compelling stories. Lopus told us that at Allia Bay someone had said that in the spring a large group of *ngoroko* in north Turkana, living in a place which translates as 'Black Gun', had raided the Merille tribe in Sudan. The story was that the *ngoroko* had killed 180 people and stolen large numbers of cattle to drive back south. Then, leaving their prizes at their *manyattas*, they promptly returned to kill another 150 Merille. While the numbers of victims might have been enhanced in the retelling I had no reason to doubt the essence of the story. No love was lost between the Merille and the *ngoroko*. Many people were killed every year.

Another story soon emerged about the pass beside Moiti where we had left our tributes in honour of those recently killed. It transpired that there had now been yet another raid in which the Shangalla had murdered a party of Borana. The dangers of this region were legion. Feeling a bit cocky that we had bluffed these brigands and were now making good speed away from them, the Shangalla stories were no longer related with fear and dread and we felt strangely jubilant. We marched on with a spring in our step.

But a solitary figure in the distance seemed to be stalking us. It became more and more unsettling as, for over an hour, it remained a constant half-mile behind us. Had the Shangalla sent someone to trail us and report our position? In which case Lopus' lakeside ruse had not worked. We were unsure and our angst bubbled up once more. Eventually we halted and the figure approached, turning out to be a young Shangalla boy of about 12.

He clearly wanted to come with us and was eager to please, collecting firewood at our midday break, then sharing our lunch before rounding up the donkeys from their grazing. But apart from the few words of Swahili he knew there was a complete language barrier between us. His name was Amede, and when we continued he came too. We did not know what to make of him, but a couple of hours later he pulled at my arm, pointed at himself, then at us, and said 'Loyangalani'. I had grave misgivings that the Shangalla would assume we had kidnapped him and seek a speedy and lethal reprisal.

The others had fallen under the spell of his charm, however, and persuaded me that he should stay with us. Looking back now this seems mad, but with our lives already balanced on a knife edge, everything was mad. He quickly settled into our march and Chukuna even passed him the spear to carry. This seemed even more crazy, handing over our only weapon to a member of the tribe keen to kill us, but before long he had speared a large mud fish in the shallows of the lake. We continued.

The shoreline of the crocs was even more densely populated than last time we had passed (astonishing that we had actually bathed there), and at Kokoi we climbed the hill to camp at our previous spot. I went to the lake for a very cautious wash and we settled for sleep. I told Chukuna that before we reached Loyangalani he must teach Amede some simple words of Swahili so that he would survive.

One of the soldiers here told us that he knew Amede's parents and that he could not come with us. The Shangalla, like the Turkana, treated their children with considerable neglect until they became of age, and Amede was tired of being left on his own for weeks at a time tending goats miles from his home, surviving as best he could. So he had run away in the best Dick Whittington tradition. At first he had worked for some Turkana fishermen, but when they moved away he seized the opportunity of coming with us to Loyangalani.

The soldiers were right to be worried about how Amede would be received in Turkana country, where many people would have blood feuds to settle, but Chukuna said he would look after him in his own home and teach him to be a fisherman. Left at Ileret, his only future would be as a raider, with an early death a strong possibility.

In the morning our attention was brusquely refocused by the game rangers telling us they had just heard on their short-wave radio of a Shangalla raiding party going up and down the lakeshore south-west of Ileret as if they were looking for someone. Thank God for Lopus' quick thinking. Without the false information he had put out, we might now be dead. Our feeling of relief quickly evaporated to be replaced by a heavy foreboding. How long would it be before they guessed and started to chase us south? We were badly restricted by the speed of our donkeys, whereas they could travel at speed. How long before they might catch us up? We must get underway quickly. Amede came on with us.

When we reached Koobi Fora we all felt unaccountably weary with an insatiable thirst so, despite having intended to soak up more miles that day, we camped there again. Amede was not used to long, arduous walks and was exhausted. Having several armed *askaris* here made us feel more secure than sleeping out in the bush. But before we slept I decided to teach Amede to write his name, which I expected him to master quickly. I failed miserably, however, because he had no concept of making marks, even as crude as drawing lines in the sand with a stick. Having scratched a large capital 'A' I asked him to copy it, but even a task so simple was completely beyond him and he drew random lines bearing no relation to it at all.

As night fell we lay on the ground listening to the game rangers' radio playing Swahili Christmas carols from 'Voice of Kenya'. It was Christmas Eve 1984.

On the radio I also heard a time check, which startled me as it turned out that my digital watch had somehow lost three quarters of an hour, and explained why the early mornings had been unaccountably hotter for the past few days. Could this also have been caused by our meteorite experience? Later when I told Thesiger about this strange phenomenon he looked at my watch and said with disdain, 'Is that one of those Japanese things? I should get rid of it. The only watch to use on trek is a Rolex if you want to rely on it under harsh conditions'. Later that year I took his advice.

Christmas on the run

On Christmas Day we were away by 7.30am, intending to find a place to camp on the way to Allia Bay, to avoid the shatteringly long march we had made when heading north. But before we left Koobi Fora, the game rangers alarmed us by saying they had just heard on their short-wave radio that the rangers' post at Kokoi, where we had slept the previous night, was now involved in a fierce gun battle with a Shangalla raiding party. This was very worrying and convinced us that they were now on our trail. I was concerned for the safety of the rangers, but hoped they would hold up the Shangalla long enough to give us a head start. They were now only half a day's walk behind us and could travel much faster than we could. It was a scary predicament.

We made good time, physically fresher after our rest, but mainly driven by our mounting anxiety. By mid-morning we were doing well and I was confident of reaching Allia Bay that evening, despite the 22 hot miles that had so exhausted me before. Now we had no choice. In order to cover as much ground as possible before the sun released its daily inferno we kept the donkeys going at a fast pace, sometimes even a brisk trot, so that despite lengthening our own stride as much as possible we found it hard to keep up with them and had to jog along behind.

This turned out to be a mistake as it fired them up with excitement, which was somehow transmitted to a small herd of about 25 zebra who came galloping up to them. We had witnessed before how donkeys and zebra feel a kindred bond, and as the zebra began their tantalising taunt of circling us at full charge, our donkeys again imagined themselves breaking out in stripes. Flushed with adrenalin they wanted nothing more than to join their wild cousins on the endless plains. The brisk trot we had coaxed them into gradually speeded up into something more like a canter, and the gap between them and us became greater and greater, while the gap between them and the zebras became smaller and smaller.

There was no longer anything we could do to control them, and eventually we watched them become part of the wild herd, growing smaller in the distance, and finally disappearing over the horizon. So there we stood, alone in this desolate place, with just the clothes we stood up in. Everything we owned was now part of a herd of wild zebra somewhere in the emptiness of the savage NFD, while a raiding party of Shangalla was gaining ground on us, intent on our demise. What a Christmas Day! Certainly more memorable than turkey and Brussels sprouts...if we lived to remember it.

Lopus and Barnaba set off to give chase and Chukuna, expecting it to be a lengthy search, filled our small water bottles from a nearby waterhole, then followed the others. I remained eerily alone with Amede, one eye on the horizon, dreading a glimpse of our pursuers. Out of sight, the others soon came across one donkey whose pannier had slipped round under its stomach and fouled its legs, forcing it to give up its frenzied bid for freedom. This they brought back to me and arranged to rendezvous by the tree we had lunched at after leaving Allia Bay on our way north, where we had made our cooking fires in trenches in the sand. They gave me hasty directions and were gone.

The donkey and I eyed each other distrustfully, it still shivering with excitement, and I full of apprehension. As Amede had stayed behind with me, I took hold of the donkey's halter while he drove it from behind. As we had noticed before, this area was dense with lion, whose tracks were everywhere in the sand, and at each stand of scrub we passed I was increasingly terrified that behind it would be a pride dozing in the shade. Certainly the donkey could smell them everywhere, becoming more and more nervous, and very sensibly not having the slightest confidence in my ability to protect us. The others had taken the spear with them and I now realised that even my hunting knife was on Chukuna's belt. We had nothing other than a slender, useless, donkey stick.

Twice, as we passed a tangle of scrub, a hare suddenly exploded from it and the donkey almost left the ground, bucking violently, eyes wild, and my heart almost leapt out of my mouth as I grimly hung onto the halter. I tried to work out a plan of what to do should we suddenly find ourselves face to face with a lion. I was perfectly certain that the donkey would not stay around for pleasantries and would be galloping away at full speed in an instant, leaving me to make my excuses to the lion. I had read that the best solution was to stand absolutely motionless. The lion might sniff me enquiringly and wander off; but had the writer ever tested this theory? I was quite sure that I would be emitting such a barrage of tantalising fear pheromones that I would be an irresistible choice on his menu. It was a most unsettling walk.

In the end I spotted the rendezvous tree with huge relief, tied the donkey to it and unloaded. The others had all the water in the donkey's loads so we sat, expecting a long, hot, thirsty wait. I wondered whether my friends would succeed in catching them and imagined having to beg the game rangers at Allia Bay for help. However, I was being unnecessarily pessimistic as, in a surprisingly short time, they arrived with all five missing animals.

Apparently the zebra were soon unimpressed by the clatter and clumsiness of the donkeys' ungainly loads, and decided they were not such desirable playmates after all. Once rejected, the donkeys had settled down to graze and waited to be rounded up again after their game. Hugely relieved, we decided to make lunch there and then, and re-used our old fire trench. But we could almost feel the Shangalla, probably not far behind us, and closing the gap quickly, so it was a hasty lunch, and after the briefest stop we were moving again.

With constant backward glances we continued at good speed. Despite our hold-up we arrived at the game rangers' post at Allia Bay an hour and a half more quickly than on our northward journey. Buoyed up by nervous energy I only felt slightly tired compared with my utter exhaustion previously. It was still Christmas Day and we were still alive – surprisingly – and determined to celebrate in style.

So it was a cruel blow to discover that there were no beers at Allia Bay, nor even any sodas. There was in fact even a water shortage, which was a much more serious problem. So Christmas would have to be postponed until we reached North Horr, about 80 miles to our south-west in the Chalbi desert. Fortunately the lady who ran the shop was full of festive cheer, and not only made us tea but also a very good meal, and then brought us water too. At least for the time being we knew we were safe here in the company of so many armed rangers. But a great debate immediately began about what to do with Amede. Some Shangalla employees knew him and insisted he stay here and be returned on the next lorry heading north. He was disconsolate and looked tearful, but perhaps it was for the best. Knowing now what our journey still had in store for us, it certainly was.

News came in that another battle was raging between the *askaris* of Kokoi Camp and the Shangalla at the place we had rested before reaching Koobi Fora. Lopus was very pleased that he had delayed them with his story of going down to the lakeshore. So was I. The rangers of Kokoi had unquestionably saved our lives by heroically delaying the Shangalla so that we could press ahead.

Despite the late hour, discussions now began concerning our intended route and whether we should follow the seasonal track from Allia Bay to North Horr; the route I had so stupidly revealed that we would take. Opinions were very divided among the park rangers as to its safety and another great debate was launched. Some thought there would be no threat, while others said, 'No, the Shangalla who are following you will take a short cut, heading south-east to get to the track ahead of you and at one of the waterholes they will ambush you and kill you'. They said that especially for the first 30 miles after leaving the park, the danger would be critical. 'But if you go that way you must sleep a long way from the waterholes. And there are many many lions there.' I hated having to make the decision, a decision that our lives might depend on. We settled down to sleep with our troubled brains churning over the risks and fears. Not my most peaceful Christmas Day...

I woke late at 6.45am on Boxing Day to find that the thoughtful woman from the shop had already brought us tea. Immediately the discussion of our route began again, with divided opinions. I suggested following a course 20 miles to the south of the vehicle track but the camp rangers said emphatically, 'You will find no water there, and trekking 80 miles to the Chalbi desert without water is not possible. It is very, very hot. You'd be lucky to survive that.' A conundrum to say the least and a dangerous one.

A couple of home guard soldiers with rifles arrived from the *manyatta* south of Moiti. I asked them if they would accompany us and they sounded intrigued, but the moment I told them our route they immediately said they needed to get back to their homes. People obviously thought it far too risky. However, I was determined not just to retrace our steps to Loyangalani. We all agreed that would be an admission of defeat, and would be thoroughly unadventurous, even cowardly. Chukuna declared that if Wilfred was with us he would say, 'Damn the Shangalla, we will take the route we had planned, and if they cut our throats in the night we will die silently like men.' My immediate reaction was less heroic: 'Bugger that!' While it might have been typical of Thesiger I found myself a little short of enthusiasm to die so easily.

The debate ebbed and flowed for most of the day, but in the end we did finally decide to follow the track and accept the risk of 'dying silently like men', in order to have access to the vital waterholes on the way. It was still a most disconcerting decision.

A man offered us a goat, but at such a high price that we refused. Luckily someone whom Lopus knew then gave us one as a present. We killed it immediately and soon it was skinned and dismembered. I discovered that, once again, the others had not mentioned to me that our rations were at an end apart from some sugar and a few rotting onions, so the shop lady kindly opened up for us and we restocked: 5 kilos of dry beans; 6 kilos of sugar; 2 kilos of onions; 1 kilo of milk powder; 2 bags of white flour to make chapattis; some packs of Sportsman cigarettes; and several packets of Mchuzi Mix and curry powder, both popular flavourings. I very much hoped this would not be the property of the Shangalla in a couple of days' time.

We had more sacks of *posho* than we could possibly eat and decided to give a sack to Amede to take back to Ileret with him. In fact he had spent a Christmas to remember, as, apart from having stuffed himself with more food than any ordinary 12-year-old could possibly eat, I had bought him a blanket and he now also stood up somewhat baggily in a selection of my clothes. We spent the rest of the day relaxing in preparation for the long, hard walk to come. I spent the time between the pages of Rudyard Kipling's Kim, a book which Wilfred claimed to reread almost every year.

Down at the lakeside, meanwhile, as I stood calf-deep in the muddy water washing my hair, I was suddenly aware of movement about five yards away from me. Startled, I leaped back, expecting the sudden thrash of a prehistoric tail as a crocodile surged at me. My heart pounded but nothing happened. I peered to see what it was, as something dark and shapeless kept breaking the surface. Still standing ankle-deep in the water I watched it, less sure that it was a crocodile, but not believing it was a fish, either.

Chukuna was nearby and I called his attention to it. After watching it for a long time he said, 'I think it's a young croc wrestling with the head of a Nile perch'. We never knew for certain, but if it was a croc I was glad it had a fish head rather than my leg. Later in the day someone gave us a huge piece of Nile perch, perhaps explaining the origin of the discarded head, so after dark we made chapattis and cooked a fish stew so enormous that none of us could finish our share.

Amede had the remains of everyone's plates tipped into his and, unbelievably, he succeeded in polishing it all off. In a life of hardship and deprivation he wasn't going to waste a single edible morsel, but how he managed it all was remarkable. Inevitably Lopus sat at a little distance upwind with his back to us, eating his goat meat, as the smell of the fish made him nauseous.

During the night the lovely rising cry of hyena started all the camp dogs barking and they charged aggressively into the darkness to give chase. Moments later the very air trembled with the irritated growls of a lion unnervingly close among the buildings next to us, and suddenly the dust flew in a furious charge straight at us. But it was only the brave dogs fleeing helter-skelter to our bedsides, their bravado now in tatters and their tails quivering between their legs. A scenario worthy of Aesop himself.

It was a restless night weighing up the risks and advantages of the route we had opted for. We were now convinced the Shangalla were intent on tracking us down and my naivety at Ileret in divulging our route south-east to North Horr could prove fatal. The majority of the rangers most definitely agreed. Yet if our pursuers had taken a shortcut south-east in order to ambush us at a waterhole on the North Horr track it may indirectly have saved our lives, because if instead they had continued chasing us south towards Allia Bay, they would probably have caught up with us while we were delayed by our donkeys wanting to dress up as zebra.

We had been told by many people, however, that whether we were being hunted or not the waterholes along the route ahead were frequent gathering places for raiders, either the Shangalla moving south or the Borana heading north. Lopus had summed up our situation: 'If we meet the Borana we can give them tobacco or food, but if we meet the Shangalla we will all be killed.' No one doubted that. In fact the area was so dangerous at that time that the Gabra Boran, whose tribal area this was, had all moved south into Rendille country, leaving it completely empty. This meant that if we met anyone on the way to North Horr they were sure to be hostile.

I churned these facts over and over. We faced a more life-threatening situation than ever before, and I hesitated to put my companions' lives at risk for the sake of my adventuresome curiosity; indeed, my own life also. I had taken a great many chances already on these treks and one day my luck would run out. But we were all young men, and the thrill of risk was in our blood. I chewed it over through the dark, sleepless hours.

Once we had all woken the next morning I announced to the others that I had made a decision. We would not follow the seasonal track south-east to North Horr but would carry on along the lakeshore to Moiti and then cut across east from there, keeping well south of this contentious track, even if it meant a cruel waterless march through stone desert. The flood of relief that swept through my friends was palpable; how brave they had been to have voted to go with me, without showing any hint of fear. A true 'band of brothers'. But it was just too absurdly dangerous. We were later to discover that this decision undoubtedly saved our lives.

Just as we were leaving I was given a bill for five shillings per person per night for all the time we had spent in the national park, which covered most of the ground between Allia Bay and Ileret. That was an unexpected blow to our coffers. I considered arguing that to pay camping fees where we had been running for our lives was a trifle harsh, but decided it was only fair to share the cost of all the ammunition fired to keep us alive. Almost instantly though, as a gesture of seasonal good will, they halved the bill.

We said our goodbyes to Amede and all shook his hand wishing him well, but the poor boy was on the point of breaking down with disappointment. As we moved off he turned his back to prevent us seeing the tears spring from his eyes but then, catching hold of himself again, he came and waved and waved incessantly as we continued our journey. I half expected him to come chasing after us.

From murderous pursuit
to deadly desolation

AFTER AN HOUR AND A HALF we reached the waterhole which supplied the game rangers' camp and, after a long time watering the thirsty donkeys, we filled all our jerry cans. Soon we left the lakeshore to make a straighter route due south through the dry landscape towards Moiti. An appalling smell began seeping from the load on the back of one donkey which turned out to be the goat meat, still wet after boiling it the day before and now absolutely putrid. Most had to be thrown out, manna from heaven for the next passing hyena.

In the evening we made an enormous meal of dried beans and *posho*, which served as supper and next day's breakfast, while Lopus built a serviceable *boma* of thorn branches by the dim light of the four-day-old crescent moon. At least the donkeys were safe there.

The next day we reached Moiti, intending to press on to the same Turkana *manyatta* where we had camped by the sweet waterhole on our way north. During our 16-mile walk that day we had failed to find any groundwater in this bone-dry country, but Barnaba dug again successfully at the Moiti *lugga* , so we camped only a mile further into the hills.

I was painfully aware that this place was infamous for frequent Shangalla massacres, but the others did not seem as concerned as I was. The donkeys were desperate to graze and, once unloaded, dashed off with determination round the shoulder of the hill. We imagined they had gone back down to the *lugga* for its better grass but when the time came to tie them up for the night they were nowhere to be found. Lopus and Barnaba took the torches and set off to hunt for them.

Two and a half hours later they returned with our charges and reported that they had caught up with them heading for the *manyatta* we had hoped to reach that night, obviously looking forward to slaking their parched thirsts again. I was amazed by their incredible memories of a landscape we had walked through two weeks earlier. Certainly much better than mine. But they would have to wait until tomorrow. While the others were away searching for them, Chukuna and I cooked maize-flour porridge and kept half for their return. Everyone was in a lighthearted mood, sure that we had dodged our pursuers, and we joked and laughed until it was time to sleep.

Next day was a slow start as we only had five miles to go. The donkeys were quite certain they knew exactly where we were going and the moment they were loaded they set off at a determined walk. The poor creatures were visibly wasted with thirst and exhaustion. In two and a half hours we reached the *manyatta*, and this time chose the ample shade of a grove of doum palms right by the waterhole on the west side of the hill. It was a good spot, and the donkeys were delighted to drink their fill at last.

When it was our turn, however, we had a shock. The water which had been so clear and sweet was now so rank that we had to hold our breath and gulp it down as fast as possible. The aftertaste was indescribable. Even in a brew it completely overpowered the taste of the coffee, and using it to wash left us smelling like a midden heap. What could have made such a difference so quickly? Had an animal drowned in it? We never discovered. But the donkeys were not as fussy as we were. Nor were the nomads from the Turkana *manyatta*, who continued passing frequently to collect it and would also look in on us to beg tobacco, as was their custom, giving me an opportunity to photograph them.

As usual it was the women who drew the water and they often sat near us for a long time, proud and attractive. As was the Turkana custom, the sides of their heads were shaved, leaving just a topknot of hair in small fine twists, and as usual they wore only skirts of goatskin. Their ears were decorated with large brass rings through holes cut all around the outer edge, some having the common aluminium leaf-shape also hanging from the top of the ears. Everyone had the traditional snake-shaped decoration through the hole cut below the lower lip, except for one girl. Perhaps this was the beginning of the end of the old traditions? However, they all had plentiful heaps of the usual bead strings around the neck and more at the wrist, as well as brightly coloured plastic and aluminium rings around the upper arm. They were a jolly bunch and we enjoyed their company. I found it easy to transport those same faces into a Western context and could imagine them in jeans and tee-shirts on a London street. We are really not so different from each other.

I was deeply touched when the senior *mzee* came to tell me that all the children whose eye infections I had treated on our previous visit were fully recovered, and everyone was intensely grateful. This was remarkable thanks indeed, which I would never have received from the Turkana on the other side of the lake, and marvellous to hear. As we talked, an enormous flock of goats was driven past and he told me proudly that they were all his own animals, but just the she-goats, with the males away in the Suguta valley, and yet more animals elsewhere. Together worth 80,000 shillings.

I was struck by the remarkable similarity of his dress and behaviour to even the poorest members of his *manyatta* and it made me realise how wealthy in animals some of these nomads might be. How different from my own culture where wealth is so often displayed flamboyantly and vulgarly. He stayed with us until evening, recounting the recent misfortunes of his village, and said that earlier in the year the Borana had raided his *manyatta* and carried off 1,200 goats. He told us that he reported the raid to the police, who spent so long asking irrelevant questions that the Boranas had long since escaped. Probably the police were scared of a confrontation, and instead descended on a few Borana villages and made a show of beating up a few innocent people.

Compared with this I could well understand the Shangalla's attitude. After being raided they would set off for reprisal, determined to shed more blood than they had suffered; two eyes for an eye and two teeth for a tooth. It was a violent world. Several old Turkana nomads had told me that things were better before Independence. Wilfred later explained that modern Kenyan bureaucracy, intended to ensure the correct process of law, could in fact be a handicap.

In the old days a British DO might simply collect a group of volunteers after a raid and set off to see justice done. If they shot the offenders, Wilfred said, 'they would just pop them down an ant-bear hole and that would be the end of that.' Popping them down ant-bear holes sounded a bit simplistic to me, and I wondered how many spare ant-bear holes there were! But what the administrative eye did not see the political heart clearly did not grieve over. It had worked.

We turned one of the *mzee*'s goats into a leisurely feast for the rest of the day, this time giving away only the head, and for the first time I tried the intestines, which proved tasty...when thoroughly cleaned. But after dark we were beset by mosquitoes so vengeful that they despised my Autan deterrent, biting us through our *shukas* and my sleeping-bag liner, and the night breeze which normally blew in to save us abandoned us to our fate. In the end, as we failed miserably to sleep, a loud rustling in the tree next to us warned us that a large snake had just woken up for a night's hunting. We beat a retreat, carrying everything up the hill, where a slight breeze held some of the mosquitoes at bay. It was a disturbed night; later we were woken by the dreadful screams of a fox as it came down the *lugga*.

I really wanted to set off east from here but they told us it would be impossible through the mountains, and they had never heard of a waterhole which was marked on my map so perhaps it had long since dried up. We were therefore forced to continue south before turning towards North Horr. So we followed the previous route – uninteresting, flat country with occasional broad *luggas*. The appalling water had left Lopus and me with severe stomach pains, which had sneered at Imodium, but which Septrin made short work of.

After 14 miles we arrived at a likely looking turning place, which would allow us a route south of the Bura Galadi Hills, and we camped at dusk close to the lake shore. Here was plenty of water to prepare for our waterless 60-mile assault on the rock desert to our east. To ensure an early start, we hobbled the two donkeys who were the ring-leaders of the escapologists to stop them tottering off too far during the night.

This very nearly proved fatal as, during the night, I awoke with a start to hear a violent din of donkeys roaring and galloping about several yards away. To my shock (and amusement) my trusted warrior friends were all sound asleep, snoring gently. I gave Lopus a shove and he was on his feet as he woke, spear in hand, with Chukuna and Barnaba immediately behind him as I struggled to pull on my shoes. We raced over to where our donkeys were bucking and kicking and saw two pairs of bright eyes in our torchlight as the hyenas turned to look at us before retreating up the *lugga*. Moments later they would undoubtedly have killed at least one of the donkeys, most likely those we had hobbled.

The donkeys were shaking with adrenalin and fear, wild-eyed and foaming at the mouth, and we brought them back, puffing and quivering, to tie to the tree next to us for the rest of the night. Soon afterwards one of the hyena called from close by, making me feel very vulnerable. The others assured me that they would not come back after discovering people with torches were nearby, but stories I had heard about the courage and cunning of these animals made me less certain. Sleep that night was light and patchy. We were very tired next day.

In the morning we found the spoor of the hyenas only a few yards away, their characteristically white faeces evidence of the amount of bone they grind up with those powerful jaws. They had certainly been back, assessing their chances.

Barnaba told us he had worked as a shepherd in this area and knew it, so he would be our guide, and we turned up the *lugga*. After an hour and a half we found a rock pool of sweet water and topped up our jerry cans. The donkeys had their final drink. This would have to get us to Furaful, an oasis in the desert where we were sure of finding water.

Soon afterwards I spotted a sleeping hare under a bush, ears flattened with eyes wide open. I was prepared, with my fighting stick in my hand, and it never woke up. The others found it hilarious, the power with which I had dispatched it, the skull smashed into tiny fragments. It certainly never knew what hit it! We hooked it onto one of the donkey's loads until lunchtime, and afterwards I was so engrossed looking for another one that I almost stepped on a sleeping leopard, if getting within 10 yards can be called 'almost stepping on'; only a couple of bounds, certainly closer than I would have chosen. Woken suddenly, it was as shocked as I was, springing to its feet with such haste that it left a stain of urine behind on the black gravel and, rather than turning to do battle, had sprinted off up the hillside; a decision I was extremely happy with. Unfortunately my camera was not in my hand, as this remains my only sighting of a leopard when on foot. Even in the game parks, leopard is always the hardest of the 'Big Five' to spot.

For some reason, at lunchtime neither Lopus nor Chukuna would touch the hare, but Barnaba and I thoroughly enjoyed it, despite having to squeeze several parasitic worms from its liver; the best meal of this safari so far.

While we ate, the devious donkeys took themselves off into the hills and were then devils to catch again. Loading them was becoming difficult, as their girth ropes were cutting in behind their front legs and, however carefully we tied them, usually managed to slip back into the same wounds, rigid with dried blood. Thankfully donkeys are long-suffering little creatures and ours were in a much happier condition than those of my last trek.

Increasingly the knot of mountains around us were unknown to the others and were either unmarked or incorrectly marked on my map, meaning that my compass fixes became largely guesswork. A dangerous position to be in. Only occasionally could we catch glimpses of recognisable peaks back at the lake. When we reached a broad *lugga* Chukuna thought it was Furaful but I was sure we were not even halfway there yet. Barnaba had been confident that we would find groundwater, but everywhere was as dry as a bone, borne out by several abandoned Borana *manyattas*. We must survive on our jerry cans.

In the evening, after unloading, I suggested hobbling the donkeys again but Barnaba said with authority, 'They will not go far. They don't know it here,' whereupon they set off at a brisk trot and soon disappeared from view. After drinking coffee, Barnaba and Chukuna set off in the darkness with torches to look for them but returned alone an hour later. This was worrying, and Lopus and Barnaba made another attempt. I watched the pinpoints of torchlight as they scoured distant hills and began to wonder what we would do if we lost our transport and their ability to carry our water in such an isolated waterless place.

After an hour and a half they returned again empty-handed. If we failed to find the donkeys it would be a hazardous journey back to the lake in temperatures close to 40°C (104°F) with only what we could carry ourselves. It seemed unlikely that Shangalla raiders would encroach into such a waterless area, but nothing was certain.

A third time they set off, now slowly and carefully tracking the donkeys' spoor and at last returned with them after over an hour. We tied the ringleaders to a lone, dead tree and the others grazed all night on the few dry wisps they could find. After a midnight feast of maize porridge we fell asleep, exhausted. It was New Year's Eve 1984.

On the first day of the New Year the donkeys were showing signs of serious thirst and there remained a 16-mile walk before we would reach Furaful. There we knew we would find water. It was going to be a hard day in this heat and over this terrain, first crossing a very wide *lugga* and then climbing hills to its east. Again our route led through broken country, and eventually Barnaba confessed that he was completely lost. Our lives depended on my compass bearings once again. When I could next get a reliable fix on mountains we recognised I found we had strayed too far south, so changed to a north-easterly course. It became increasingly clear that my map was more than a little vague in this remote place, drawn with more imagination than evidence. You put absolute faith in a map, so when it is inaccurate it is a dangerous ally indeed.

After passing more abandoned *manyattas* we ate the last of our goat meat and refilled our small water bottles again from the fast-depleting jerry cans. In extreme dry heat it is extraordinary how much water you need to drink, and how seldom you ever have to pee, if at all, passing all moisture out as sweat. But when you do pee, the urine can be so concentrated that it burns the urethra. In *My Kenya Days* Thesiger tells us that the American explorer, Donaldson Smith, who made a circuit of Mount Kulal during his expedition of 1894-95, had described the stony desert north of the mountain as, 'four days of torment, marching through a fiery furnace with the sun's rays beating down with relentless fury.' It was a very accurate description.

A seductive mirage danced in front of us while a strong wind blessedly mitigated the full virulence of the sun. We came onto a jumble of strewn boulders which tilted and rolled beneath our feet and greatly tired the poor, desiccated donkeys, making our progress increasingly slow. This continued interminably so we swung off to the left to escape from it and found ourselves crossing flat sand between the hills.

From here we had magnificent views south to Mount Kulal and beyond to where the distant pale silhouette of Mount Nyiru dominated the country south of the lake. The day seemed endless and my heart thundered in the heat. At last, crossing a small hill, watched by a lone Grevy's zebra, we looked down into the valley of the Furaful *lugga*. Thank God. We had reached it at last and both we and the donkeys would soon be able to drink our fill. We sat in the shade of a thorn tree and rested, slaking our thirst on most of what was left of the water in certain knowledge that there would soon be more than enough for us all.

When we reached the doum palms of the oasis itself, to our increasing horror we found that all the waterholes were bone dry. We trudged dejectedly along the *lugga* from one small depression to the next, driving the steel haft of the spear into the sand to test for moisture. All dry. Eventually our spirits lifted when we found a hole dug half into the bank of the *lugga* with damp gravel at its base. We started to dig deeper but found immediately that it stopped on a bed of rock. It had nothing more to offer.

Although there were many *manyattas* along the riverbed, all were deserted. However, the sand was covered with countless tracks of camels, goats and people, and we realised uncomfortably they must be the tracks of recent raiding parties returning with their spoils. We knew there must be water somewhere, yet the holes had been refilled to hide them and prevent evaporation, and search as we might we could not find any clues. As Chukuna said, 'Even a yard to one side of a water source the sand can be quite dry.' Water is a quixotic element which plays games with us and laughs at our pain. Our dream of camping here and even spending a day recuperating had vanished, and we knew that we must now continue into the night to Gus, another little oasis more than 10 miles to our east. Only four litres of water remained. Even though there was some grass here, the wretched donkeys were too exhausted and thirsty even to attempt to graze, and just stood motionless in their anguish.

We resumed our march and doggedly dragged ourselves back across the black gravel flats towards the low hill which marked the direction of Gus. We walked as automatons, with little conversation, and the donkeys plodded along in absolute dejection, with heads hung down and every right to curse us.

After several miles we came onto the Loyangalani to North Horr road, a dirt track only passable in dry weather. Here it was joined by an even less serviceable rough piste leading north to join the seasonal track from Allia Bay to North Horr; the one that we had decided not to follow due to the probability of a Shangalla ambush. We barely noticed the passing miles. Numb and parched, we crawled into Gus as the last smear of light seeped from the sky, replaced by a strong, clear moon. Water was all we could think about.

Blocked by bandits
(yet again)

GUS WAS A TINY settlement of nine mud-walled, corrugated iron-roofed buildings, two of which were *dukas* and the rest for the administrative police, only marked on my map because of the large waterhole on which it sat, and surrounded by a cluster of hemispherical brown huts of the Borana tribe.

The moment we arrived a group of policemen greeted us and began questioning us about where we had come from and whether we had seen any signs of people or their footprints. We described the prints in the sand at Furaful and they told us that a large party of over 100 Shangalla raiders had been spotted on the track from Allia Bay to North Horr and all the Borana of that area had fled south with their animals. These raiders had been seen two days before, exactly when we would have been there. If we had, we would not be alive now.

I thanked God for my change of heart and our altered route. Had they been searching specifically for us? If not, it was an uncanny coincidence. But either way we would be dead. They told us that next day a detachment of administrative police would be driving up to hunt for them, and I ungenerously hoped they would shoot the lot. I still wanted to get to North Horr and reassuringly they told us that the road there from Gus was always safe because there were no flocks to be raided in the Chalbi desert. But they also told us, 'People only walk at night in the Chalbi to avoid the heat. A man without donkeys can leave before sunset and arrive at North Horr by midnight, covering the 25 miles at a brisk pace'. So we decided to rest for a day and then carry on. But now, water was all we wanted.

The idea of walking by night was disappointing, as we would not see a thing of the Chalbi. Some parts are salt desert, but I did not know which. I had only been in extensive salt desert in southeast Iran in 1969 and it had been an eerie sight. I suggested to the others that we leave the donkeys here to recuperate and that we make the walk alone. But first, sleep! The end of New Year's Day was celebrated with two chapattis and a cup of coffee each before we collapsed, completely spent. All night a strong wind blew, covering us with desert sand, which glued our eyes shut and filled our mouths and noses. But we were far too tired to even notice or care.

Despite our exhaustion it was marvellous that everyone was still in good spirits. There had been no irritation between any of us. I was very lucky to have such an extraordinary group of companions – courageous, unflinching and always quick to see humour. I could not possibly have asked for better colleagues, of any nationality, race or colour. We had become a close-knit band. Chukuna was now 24 years old; Barnaba 26; Lopus 32; and I was 33 – all equals. We discussed which route to take for the rest of our safari, and decided that from North Horr we would return to Loyangalani via Mount Kulal, arriving at its northern peak, Arabel, and then crossing the long mountain by a pass which the map showed bisecting its centre.

As so often happened on my walks, no sooner was a plan hatched than it was dashed by force of circumstance. Almost immediately, we heard that a raiding party had been seen on Kulal, and the police suspected that it was the same band of Shangalla brigands that had been on the track from Allia Bay to North Horr. Soon afterwards police from Loyangalani arrived in Gus, where they awaited a contingent from North Horr arriving on camels. When this group appeared, two and a half hours later than expected, they couched and unsaddled their camels and transferred to lorries, leaving together to do battle with the raiding party on Kulal.

We slept during the day and left at 8.15pm after another worrying hunt for the two escapologist donkeys. Barnaba, who had the tireless legs of a nomadic shepherd, streaked away in front of us and several times we asked him to slow down. Even so, we could barely keep up. It was a boring walk and despite a full moon we could only see vague silhouettes of hills and thorn trees. Every hour and a half we rested for ten minutes, but each time we restarted our conversation petered out. We were weary and aching, our feet falling into time on the black gravel of the road. Legs felt like old pieces of machinery long overdue for lubrication.

By midnight we had only covered 15 of the 25 miles and were worried when we noticed a single light was gaining ground behind us, but it turned out to be the only working headlight of a Toyota pick-up from the Loyangalani camp site on its way to exchange empty beer bottles for new ones. Feeling a bit guilty that I was cheating, I hopped in the back with the others. We soon regretted our decision, as the driver was very drunk and we careered all over the place, often turning off the track into the desert to pick up yet more speed, bucking over sandy ridges and sometimes taking violent evasive action to avoid patches of scrub, almost rolling over. Surprisingly, we arrived at North Horr half an hour later without mishap and climbed out unsteadily.

The place was fast asleep and we walked between Borana huts in the absolute silence until lying down to sleep at the base of a large sand dune. Mosquitoes immediately attacked us with such ferocity they might have had a vendetta against us. The more we writhed in our torment, the more the sand stuck to our sweaty bodies. Just as we finally lost consciousness an icy wind blew in from the desert, and we were awake again in the penetrating cold. With no blankets and just thin *shukas* it was a wretched night.

In an uncomfortable dawn we set off to find a friend of Chukuna's, only to discover that he had moved to Marsabit. So we wandered off to the El-Beso Hotel, a scruffy little tea house run by probably the idlest woman in the entire Borana tribe. We ate the few stale mandazis that she had, washed down with tea. We pre-ordered lunch of meat and rice, although she did her best to put us off, moaning that she would have to go out and buy the ingredients.

The main street was just a stretch of sand between an assortment of cement-faced shops, all surrounded by the *manyattas* of the Boranas and some clumps of palm trees. The only other features were a mosque, the mission compound containing a small hospital, the police station with its lines of barracks, and the DO's office (*see photo 38*).

Chukuna told us that his birthday had been one of the days between Christmas and New Year – he did not know which – so we went to the little bar at the end of the street to celebrate all three events with the inevitable hot beer before our lunch. We had guessed that it might be a frugal offering, which it certainly was, but the bill was not so frugal – a hefty 70 shillings. We had nowhere to lay our heads that night so, in desperation, we went back to the police station and pleaded with the charming sergeant on duty to give us an empty cell. The life of a vagrant! It was a small space with just a concrete floor, but was at least clean. We invested in a spray can of Doom which 'Kills all doo-doos dead' and felt suitably armed for the coming mosquito battle.

After more tea at the El-Beso we returned to the bar for a nightcap. A young man there introduced himself as Sharif Abdul, son of the imam of the mosque. 'I am here on holiday from my job in Jeddah, where I am chauffeur to the Saudi minister for the PTT [Post, Telephone and Telegraph].' What an extraordinary juxtaposition of two contrasting worlds. 'I'm trying to find a lift to Loyangalani,' he told us, 'and if I find one I'll ask if they can drop you off at Gus as we go past. But tomorrow you must come to lunch with me.'

We cannot have been very desirable guests, long since having forgotten what a civilised human being should smell like, so his offer was more than a little public-spirited. As we walked back to sleep at the police station we woke up a shopkeeper and bought some tins of baked beans and four packets of biscuits, which served as our supper. Then to our cell, where Lopus immediately seized the can of Doom and blasted the place with wanton enthusiasm.

At 11pm the mosquitoes arrived through the bars in battle array, and this time we were prepared. I reached for the aerosol, but after one short squirt it was empty. Lopus had used it all up before the creatures had even arrived! I could have wept, but had to accept another night of torture by proboscis. This time I put up a white flag from the start and lay with my chest and arms uncovered as a ritual sacrifice. Perhaps the complete acceptance of my fate did the trick and I was soon sound asleep. My memories of North Horr are certainly not fond ones.

At 7.30am Chukuna took us to a large pool where we did our best to rejoin the human race in terms of personal hygiene. This pond was a delightful place in the middle of a grove of palms, gently swaying in the breeze with the elegant romance of a Caribbean beach. Below them the clear water threw back lovely reflections of their green tracery against the clear sky. By this late stage of the trek the unforgiving roasting had turned my skin almost as dark as that of my companions. No wonder everyone thought I was a Somali.

For want of choice we went back to the El-Beso for breakfast. The lazy, fat woman was very slowly making mandazis, which we ate as fast as she produced them. The news reached us that a Toyota pick-up was about to set off for Loyangalani delivering maize flour for a charity, so we went to investigate. It turned out to be already overloaded with sacks, people and a very disapproving cow, so we watched it set off painfully, with its suspension even more deeply distressed than the poor cow.

Lunch with Sharif Abdul was delightful, a feast of meat, potatoes and rice, laced with hot chillies, which the Arabs love and Africans often do not, so I pinched those that Lopus and Barnaba could not eat. Unfortunately lunch came to an abrupt end when someone dashed in to whisper to Sharif, who announced, 'There are two police lorries leaving shortly which might take you,' so we dashed off to reserve our places, with a 50-shilling bribe to the corporal in charge. They were on their way to Arabel on Mount Kulal to reinforce the police already battling the Ethiopian raiding party.

Apparently there had been a fierce gunfight during the night and a Turkana policeman whispered to me, 'We bombed them very hard.' He told us that these raiders were not Shangalla after all but another tribe, perhaps even more ruthless, called the Amakoke (about whom all my researches have drawn a blank), an Ethiopian branch of the Borana tribe, who had come raiding their Kenyan cousins. They had come in force – at least 200, though some thought twice that number. Certainly a sufficient strength to have forced them to travel in two groups.

It was spine-chilling to be told that they had camped at Furaful on the very night we had intended to sleep there, and must have arrived no more than two hours after we had left. Thank God we had been unable to find water and so had not made camp. A terrifyingly close shave. There was not a shadow of doubt that we would have been killed if they had found us, because the Amakoke, like the Shangalla, gained social stature from the numbers they killed. Unlike the Shangalla, however, the Amakoke actively followed a practice common among certain Ethiopian tribes of cutting the testicles from their victims as trophies to prove how many they had killed. By comparison, the Shangalla suddenly seemed rather civilised! Such a trophy from a white man might have been highly prized. I tried not to dwell on this alarming thought and crossed my legs proprietorially.

About 40 policemen were keeping them holed up at Arabel, with more on the way. It was clear that our ambition to finish our safari by crossing through Kulal was now out of the question, and so, yet again, my plans had been disrupted by the activities of brigands in this savage wilderness. The fact that this large band on Kulal had turned out to be Amakoke meant of course that there was still a raiding party of at least 100 Shangalla unaccounted for in this area, who could be anywhere and still might be on our route to Loyangalani. But there was little we could do about that, other than just hope for the best. The driver of our lorry strongly advised us to load our donkeys as soon as we reached Gus, and walk all night to return to Loyangalani as soon as possible, because the dangers were mounting rapidly.

This time we took a quite different route, ignoring the road completely and heading in a straight line across-country, making the lorries lurch and wallow over the uneven ground. Unfortunately the salt flats must have been further east and we saw nothing but sand and scant scrub. As the sun slipped out of the western sky we reached the indistinct track leading down to Kulal and were dropped off to walk the remaining miles to Gus while they continued to join in the 'bombing' of the Amakoke.

It was dark when we arrived an hour later to find only two men remaining at the police post, and everyone else now fighting at Arabel. After talking with them we decided to spend a day or two resting here before setting off. It was strange how we had all missed our donkeys, who now symbolised our curious peripatetic home. We bought a goat for 100 shillings, which we killed and cooked before sleeping, putting half the meat in a sack which we strung up in a tree. We then slept so soundly that no one heard the pariah dogs of Gus raiding us during the night and eating the rest. We were more tired than we had realised and gratefully relaxed next day, washing clothes, and preparing for the last two-day trek to Loyangalani.

The end of an odyssey

AFTER THEIR FOUR-DAY rest and recuperation with good grazing the donkeys were even starting to look quite fat and healthy. They were also lively and unimpressed by our plans to continue, and we had our work cut out to catch and reload them with their hated burdens. It was January 6th. Apart from the Amakoke threat, no one knew what had become of the large band of Shangalla. It was all rather dodgy. There seemed to be various possible outcomes: the Amakoke would be killed or captured; they might flee back north, directly towards us; we might easily bump into the missing Shangalla; or possibly we would just carry on without incident.

We were potentially between two huge raiding parties. Everyone pressed us to get to the safety of Loyangalani as soon as possible, but strangely, having survived for so long under constant threat of attack and certain death, while hardly gung-ho, we had become somewhat inured to the risks. As we continued south-west, the driver of a Fisheries Land Rover carrying the mayor of Loyangalani stopped to tell us that the battle with the Amakoke was still raging. We hoped it would continue.

We stopped wearily for our midday break gazing out on a breathtaking view across the lake. As we approached the coastal strip we found fresh grazing had brought herds of goats, cows and camels, with *manyattas* which had moved from Loyangalani. Everyone was talking about the battle on Arabel.

Barnaba recounted, 'When I was a small boy looking after cows on the slopes of Mount Kulal we heard shooting. With my friends I ran to the police post at Loyangalani. The police refused to believe us and questioned us all afternoon. I now realise they were scared of going. Only when some Turkana nomads arrived with the same story did they take action, much too late. The Shangalla had already killed 42 people.'

The profile of Mount Kulal slowly altered as we walked south, the afternoon sun picking out the peaks and valleys of its long, western flank. Maybe we were too far away to hear the shooting, but all was silent. The day was drawing to its end, as was our safari, and we approached the lengthening shadows of the rocky hill above El Molo Bay. Leaving the road we found many friends among their *manyattas*, eager for stories of our trek as we drank tea with them. Any tales involving raiding parties always commanded an attentive audience, and they listened spellbound and incredulous as we described our stay inside the very heart of the enemy camp at Ileret.

We were now so close to Loyangalani that we all decided to carry on and finish our trek that day. So it was quite dark when we continued, retracing the first day's walk and crossing the hills at the airstrip. We at last picked up the twinkling lights of the little town. Weary from the long day's walk of 26 miles we camped at the first tree we came to on the edge of town, tethering the donkeys for the night until their owners could collect them in the morning.

There I divided up the equipment between my friends and made up the wages. I had promised 25 shillings a day but increased this to 30 a day for the 30 days. Then, still having sufficient cash, I made this up from 900 to 1,500 shillings each, a substantial sum in the context of their lives. They had been the most steadfast, courageous and entertaining companions and had earned my profound respect. Without them not only would this trip have been impossible, but also, without their intelligent judgement and stoic loyalty in very dangerous circumstances, the outcome might have been tragically different. I hope that if any of them are still alive as I write this, they remember it with the same tingle of excitement and affection as I do. What incredible young men.

The end of every trek always saddened me by its abruptness – Alice stepping back out of her looking glass, the door closing suddenly on the wild and exotic world we had explored together, life normal again. There were no lengthy goodbyes, just a return to reality. Everyone was very tired and needed to go home at the end of this 450-mile walk.

Barnaba and Chukuna went off with their bags to sleep with their families and Lopus and I settled down for my final night by Lake Turkana. It was the last time I was to see that remarkable Jade Sea, around which I had spent so much time and covered about 1,200 miles. I have never been back.

The next day Lopus set off for his home on the edge of the Rendille deserts and I was sure that he would use his money wisely to build up his herd of camels and prosper. Barnaba would no doubt invest in goats and also do well. But I was saddened to meet Chukuna in the morning, still bleary after a reckless night drinking changaa, and to hear that all his money had already been begged from him. This highly intelligent and delightful young man had been irreparably damaged by his lengthy incarceration. I had hoped that this safari would have been the start of a new life for him, but it was not to be.

Next day, thirteen and a half hours perched on top of a lorry-load of dried fish, cold, dusty and cramped, left me with a smell which took days to wash away. At Baragoi I saw, walking dejectedly along the street, the sub-chief whose wealthy *manyatta* I had stayed in on my previous trek. He had, of course, heard about the death of Ayoko, and he had himself since been devastated by raiders, leaving him destitute and penniless. I was deeply saddened by this tragic end for such a dignified and generous man. Nothing was certain in this wild, tribal world.

Once again, I enjoyed watching Lawi's *morans* driving his goats to water (*see photo 40*), and one day, in a nearby *manyatta*, I was introduced to two delightful girls who had endured clitoridectomy just the previous day. They were still surprisingly buoyant, and keen to have their photograph taken with a couple of fine-looking *morans* (*see photo 39*).

I stayed a few more days at Wilfred's camp. He hugely enjoyed lengthy discussions about the hardships and perils of the trip. I was proud that he had accepted me as a traveller of the true sort, and we had become close friends. While I had been away he had at last finished the final edit of his great autobiography, *The Life of my Choice*, painstakingly written in longhand on a thick bundle of papers over several years. He was keen to get it to his London publishers, Collins, as soon as possible, as they were pressing him for it. He now entrusted it to me to take back for him. I appreciated the honour and gravity of this task as, should I fail, it would be impossible for him to start again.

As he handed it over to me he said, 'John, if you lose this I'll cut my throat and I'll haunt you for the rest of your life!'

I kept it on my person until, with relief, I passed it to his grateful editor a couple of weeks later in London. As soon as the book was published, Wilfred signed a copy for me and I enjoyed being able to read it at last.

We continued to meet for lunch whenever he was in London, and eventually the day came when he had to make the ghastly decision to return permanently to England rather than end his days in the bush, as he had fancifully imagined. The memory of this great explorer and his inspirational friendship has been a pillar of strength to me all my life; proof that anything is possible with determination and courage. So, also, has the memory of my three indomitable companions and this final trek into the stronghold of the Shangalla – that veritable hornets' nest.

'Life followed ancient patterns, as life does;
new friends joined us and old friends went.
Like shadows in the memory,
they drifted in and out of our story.
We watched them go.
One should not cling to shadows.'

Kuki Gallmann (b. 1943)
I Dreamed of Africa

Tying Loose Ends

I RETURNED TO ENGLAND with a heavy heart, knowing I had completed my treks around that extraordinary lake. Those walks have had a life-long influence on me. A land of such cruel physical landscape and such brutal temperatures, thirst and famine. A land where life often seemed savage in the extreme. Yet, behind their different customs and exotic costumes the people were so remarkably like us. Human beings are not so very different from each other. We might describe the way they lived as savage, but surely the savagery of the West, where the fountain pen or computer keypad can inflict more damage than a spear or an AK-47, can be much more dangerous. Human aggression and greed knows no bounds, whether dressed in a ragged loin-cloth or an Armani suit.

I have never been back to Lake Turkana but I did return to Samburu a few years later at the invitation of Wilfred, Lawi, and

Kibriti. Kibriti had suggested that he take me down to Lake Baringo, a favourite place of Wilfred's for watching game going down to drink. But when I arrived at Maralal, I was sorry to find Wilfred absent, having been invited to an exhibition of his remarkable photographs of the deserts of the Empty Quarter of Arabia. He no longer lived at Lawi's guest house and I suspected that friction with Lawi's new wife had made him an increasingly difficult guest. In his autobiographical rollercoaster, *Eye on the World*, Thesiger's old friend Gavin Young mentions that he 'has the prima donna's sharp tongue.' So he now had a room in Laputa's house, also on a hillside some distance from Maralal. In his absence Wilfred had left instructions that I was to be given his bed. This was a proper bed, unlike his previous austere sleeping quarters, although I very much doubted whether anyone had bothered to change the sheets, and I expect that on his return he probably found mine still there to greet him. He would not have cared.

Maralal was already changing, not always for the better. Lawi was now the Mayor and had gained a lot of prestige as well as weight. His athletic young-warrior physique was now little more than a memory. He had established an off-licence store which did a roaring trade for all the wrong reasons, making cheap liquor available to people who previously were content with the local, less alcoholic and inexpensive *pombe*. His customers had only one ambition, to become comatose as quickly as possible, and the two bestsellers were cheap sherry and cheap vodka. It was clearly putting people into penury while making Lawi a handsome profit. Very sadly Chukuna was now one of those drunks, and although we enjoyed some great reminiscences when he was sober and his memory was sharp, he was often in alcoholic oblivion.

Lawi and Laputa had also become heavy drinkers, although Lawi always maintained his poise and dignity. This was sadly not true of Laputa, who was often too drunk to get home. I wondered whether Wilfred was aware of what was happening; maybe he preferred not to face the truth. Lawi was the apple of his eye, his 'adopted son', and he would have been deeply hurt.

I suspected Laputa was now also finding him a difficult house guest. One night, when Wilfred's self-appointed bodyguard Lopego was away, masked men entered the house, locked Laputa in his room, and then beat Wilfred savagely with clubs on his arms and legs, leaving him black and blue, but avoiding his head, and breaking no bones. They obviously had not intended to kill him, yet it was a cruel attack on an elderly man. Afterwards I heard it whispered that the attack might have been with Laputa's knowledge, an attempt to dissuade Thesiger from staying there. I very much hoped not. In any event Wilfred did not take the hint.

Lawi and Laputa both died in the mid 1990s (perhaps due to alcohol), a profound sadness for Wilfred. All his life he had needed human company and was prone to loneliness on his own. Having withstood the nighttime attack, it was these losses that eventually drove him from Kenya, to spend his last years in England. He had always wanted to die in Maralal, in the wilds he loved best, the place he called his 'Sanctuary'.

A lot has been claimed or guessed about Thesiger's sexuality, particularly since his death. In today's society it is hardly relevant and I do not intend to add to these speculations other than to repeat what Lawi once told me, saying that almost every visitor from England would at some stage ask him whether Wilfred was homosexual. Lawi found it a strange question and told me that, having lived alongside Wilfred ever since he was 12, he had never witnessed a single incident to corroborate it. I personally also had no evidence to suggest it. Beyond that, it is none of my business. Throughout his life he had little close association with the opposite sex and I think he felt uncomfortable in the company of young women. However, he once took me to tea in the Nairobi apartment of a remarkable old lady, a lifelong friend, who had owned a very large ranch near Machakos. It was easy to feel their mutually affectionate rapport.

As he had promised, Kibriti organised a motoring safari for me in his Land Rover. In the Samburu National Reserve I was shocked to see how little game remained. We then drove down to Lake Baringo, where we pitched a couple of tents on its grassy banks for a few nights. I found it strange having a tent to myself, while everyone else mucked in together, and I wasn't sure I liked being treated with such alienating respect after all the weeks I had lived in the bush wedged alongside my companions. One night a hippo tripped over the guy ropes of my tent, making it shudder violently, its great feet less than a yard from my head. Hippos scent-mark their territory by defecating while flicking their tails to spread their dung far and wide, and in the morning my tent was heavily 'pebble-dashed'. Kibriti suggested with a wry grin that it was a significant message to tell me I was not welcome on its patch.

I guessed Kibriti was growing apart from Wilfred's other protégés due to his indifference to alcohol, which proved a blessing for him. While Lawi and Laputa were both highly literate Kibriti never learnt to read, although astute at business, carrying all the figures in his head. He became a pillar of the establishment and chairman of the board of governors of a local school, despite his illiteracy. His own children tried to teach him but he never picked it up.

I went down to the coast to stay a few days with Moh'd Abeid, as he was now very elderly and frail and I knew that this would be my last chance. I then took a six-seater plane up the coast to Lamu, the lovely little island settlement which so much resembled the old Stone Town of Zanzibar; streets just wide enough to allow the passage of a loaded donkey. There was only one car on the island, a

Land Rover belonging to the DC, little used as there were almost no roads large enough to take it. I had been there before and had loved it and was not surprised to discover that it was Wilfred's favourite destination at the coast. I was lucky to be introduced to the best dhow captain on the island, Shariff, and spent a long day at sea with him in his small dhow *Tabassam* during a wild monsoon storm, returning by moonlight. It was a thrilling end to this last visit and a few days later I was back in England.

Soon afterwards I was sad to hear that my friend Omar El-Haj had left his beautiful house in Nairobi. He had always worried that he had made it too desirable and that envious eyes in positions of power might oust him from it. Instead he began spending his time in Zanzibar, where his family still owned several houses, and later my wife and I stayed with him there during our honeymoon. It was a magical experience, once more on the island of my birth, where my father had spent most of his working life. We even found his old office on the edge of the Stone Town, his desk exactly as he had left it, nothing changed in the intervening 35 years except for a thick layer of dust.

Wilfred and I kept in regular contact and I still lunched with him from time to time when he was in London, sometimes a very simple snack at his flat now that his devoted housekeeper Molly was too elderly to look after him, otherwise at one of his clubs, such as the Special Forces Club. He died in 2003 at the age of 93, his reputation now enshrined in the history of desert exploration alongside those he had venerated, Doughty, Lawrence and Burton. His life was remarkable, the last of the 'Victorian' explorers, and I was very lucky to have known him.

During those four treks I discovered a great deal about life in what was the extraordinary wilderness of the Northern Frontier District. Equally, I discovered a great deal about myself; no significant bravery or spectacular heroics. Perhaps, as Apsley Cherry-Garrard had written long before (see 'To Begin at the Beginning'), I had been sufficiently 'fearful [to] do much'. I recognise how much I owed to the peoples of the NFD. People no worse and no better than me, in many ways remarkably similar, just living in another world, quite different in time and place. A world that has now changed.

I also recognise the enormous debt I owed to our indefatigable donkeys who put up with so much hardship and misery to achieve what we asked of them.

So I would urge young people to leave their smart phones at home and go to explore the wild places of the world before they, too, are changed forever, integrating with the local people and their harsh lives. But tread lightly, go with humility, not to preach or change things, just to observe and learn. Do you have the right to assume superiority? We are the ones who are destroying this planet, not them. You will never regret it, and it will become a foundation stone on which to build the rest of your life.

Today, on the internet, I see navigable roads, airstrips, health clinics, organised safaris and local people usually wearing western clothes. It would be foolish to think the land I travelled through would remain the same, and no doubt the lives of its people are safer with better health care, education and links to the outside world. Raiding still persists in some areas, but I now see scientific research stations and tourist accommodation in places where they would previously have been murdered in their beds. It is even believed that under Turkana's rocky landscape lies Africa's largest oil field, and a wind-farm of 365 turbines is already being built east of the lake. But I feel a sadness for the loss of its wildness, its savagery and the thrill that extended back through millennia.

A cloying sameness now stretches across the world with the dominance of our culture. The modern world has arrived, progress accelerates, and nothing will ever be the same again. Exports as far afield as the Congo have decimated fish stocks in Lake Turkana. In December 2016 the 'Gibe III' dam was inaugurated across the River Omo in Ethiopia, the source of 90% of Lake Turkana's inflow, with 'Gibe IV' and 'Gibe V' already in progress. Experts warn that this could threaten the very existence of the lake and its tribal people. Already the lake has shrunk dramatically, Kalokol is now a long way from the shore, with the fishing lodge left high and dry. Mugurr must now be a harmless mountain far from the water's edge.

Life moves on and leaves its memories behind; my days around Africa's jade-coloured sea, remote in a land of shattered rock, isolated from the modern world with the quiver of excitement running through its wildness. I still look back on its arid solitude and see in my memory the visions of those immense skies of implacable blue, wild lightning storms, glorious flaming sunsets, and images of a solitary warrior in a vastness of dust and pulsating heat; a time of danger and extremes, home to fascinating peoples in a different world. But our brothers and sisters all. My memories are no longer private places, now shared with you, and I hope that you have enjoyed footing beside me across those far-flung lands, sharing memories of people and places already fading into history. The history of our world.

Brief History of East Africa

IT IS USUALLY CLAIMED that Africa contains the birthplace of Mankind, eventually spreading to populate the world.

During the first century AD East Africa was trading with India, and by 700AD Arabs from the Persian Gulf sailed on the monsoons to trade with the interior of Africa through Zanzibar. In the 13th century ivory and gold was bartered for Chinese porcelain and Islamic pottery, iron was smelted and substantial stone buildings erected. By the 15th century the East African coast was prosperous, but Islamic rather than African. As a collection of disparate states it was overthrown by the Portuguese invasion of 1498, but in the 17th century the Omanis conquered Mombasa and Zanzibar, and for 100 years Portuguese and Omani influences ebbed and flowed. The Omani Sultans of Zanzibar finally dominated until the revolution of 1964.

In the early 19th century the British appeared, siding with the Omanis, to protect their trade routes to India. An Indian workforce was encouraged, with European and American traders soon following. The 'Scramble for Africa' was underway.

Inhospitable terrain inland restricted European involvement to the coastal strip until the Victorian era of exploration, although Arab slaving caravans already extended as far as the River Congo. The export of slaves was nominally ended in 1822, but actually continued for some years. After the first 19th-century explorers, such as Livingstone, Burton and Speke, a flood of others followed. At the same time the first Christian missionaries began to journey into the interior of East Africa.

What was happening amongst the tribal people of the hinterland is harder to know due to the lack of written records, so oral traditions are vital such as what Lopus explained to me (Trek 4). In the area relevant to this book, it seems that Nilotic peoples had moved south at the end of the 15th century, the ancestors of the present tribes, displacing earlier Cushitic peoples who had dominated the area for two thousand years.

By the middle of the 19th century, trade routes from Abyssinia reached south, almost to Lake Turkana, and routes from Mombasa stretched north towards it, but the inhospitable volcanic deserts around the lake dissuaded traders and explorers from entering Turkana tribal lands. Lake Turkana itself was quite unknown to the West until 1888.

East Africa became dominated by Britain and Germany until WWI when Britain prevailed. Its colonies and protectorates became independent during the first half of the 1960s, although Turkana district remained a restricted zone for several more years due to its dangers.

The newly autonomous Kenya grasped her Independence in 1963 jealously and sometimes bloodily. Seventeen years later

I set out on these treks. Visitors needed a new understanding and respect for her rights and challenges, coming as equals, not superiors. As such I made closer friendships with my companions, was better integrated, understanding their strengths, weaknesses and fears and completely forgetting our colour difference. I learnt a great deal from them, and frequently admired them.

Glossary

Askari
A soldier or guard.

Boma
A fence or barrier to hold animals. Usually made of cut thorn branches, but occasionally a living hedge. It usually encircles the *manyatta*.

Borana/Boran
This tribe originated in Ethiopia and many settled in the NFD around Marsabit. Both words are used, but correctly they are the Borana. The confusion arises simply because the final 'a' is not pronounced.

Changaa
An illegal, impure distilled spirit made from maize flour, popular in towns. Rather similar to the old Irish poteen. Changaa means 'kill me quickly' which it more or less does.

DO, DC
Administrative ranks left over from the British colonial system. A District Officer was responsible for a smallish area, and several may be under the control of a District Commissioner. More senior still was a Provincial Commissioner who administered the entire province.

Doum palm
Hyphaene thebaica. A palm tree associated with Arabia and the northern half of Africa. Known in Turkana as *ekingoli*. Its black fruit is edible and used as decoration.

Duka
Village shop, usually run by Somalis.

Fighting stick
Weapon carved from a species of acacia tree, with a knot of harder wood at the end which curves to one side. Invariably carried by all Turkana men.

Fucidin
An antibiotic ointment.

GSU
General Service Unit, a paramilitary wing of the Kenyan police force first established in 1948 and renamed GSU in 1953. It was used particularly in the Shifta War of 1963-67 and afterwards, and

at the time of my treks it and the Administrative Police were the main forces active in the NFD.

Head stool

A curved seat, sometimes oval but usually rectangular, carved from one piece of wood with a single or double leg widening to a base. Carried upside down by a piece of string or rawhide threaded through the leg. Used as a support to protect the head decoration when lying down, but also to sit on or tuck under a knee or elbow when reclining. Invariably carried by all Turkana men.

Laibon

A seer, or medicine man.

Lugga

A bed of a stream or small river, usually dry. The term was always used on the east and south side of Lake Turkana, but I never heard it on the west side in Turkana District.

Manyatta

A homestead or hamlet, consisting of a group of huts often set within a *boma*.

Matatu

Van converted into a taxi, with simple wooden bench seats, into which as many people as possible were squeezed. They were poorly regulated and maintained and often involved in accidents.

Mboga

(Pronounced mboka) A stew of meat and/or vegetables used to flavour *posho*.

Mchuzi mix
A dry bouillon or mixture of spices and herbs, commercially produced in small sachets, to add to cooking. Very popular with tribal people in the NFD.

Morans
Warriors, a strictly designated age group.

Msungu
A white person. Plural 'wasungu'.

Mzee
A mature man, or old man. The age grouping after the *morans*.

NFD
The Northern Frontier District was formed in 1925 from the southern half of the former Jubaland, which had been divided with the Italians. Until 1934 access was restricted to those with special passes. Turkana continued to be a restricted area until several years after Kenyan Independence in 1964. It was always a dangerous and lawless area of the country.

Ngoroko
In the days when I was in the NFD the ngoroko were lawless bands of Turkana rogues and disaffected young men. They lived by raiding *manyattas*, stealing herds and flocks, and generally raping, pillaging and murdering. They operated in groups of often only a handful but occasionally of hundreds. They raided their own tribe but would also attack across tribal or national boundaries. The term came to be used nationally for all groups of brigands, sometimes allegedly controlled by politicians and senior police officials, masquerading as Anti Stock Theft Units and Administration Police Patrols,

stealing flocks and herds, trafficking arms and drugs, organising assassinations, and poaching elephant tusks and rhino horn.

Panga
A short, stout machete with a curved blade.

Pombe
A homemade beer made from maize flour fermented with sugar or honey.

Posho
The staple diet of East Africa. Maize flour cooked with water to make a thick dough, often eaten with a stew of meat and/or vegetables (see **mboga**). Synonymous with *ugali*. 'Porridge' is used to describe a thinner version of posho sweetened with sugar and eaten with a spoon.

Shifta
A word meaning 'bandit' adopted in Kenya to describe those Somalis fighting in the North-east who wanted to make this area part of Greater Somalia. This led to the 'Shifta Wars' (1963-67), after which bands of Shifta would roam the NFD as far as Lake Turkana stealing animals and murdering wherever they could.

Shuka
Rectangle of cloth, used as the most minimal item of clothing, popular amongst the tribes of the NFD, as it provided a splash of much-loved colour. Red was particularly favoured.

Sufuria
Cooking pan made of spun aluminium, usually without handles.

Swahili
Indigenous people of the East African coastline, whose heritage mixes African and Arabian blood lines. The Arabian line is usually from Oman or the Hadhramaut. Kiswahili is the original language spoken on the coast, while a colloquial version is spoken throughout East Africa, which in British times was known as 'kitchen Swahili'.

Targilla
Tuareg unleavened bread, baked in the Sahara in hot sand under a fire.

Thumb knife
A ring of steel which curls up to form a small crescent shaped blade. Sometimes worn on other fingers.

Toto
A small child.

Tyre sandals
Soles made from vehicle tyres with straps cut from the inner tube and nailed into its thickness, crossing over the foot. The standard footwear of the NFD, replacing earlier sandals of animal skin.

Wrist knife
A steel disc with a central hole into which the wrist is slipped through a narrow opening. Sharpened around the edge for fighting or jointing and skinning animals. Generally worn on the left wrist.

Acknowledgements

This book has taken a long time to write, both during our years in France, and since returning to UK. I owe thanks to many people for their encouragement and for critical comments about earlier drafts, including especially: David Crane; James Hart; Karen Holdich; Richard Holmes; Jerry and Jane Hopkinson; David Moss; Anthony and Victoria Pakenham; and Sarah Pakenham. Also to my cousin Richard Henderson who scanned my colour slides to produce these images.

I very much want to thank my publisher, Dan Hiscocks at Eye Books, and his team, who have unswervingly supported this book, and in particular my editor, Clio Mitchell, whose indefatigable attention to detail has forged it into its final shape.

Most of all I must thank my wife Mo for her comments, criticism and corrections over several years, and her constant support, even when it seemed an uphill struggle. She has also produced the many delightful line drawings which help describe the book.